The World Atlas Of
MOTOR RACING

THE WORLD ATLAS OF
MOTOR RACING
JOE SAWARD

ARTWORK
JIM BAMBER

MALLARD PRESS

Title-spread pictures Colour drawing is of Jarama circuit, north of Madrid. In the photograph, from the 1989 running of the classic Sebring 12-hour sportscar race, the Cobb/Nielsen Jaguar XJR-9, which took second place, leads the Wollek/J. Andretti/Bell Busby-Porsche 962, which later retired.

Author's Note

Writing any book on the racing circuits of the world is a huge task. Visiting them all would be impossible. Thus, I have relied heavily on two men who have been there, seen it and done it. I make no apologies for constantly referring to the words of Denny Hulme and David Hobbs, who between them have raced on an unbelievable number of circuits around the globe. Other drivers have commented on their favourite tracks, but Denny and David are the backbone of this book, able to compare circuits. Research has involved several hundred books in various languages, thousands of magazines and endless conversations. Particular thanks should go to the following for their help, encouragement, patience, accommodation, finance or, in some cases, comfort while this book was being written and at various stages beforehand when, without their help, the author would still be stuck, starving, at some obscure racing track in south-west France. They are, with the exception of the first two, in aphabetical order; and if any have been missed I apologise for it: Denny Hulme, David Hobbs, Kuni Akai, Gary Anderson, Gerhard Berger, Peter Brock, Michael Brown, Emma Burnett, Tommy Byrne, Bob Costanzo, Kelly Davis, Ruth Davis, Gwyn Dolphin, Mike Doodson, David Draper, Chris Economaki, Peter Flohr, Peter Foubister, Ian Gamble, Allan Grice, Will Hagon, Rachel Harry, Mal Hemmerling, Bob Holden, Will Hoy, Mark Hughes, Bob Jennings, Alan Jones, Bruce Jones, Eddie Jordan, Gordon Kirby, Charly Lamm, David McKay, Katie Montague-Johnstone, Wayne Munro, Kris Nissen, Win Percy, Nelson Piquet, Emanuele Pirro, Suzanne Radbone, Roberto Ravaglia, Nigel Roebuck, Tony Schulp, David Segal, Jeremy Shaw, Graham Smith, Quentin Spurring, Kees Van der Grint, Fred Vogel, Tom Walkinshaw, Andrew Whyte, Bryn Williams. And the staff of *Autosport* in London.

Acknowledgements

The publishers would like to thank the following organisations and individuals for their kind permission to reproduce the photographs in this book:

ADAC-Berlin 60 bottom; Aston Publications Ltd 164—5, 197 bottom; Auto Racing Memories 2—3, 146 top; *Autosport* 18—19, 19 right, 24, 25, 32, 38—9, 46, 47 top, 53, 55 right, 57, 67 left, 69 bottom, 71 top, 73, 85, 88, 91, 92, 93, 99, 105, 109 bottom, 110, 114, 115 right, 116 left, 118—9, 119 right, 120 right, 122, 123, 124 top, 125, 127 top, 128 bottom, 129 bottom, 143 bottom, 144, 147 top, 149, 154, 155, 167, 171, 176—7, 178 bottom, 187, 188—9, 194, 200—1, 202, 204, 208 top, 213, 218, 219; Charles Briscoe-Knight 22, 23, 89, 94 top, 161 top, 162, 169, 184—5, 190; Malcolm Bryan 68 bottom; Charlotte Motor Speedway 153; Colorsport 31, 76 bottom; /Baudin 92—3; /Compoint 21, 175, 186, 205; /de Nombel 14, 39 right, 43 below, 55 left, 67 right; /Duomo 163 bottom; /Focus West-Bob Beck 134 top; /Marguerat 38; /Taillade 48, 78, 103, 120 left, 127 bottom; /David Taylor 134 bottom, 138; Courtesy Daytona Speedway 143 top; Förenade Bil Import AB 97; David Hodges 6—7, 8—9, 10—11, 20, 28 left, 33, 34, 35, 37, 40, 41, 42 bottom, 43 top, 45, 49, 50, 51, 52, 56, 58, 59, 60 top, 61, 62, 63, 70, 71 bottom, 72, 75, 100, 101 top, 104, 106, 107, 108, 109 top, 112, 128—9 top, 129 right, 130, 131, 135, 139, 145, 146 bottom, 152, 173, 174, 178 top, 188, 197 top; Leigh Jones 121; Laguna Seca 147 bottom; LAT 69 top, 74, 80, 81, 96, 115 left, 136, 180, 181, 183, 210, 211, 212, 220, 221; Linear Photographs 206, 208 bottom; The National Motor Museum at Beaulieu 42 top, 116—7 top, 117 right, 124 bottom; Nürburgring GmbH 64; Bill Oursler 166; Pemberton Publicity Services 198 bottom; Road America 151; Road Atlanta 157, 158, 159; Nigel Snowdon 140, 192, 196, 198, 215; Toyota Grand Prix Long Beach 161 bottom; Bryn Williams 15, 28—9, 47 bottom, 76 top, 77, 83, 84, 87, 94 bottom, 101 bottom, 163 top.

Many of the circuits, associated companies and photographers have also provided material for artwork reference, for which we are extremely grateful.

MALLARD PRESS

MALLARD PRESS
An imprint of BDD Promotional Book Company Inc.
666 Fifth Avenue
New York, NY 10103

"Mallard Press and its accompanying design and logo are trademarks of BDD Promotional Book Company Inc."

Copyright © 1989 The Hamlyn Publishing Group Limited

First published in the United States of America in 1989 by The Mallard Press

ISBN 0792—45017—5

Printed in Italy

CONTENTS

INTRODUCTION

For most people, motor racing is something to watch on television or read about briefly in the papers. It's exciting, something a little different, a little glamorous. Those with deeper interest turn to the specialist weekly publications, while thousands now flock to the track to follow the sport. These are the lucky ones, for no matter how many words or pictures you see, there is nothing to compare with visiting the great circuits of the world. It offers experiences which cannot easily be conveyed by words. Each track has different sights, smells and sounds — and different ghosts.

You cannot reproduce the shiver up the spine as you walk through the old pits at the Nürburgring; or the thrill of hearing the roar of the *tifosi* in full song at Monza. How can you explain in print the feeling you have when the ground shakes as 40 NASCAR stock cars thunder past at 200mph at Daytona?

You have to be there, you have to see the banking at Monza; you have to marvel at how steep the road is at Bathurst, or how close the cars go to the barriers at Monte Carlo; you have to see 400,000 people crammed in at Indianapolis to believe it is really possible. Spa doesn't really come alive until you've experienced the swirling clouds and felt the rain trickling down your neck. Le Mans is never quite complete unless you have been to the kink on the Mulsanne in the middle of the night and been left dazed by the laser show of the headlights in the darkness.

Each circuit has its own peculiar atmosphere, its own quirks and tricks which must be mastered by the drivers. Across the world there are racing circuits of all shapes, sizes and forms.

They range from the highly professional, highly safe, permanent venues, to the hairy-chested-hero street courses that are used for one weekend a year. Still more great circuits have gone, swallowed up by urban expansion, deserted through lack of finance, or closed down for being too dangerous.

In the modern age, motor-racing venues must be safe for both drivers and spectators. Gone are the days when you could distribute a few hay bales around a town and unleash racing cars to dodge between street lights, manhole covers, kerbs and shop fronts. The sport cannot afford disasters like that at Le Mans in 1955 when a Mercedes flew into the crowd, killing many more than official figures have ever admitted.

Motor racing today takes place on extremely safe, closed racing tracks. Hurtling round in their high-powered machines, the drivers are safe in the knowledge that if they lose control, there are numerous precautions to help them and others to avoid injury. The modern racing circuit has huge run-off areas. There are sandtraps which help to slow the cars and tyre barriers to cushion impacts. Debris fences are built high to catch wreckage thrown off cars in collision. Motor racing will never be completely safe, but the percentages have been dramatically reduced.

It wasn't always like that. One man

The front-row line-up for the inaugural Indianapolis 500 in 1911. Left to right: National, Interstate, Simplex and Case; the Stoddard-Dayton pace car at right seems reluctant to start.

Brooklands was the world's first purpose-built autodrome. Seen here are cars in the Double Twelve, a 24-hour event which avoided night racing and was run three times, 1929-31. Note how the faster cars ran higher on the banking.

whose career spanned the transition from the wild and dangerous days to the modern sanitised era was Denny Hulme, World Champion of 1967. He dodged trees and houses with the best of them on his way to the top before becoming a leading light in the movement to make racing safer. 'We didn't know any better in the old days,' he remembers. 'Now we've got the most incredibly hygienic circuits you have ever seen. Some people criticise them. They say it's terribly boring motor racing. Yes, compared to the old Nürburgring, I suppose it is. But, I tell you, it's better than going to a funeral every Tuesday morning.' Until the end of the 1960s, the drivers took what today we would consider to be unbelievable risks — and there were many funerals.

Motor racing developed from the city-to-city competitions in the 1890s. These drew thousands of curious spectators, who didn't understand that the strange machines were potentially lethal. On the dusty cross-country roads the drivers had to dodge trees, houses, spectators, dogs and farm animals. This crazy situation culminated in an unholy slaughter on the roads between Paris and Bordeaux in 1903. This could not continue. Racing switched to closed circuits, which cut down the possibilities of unseen dangers, making the policing much easier.

The first circuit race is generally accepted to have been the Course du Catalogue at Melun, to the south-east of Paris in 1900, which was run on closed public roads around a 45-mile triangular course. This was only a small, local event, and it was not until two years later that the Circuit des Ardennes in Belgium — all 53 miles of it — became the first international closed racetrack. These early circuits

were huge; but as racing developed and the demand for improved safety grew, the circuits, while remaining on public roads, got smaller. Today, it is unusual to find any circuit more than five miles long. The switch away from inter-city road races was a worldwide movement — with the exception of South America, where there are still *Turismo de Carretera* races on the roads and there is still an alarming number of fatal accidents to spectators.

The traditions of the various continents have been very different since the early days and men have raced more or less anywhere it is possible to do so. One significant early development in Europe, America and Australia was the construction of oval speedways — at Brooklands (1907), Indianapolis (1909), Sitges-Terramar (1922), Montlhéry (1924), the Melbourne Motordrome (1924) and Maroubra (1925). Brooklands was the first purpose-built motor-racing facility in the world. The age of improvisation was over — or so it seemed. The idea of Hugh Fortesque Locke-King, Brooklands was designed by Colonel Capel Holden and was virtually oval in shape, with concrete banking. Situated just 20 miles from London at Weybridge, Surrey, it was easily accessible for the crowds. The track was the centre of British racing for many years, until it was requisitioned during the Second World War by Vickers-Armstrong. It was sold to the company after the war and racing on the site ceased, though parts of the banking remain today.

Indianapolis still operates to this day — the world's longest-surviving permanent racing track. It was a huge and utterly remarkable undertaking. Built from some 3.2 million bricks, the track formed a 2.5 mile rectangle with four distinct, slightly banked corners.

The expense of such projects was enormous and alternatives were sought for American racing; soon clay ovals and wooden speedways flourished across the United States.

Horse-racing courses had had dirt tracks and clay ovals from as early as 1902. It was on these that the legendary Barney Oldfield and his contemporaries raced, starting a tradition that is still strong, with thousands of clay ovals in existence across America. The tracks have come and gone: Empire City, Grosse Point, Ormond Beach, Ascot, Duquoin, Springfield, Langhorne, Terre Haute — famous and evocative names to the older drivers and racing fans.

Board tracks were a passing phase, starting in 1910 with the construction of a wooden speedway at Playa del Rey, California. Beverly Hills had a track built with film money, and in the east there were others at Uniontown, Altoona, Atlantic City and Sheepshead Bay. But they were expensive to

Montlhéry autodrome has a symmetrical banked oval (sweeping away to the right in this shot) connected to a road circuit of variable length. The broad pits apron is visible at lower right.

Permanent circuits were rare in Europe until the 1920s when the Nürburgring opened. Monza and Montlhéry had both road and oval tracks — as did Brooklands by this stage — but here was something new, the purpose-built road circuit, closed to traffic when not in use. Closed public-road courses were common, with Spa starting up in 1924, Solitude in Germany the following year, and Monaco in 1929. The same year Le Mans circuit, which had been the venue for the 1921 French Grand Prix, took on something close to its modern guise.

The concept of the permanent circuit was still unusual, though, and racing went on wherever it could. There have been numerous cases of beach races, up-and-down blasts on dual carriageways and on the perimeter roads of horse-racing tracks, with the latter having all the necessary spectator facilities.

The daredevils of racing, of course, enjoyed other dangerous pastimes and, not unnaturally, runways and perimeter roads at airfields were seen as suitable places to race. The first such event was held at Mines Field in California in 1934 but it was not until after the Second World War that dozens of disused airbases suddenly became available. Tracks such as Silverstone and Sebring developed from these beginnings, while others remained as airfields where racing was tolerated, as with most of the tracks used today in Germany.

Street racing continues around the world, notably at established circuits such as Pau and Monaco, although in recent years street races have been common in America; even Britain, for so long against such things, has adopted changes in the law to allow Formula 3000 cars to compete on the streets of Birmingham. Less satisfactory, however, has been another American trend — car park racing. Still, it goes to prove that if you want to race badly enough, there is always somewhere where it can be done.

run; and, being susceptible to fire and weathering, some were torn down, some burned, some just rotted away.

American road racing started in 1904 with the Vanderbilt Cup races on a 28-mile road course on Long Island, outside New York, in the south at Savannah, Georgia, with the first of the American Grand Prizes in 1908, and in Illinois with the Elgin races from 1910. Road racing was less common in the United States than in Europe — although in Britain the use of public roads was banned by Parliament.

AUSTRIA Österreichring

One of the most beautiful and challenging of the modern Grand Prix circuits, the Österreichring (also known as Zeltweg) is Austria's premier racing track. Hidden away in the mountainous Styrian region of central Austria, to the north of Klagenfurt, the Österreichring was built in 1969, replacing an old airfield track at Zeltweg, which can still be seen below the new track in the valley of the River Mur. The original Zeltweg was L-shaped, laid out between marker cones and hay bales on the bumpy concrete runways of a military air base. It was dull and unpopular with the drivers from its very beginnings in 1958. The enthusiasm of the local organisers, however, meant that the airfield hosted international meetings from its inception. The first race was an international sportscar event won by the Porsche of Wolfgang von Trips, chased by Jean Behra. A year later, the feature race at Zeltweg was for Formula 2 cars, and in 1960 a second F2 race was won by Stirling Moss.

The Austrian organisers were not satisfied: they had set their hearts on a Formula 1 World Championship event. As a step towards this they held a non-championship F1 meeting in 1961 with Lotus driver Innes Ireland triumphing. Two years later Zeltweg repeated the exercise, this race being won by Jack Brabham. At last the Austrian aspirations were fulfilled — Zeltweg played host to a full-blown Formula 1 World Championship Grand Prix in 1964. The rough surface, however, was too much for the Formula 1 cars of the day and car after car fell by the wayside, leaving Lorenzo Bandini (Ferrari) to score his one and only Grand Prix victory.

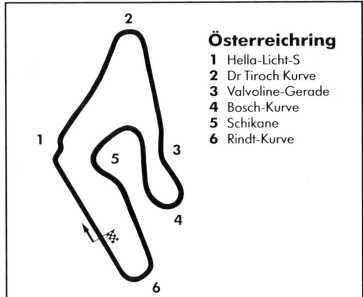

Österreichring

1 Hella-Licht-S
2 Dr Tiroch Kurve
3 Valvoline-Gerade
4 Bosch-Kurve
5 Schikane
6 Rindt-Kurve

Not unsurprisingly, Formula 1 did not return and Zeltweg had to switch to sportscars, local rising star Jochen Rindt winning in 1965 in a Ferrari. By then, however, work had begun on an ambitious new track and, once replaced by the Österreichring, Zeltweg was quickly and quietly forgotten. The new track was a magnificent high-speed circuit, sweeping, rising and falling in a natural arena on the mountainside overlooking the valley. The circuit is 3.67 miles long with a series of fast and testing corners. It quickly emerged as one of the fastest of all the Grand Prix tracks.

The startling thing about going to the Österreichring, if you have previously seen it on television, is that you realise just how much the cameras flatten out the track. The hill that rises from the pits straight to Hella Licht corner is very steep. The corner is

The fast sweeping curves of the Österreichring in a setting of wooded hills — a combination that makes for exciting viewing in unusually attractive scenery.

blind, the cars bursting over the brow. Originally, this was a fast righthand sweeper, but following the accident in 1975 which led to the death of American F1 driver Mark Donohue, a chicane was built to slow the corner.

From Hella Licht, with its wooden grandstands, from which you can see much of the circuit, the track runs fast along the side of a hill, out of sight of the main bowl, to the sweeping and slightly uphill Dr Tiroch-Kurve. This corner is followed by a steep rise between the trees before the track emerges for the high-speed run across the top of the bowl, through a fast left-handed kink towards the Bosch-Kurve, a remarkable swooping corner, round and down with next to no run-off area. There follows the oddly cambered Texaco Schikane section which appears easy, but which catches out many — most notably the Ligier of Andrea de Cesaris in 1985 which cartwheeled dramatically through the corners, the Italian emerging unscathed — only to be fired by his team boss!

From there the track rises again over another brow and into the long, sweeping Rindt-Kurve, which sweeps down to the start/finish straight. 'The

circuit is one of the nicest in the world,' says local hero Gerhard Berger. 'Of course, it is my home circuit and I have driven here a lot, so I am bound to say that; but you talk to any Formula 1 driver and they will say the same thing. I don't think it is dangerous, and every one of the corners is good.'

The circuit, however, has not been kind to his compatriots. The first Grand Prix there took place in 1970 — Jochen Rindt's year — but the Austrian, despite taking pole position that day, had to give way to the Ferraris of Jacky Ickx and Clay Regazzoni, which raced home to a 1-2 finish. Odd though it may seem, the Österreichring is a Ferrari track, the fans pouring north from Italy to see the races; but they haven't seen a Ferrari victory there since 1970. In 1971 Swiss driver Jo Siffert struggled to keep his BRM ahead as Emerson Fittipaldi's Lotus closed in to finish just a few seconds behind at the flag. The Brazilian returned to win the following year and Ronnie Peterson gave Lotus another victory in 1973.

The Grand Prix of 1975 will be among the Austrian GPs best remembered by Formula 1 fans. There was Donohue's crash in the warm-up and

then, in the rain, chaos and victory to the March of Vittorio Brambilla, who spun off and crashed while acknowledging the chequered flag! A year later there were almost no spectators at all. A few days before the race Niki Lauda was grievously hurt at the Nürburgring and his Ferrari team stayed away from Austria. It was a shame for there was a good race in which John Watson scored his first Formula 1 victory, the only GP win for the Penske team.

The odd winners continued, Alan Jones scoring the Shadow team's sole GP victory in 1977 and Elio de Angelis (Lotus) holding off Keke Rosberg by a whisker to win his first Grand Prix in 1982. At last, iin 1984, an Austrian finally won his home race when Niki Lauda's McLaren outpaced the field. Since Lauda's retirement, Berger has tried to win the race, but he too has had to struggle. After the 1987 event, which had to have two restarts because of accidents, the Fédération Internationale du Sport Automobile (FISA) dropped the race from the calendar. Major improvement work took place in 1988 and the Austrians hope that they will soon have a Grand Prix once again.

Salzburgring

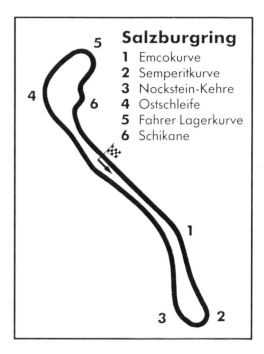

Austria has one other permanent circuit today, the Salzburgring, hidden away in the hills of the Salzkammergut on the road from the beautiful city of Salzburg towards the lakeland and the spa town of Bad Ischl. Better known as a motorcycle track, the circuit once held international Formula 2 races, although in later years it could manage no more than the European Touring Car Championships. It runs down one side of a valley to a hairpin with a return leg higher up the hillside on the opposite side, with a particularly interesting corner above the paddock. The track has little room for expansion and inevitably has slipped from the international scene.

The Salzburgring and Zeltweg are the only tracks still used, although previously there were international races at Innsbruck and at the airfields of Tulln-Langenlebarn and Aspern.

The Salzburgring is hemmed in by the Salzkammergut hills. Here a Rover speeds on the return leg in a European Touring Car race.

BELGIUM Spa-Francorchamps

When racing fans talk of Belgium, it means only one thing — the world-famous Spa-Francorchamps circuits. In its old form and today in a newer, truncated layout, Spa has been and remains one of the greatest road courses of the world — and certainly one of the fastest.

Spa was the idea of Jules de Thier, who mapped out a course on the country roads through the Ardennes hills and forests in 1924. Roughly triangular in shape, the course ran from Francorchamps to Malmédy to Stavelot and back to Francorchamps. Racing was not new to the Ardennes in 1924. The hills had been the home of the Circuit des Ardennes, one of the earliest races held on a closed 'circuit' from 1902, when Briton Charles Jarrot won the first, to 1907, when the courses at both Bastogne and Arlon slipped into history. Until the racing circuit appeared, the reputation of the town of Spa had been based on its natural springs. It was (and still is) a resort, a watering-hole for the rich and famous.

Today the hills around Spa are still full of tourists, pottering about between the grandeur of the buildings of the town, the noise of the fun park by the waterfalls at the nearby Coo, the chilling memorial to the Malmédy massacre or, if they manage to find it, the tiny Spa racing museum in Stavelot. They will drive past the new modern pits and will recognise perhaps that they are on a famous racing track. Down near the Eau Rouge restaurant the road diverts in a sweep to the left — Eau Rouge corner is not a place for everyday traffic. Probably without knowing, they will rejoin the track and, climbing up

through the trees to Les Combes, may be unaware that they are on revered tarmac. There is a reminder at the top of the hill, for off on the right is the new track, with its red and white kerbing, disappearing away through the chicane they call the 'Pif-Paf Malmédy'. Ahead, around the sweeper

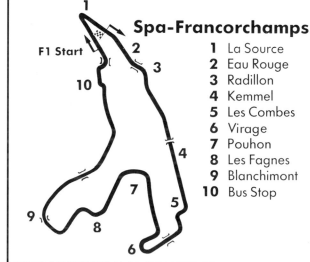

Spa-Francorchamps

F1 Start

1	La Source
2	Eau Rouge
3	Radillon
4	Kemmel
5	Les Combes
6	Virage
7	Pouhon
8	Les Fagnes
9	Blanchimont
10	Bus Stop

Spa-Francorchamps Formula 1

1950	J.M. Fangio (Alfa Romeo)
1951	G. Farina (Alfa Romeo)
1952	A. Ascari (Ferrari)
1953	A. Ascari (Ferrari)
1954	J.M. Fangio (Maserati)
1955	J.M. Fangio (Mercedes)
1956	P. Collins (Ferrari)
1958	T. Brooks (Vanwall)
1960	J. Brabham (Cooper)
1961	P. Hill (Ferrari)
1962	J. Clark (Lotus)
1963	J. Clark (Lotus)
1964	J. Clark (Lotus)
1965	J. Clark (Lotus)
1966	J. Surtees (Ferrari)
1967	D. Gurney (Eagle)
1968	B. McLaren (McLaren)
1970	P. Rodriguez (BRM)
1983	A. Prost (Renault)
1985	A. Senna (Lotus)
1986	N. Mansell (Williams)
1987	A. Prost (McLaren)
1988	A. Senna (McLaren)

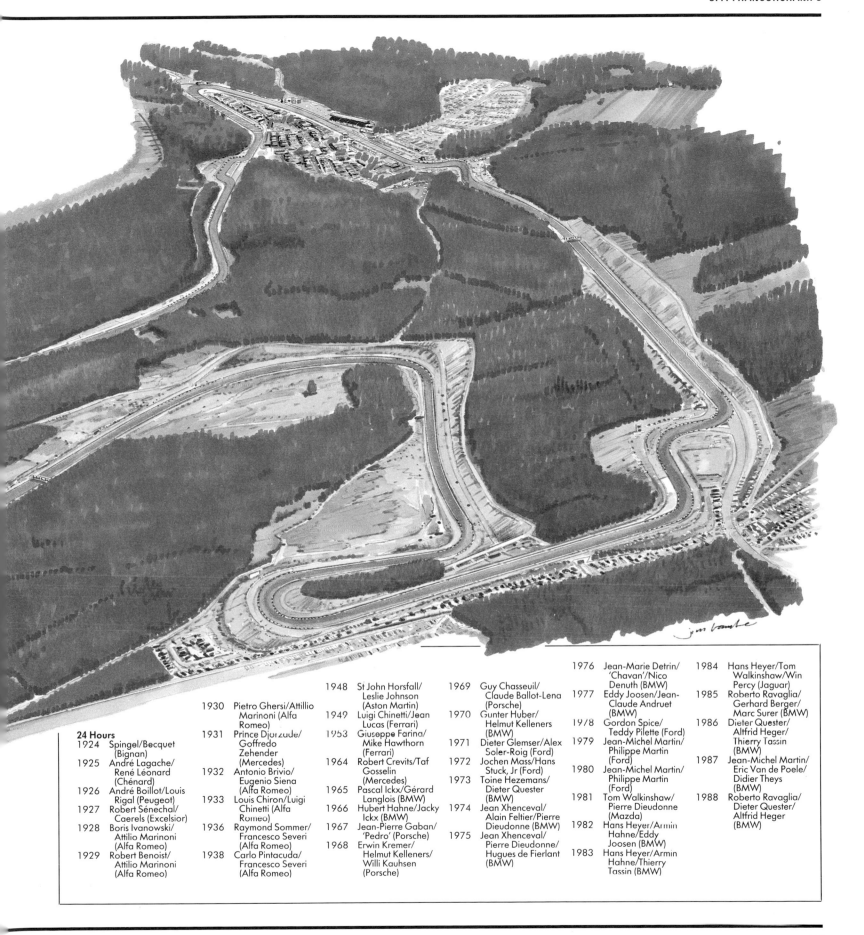

24 Hours

1924	Spingel/Becquet (Bignan)
1925	André Lagache/René Léonard (Chénard)
1926	André Boillot/Louis Rigal (Peugeot)
1927	Robert Sénéchal/Caerels (Excelsior)
1928	Boris Ivanowski/Attilio Marinoni (Alfa Romeo)
1929	Robert Benoist/Attilio Marinoni (Alfa Romeo)
1930	Pietro Ghersi/Attillio Marinoni (Alfa Romeo)
1931	Prince Djorzude/Goffredo Zehender (Mercedes)
1932	Antonio Brivio/Eugenio Siena (Alfa Romeo)
1933	Louis Chiron/Luigi Chinetti (Alfa Romeo)
1936	Raymond Sommer/Francesco Severi (Alfa Romeo)
1938	Carlo Pintacuda/Francesco Severi (Alfa Romeo)
1948	St John Horsfall/Leslie Johnson (Aston Martin)
1949	Luigi Chinetti/Jean Lucas (Ferrari)
1953	Giuseppe Farina/Mike Hawthorn (Ferrari)
1964	Robert Crevits/Taf Gosselin (Mercedes)
1965	Pascal Ickx/Gérard Langlois (BMW)
1966	Hubert Hahne/Jacky Ickx (BMW)
1967	Jean-Pierre Gaban/'Pedro' (Porsche)
1968	Erwin Kremer/Helmut Kelleners/Willi Kauhsen (Porsche)
1969	Guy Chasseuil/Claude Ballot-Lena (Porsche)
1970	Gunter Huber/Helmut Kelleners (BMW)
1971	Dieter Glemser/Alex Soler-Roig (Ford)
1972	Jochen Mass/Hans Stuck, Jr (Ford)
1973	Toine Hezemans/Dieter Quester (BMW)
1974	Jean Xhenceval/Alain Feltier/Pierre Dieudonne (BMW)
1975	Jean Xhenceval/Pierre Dieudonne/Hugues de Fierlant (BMW)
1976	Jean-Marie Detrin/'Chavan'/Nico Denuth (BMW)
1977	Eddy Joosen/Jean-Claude Andruet (BMW)
1978	Gordon Spice/Teddy Pilette (Ford)
1979	Jean-Michel Martin/Philippe Martin (Ford)
1980	Jean-Michel Martin/Philippe Martin (Ford)
1981	Tom Walkinshaw/Pierre Dieudonne (Mazda)
1982	Hans Heyer/Armin Hahne/Eddy Joosen (BMW)
1983	Hans Heyer/Armin Hahne/Thierry Tassin (BMW)
1984	Hans Heyer/Tom Walkinshaw/Win Percy (Jaguar)
1985	Roberto Ravaglia/Gerhard Berger/Marc Surer (BMW)
1986	Dieter Quester/Altfrid Heger/Thierry Tassin (BMW)
1987	Jean-Michel Martin/Eric Van de Poele/Didier Theys (BMW)
1988	Roberto Ravaglia/Dieter Quester/Altfrid Heger (BMW)

The line of one of the most famous corners in racing, Spa's Eau Rouge, has changed little in post-war years, although the track is now lined with safety barriers — and many more advertising hoardings. **Above** Mike Hawthorn in a Cooper-Bristol in the 1952 Belgian GP. **Left** The field setting off in the Spa 24-hour Race, which for many is the high point of the season in saloon-car racing.

that was the old Les Combes corner, is Burnenville, the sweeping downhill section through the village towards Malmédy.

A motorway has been built over the old track at Malmédy, but if you pass the junction, keeping the new motorway to your left, you will find yourself on a long straight piece of road, heading towards the fearsome Masta kink. There is something evil-sounding about the name and, arriving there and threading between the houses, you will realise why this had such a reputation. Ahead now is the slightly banked turn at Stavelot, leading on to the long, fast blast through the trees up towards where the new track rejoins the old and to Blanchimont and the absurd chicane they call 'The Bus Stop'. Suddenly you will be back where you started at La Source hairpin. This is what motor racing was all about. A lap speed of 160mph, danger lurking around every corner, cambers, gradients and houses to dodge. When it was announced that the old track was to be rebuilt because it was too dangerous, the racers feared an artificial track but, remarkably, the new section retained the character of the old, sweeping from

Les Combes down through Rivage to the fast downhill left-hander at Pouhon. 'It is the perfect track,' said Keke Rosberg when it opened.

They used to talk fearfully of Masta and of Burnenville and mentioned Stavelot with slight awe, but the corner to beat them all is Eau Rouge. 'What a corner!' says Formula 1 star Gerhard Berger, 'There is nothing like it. The best in the world, for sure.' Nothing can compare to dusk on the first qualifying day for the annual Spa 24 Hours, as the big touring cars hurtle down the hill past the pits towards Eau Rouge in the twilight, headlights ablaze. The track flicks left, bottoms out and then soars majestically to the right, steeply uphill to the fast left-hander at Raidillon.

There have long been three major races in Spa's calendar: the Grand Prix, the 24 Hours and the 1000 km. For many the 24 Hours is the best event of the year, with an atmosphere which Le Mans can never match. To win at Spa in a touring car is the ultimate single achievement in that form of the sport. The Spa 1000 has become a classic, with Brian Redman a five times winner.

There is history all around the track. At Eau Rouge you stand and remember Stefan Bellof, the World Sportscar Champion of 1984, killed, where the road begins to rise, in the Spa 1000 of 1985. You remember the rain-sodden Formula 2 meeting of 1982 when five cars skated off the track to destruction. When it rains at Spa

Spa night scene: the pits and control buildings, with the view downhill towards Eau Rouge, during the 24-hour Race.

— and it does all the time — a stream runs across the track at the bottom of the hill.

Even the best could not avoid the danger of Spa: Stirling Moss was badly injured away out the back and Jackie Stewart became safety-conscious there. This was the track — and thankfully the only one in the world — on which two drivers were killed in the same Grand Prix; and then during the 24 Hours of 1973, there were three deaths in the night.

'I went back there recently,' remembers Denny Hulme, 'and it was unreal, unbelievable that we ever raced there. I couldn't believe that bit of banking at Stavelot. Sure, it was nice to drive, really high speed; but dangerous, so dangerous. I had a big

lose at Spa one year in the wet. It was raining and I was puttering back to the pits. I knew the leaders were coming, so I parked the car, climbed out and waved, then got back in and drove it a bit further round. I wasn't going to be going slowly on the track with all those lunatics going by in the spray.'

The last Belgian GP on the old circuit at Spa was in 1970. After a year without a race the race alternated between Zolder and an artificial new circuit at Nivelles, political pressure demanding that the Flemish and Walloon territories each be satisfied. Nivelles, close to Brussels, was flat, safe and utterly dull and the Grand Prix teams hated it. It was used just twice for Formula 1 before fading away with financial troubles.

The Ardennes hills make for good viewing at Spa. Here spectators look down to the fast left-hander at Pouhon; in the background is the complex of buildings in the start/finish area on the far side of the circuit.

Zolder

When Nivelles disappeared, Zolder became the home of the Belgian GP, with Jackie Stewart winning the first in 1973. Deep in the Flemish-speaking part of the country, the Omloop Terlamen is near the town of Hasselt, north-west of Liège, and close by the village of Zolder. It is set in a thickly wooded area, dotted with lakes, through which the mighty Albert Canal carves its route. Built in the early 1960s and opened in 1965, the track undulates through pine-covered sand hills. The tall pit building and the steep-sided grandstand opposite create a tunnel of noise, bouncing back and forth. The first major international event, the Limbourg Grand Prix for F2, cars took place in 1966, and was won by Jack Brabham; and Zolder served its apprenticeship before finally getting a chance to stage a Formula 1 race.

Originally it was a sweeping track, but the addition of chicanes has made it less interesting than it once was, and now it is considered hard on both cars and drivers. To them it is dreary, a place of drizzle and mist, with none of

Below Part of the 1981 Belgian GP grid poised for the start at Zolder.

Zolder Formula 1

1973	J. Stewart (Tyrrell)
1975	N. Lauda (Ferrari)
1976	N. Lauda (Ferrari)
1977	G. Nilsson (Lotus)
1978	M. Andretti (Lotus)
1979	J. Scheckter (Ferrari)
1980	D. Pironi (Ligier)
1981	C. Reutemann (Williams)
1982	J. Watson (McLaren)
1984	M. Alboreto (Ferrari)

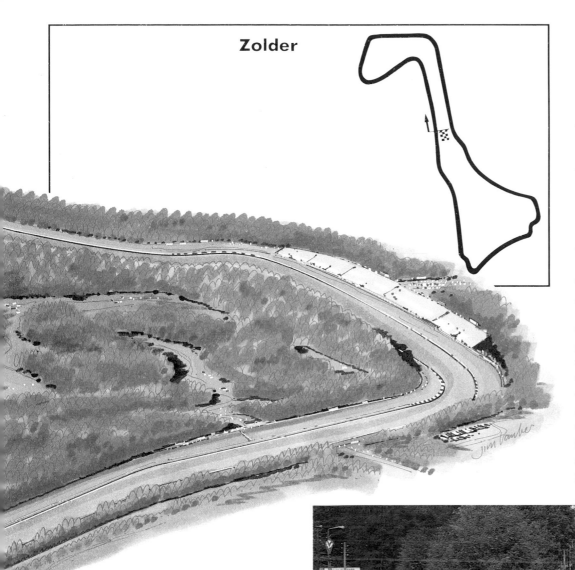

Zolder

the glamour and panache of Spa. In recent years the lack of enthusiasm among the drivers has become an antipathy. 'There's nothing wrong with Zolder that a bulldozer wouldn't fix,' commented Tom Walkinshaw, now Jaguar sportscar team boss, one year. 'They could use it as an artillery range, only the marshals would probably tow the tanks away!'

As a Grand Prix track, Zolder witnessed back-to-back victories for Niki Lauda in 1975-6, Gunnar Nilsson's only F1 victory in 1977 and in 1980 the first victory for a bright young charger called Didier Pironi, who would go on from Ligier to better — and worse — at Ferrari. As Hockenheim will forever be remembered as the track that killed Jim Clark, so to the modern generations Zolder is where Gilles Villeneuve died, hurled from his wildly cartwheeling Ferrari when on a flying lap in qualifying for the 1982 Belgian Grand Prix. By then Pironi was his team-mate. A fortnight before, the two had fallen out during the San Marino GP and Villeneuve had sworn never to talk to Pironi again. There is a

Chicanes had to be introduced at many circuits in the 1980s, invariably to slow cars. Some were laid out sensibly; others gave drivers no option but to file through. This Zolder example, seen in the 1981 GP, allowed cars little opportunity for overtaking.

A Tyrrell negotiates the first chicane at Zolder.

monument to Villeneuve at the top of the pit lane and, at most meetings, if you make your way out to the corner they now call Villeneuve, you will see flowers placed beside the track.

After Villeneuve's death Zolder faded dramatically from the international scene. The rebuilt Spa opened the following year and the Belgian Grand Prix was whisked back to its spiritual home. Zolder went into decline. Major changes were made in 1986 including the new Villeneuve chicane, the reprofiling of many of the corners, extra kerbs and concrete barriers. The plan was to win the Grand Prix back from Spa, but it didn't work, despite the disastrous 1985 race at Spa when the newly laid surface broke up, causing the postponement of the Grand Prix until later in the year — a unique happening in the modern era.

If the Belgian GP has had a disjointed history, the Grand Prix des Frontières at **Chimay** (south of Charleroi) has been one of the most consistent in Europe. Started in 1926, the race had an unbroken run until 1939, restarted immediately after the war and did not miss a year until 1964. In its long history Chimay was disputed by various classes ranging from Formula 1 in 1949 and 1954, to sportscars, Formula Juniors and ultimately Formula 3. The traditional Whitsun event took place on a 6.75-mile track made up of closed public roads. The track, absurdly dangerous for the modern era, was long, fast and had ditches beside the roads! It was a place for heroes and David Purley, one of the bravest of the brave, always excelled there. Chimay fell victim to progress, although the track is still used intermittently for the Belgian Production Car Championship.

There have been several circuits laid out on the streets or in the parks of **Brussels**, but none has endured. One held a Formula 2 Brussels GP in 1949 and another, at Heysel, did similarly 11 years later. Heysel went on to stage a pair of non-championship Formula 1 events under the Brussels GP banner in 1961-2 with Jack Brabham and Willy Mairesse winning. In the 1930s **Antwerp** held a pair of sportscar events and there were various post-war street races for F2 cars at **Mons, Namur** and **Mettet**.

In the late 1960's, looking for other venues, the Belgians turned briefly to the airbase at **Coxyde** in the dunes outside Ostend where, in 1969, Trevor Taylor won an international Formula 5000 event. Across the border in **Luxembourg**, there have also been a number of street races dating back to the first Luxembourg GP in 1939, won by the Bugatti of Jean-Pierre Wimille. After the war the event was held for Formula 2 cars on the Findell street track.

The Brussels Grand Prix was a short-lived non-championship street race on the Heysel circuit. Here Jo Bonnier and Dan Gurney in Porsches lead the 1962 event.

EASTERN EUROPE

Brno

In the hills to the west of Brno, the major city of central Czechoslovakia, is a network of public roads which hold a special place in the history of motor racing. This was the site of the last of the great road-racing tracks of Europe, not as well known as Spa or the Nürburgring, but just as spectacular. The old track has gone now but, on the way from the city to the massive and rather clinical new Automotodrom, you pass the decaying pits of the old circuit. Few westerners saw cars in action on it, but those who did will not forget it.

Returning to Brno, you forget about the new track and, like it or not, find yourself following the old road. The old barriers are getting overgrown and are falling down, but you can still catch the feeling of the place. This was one of the great tracks. It survived longer than the other great road circuits, but in 1986 it had to be closed down. It was terrifyingly fast, with a little bit of everything. This was the place that would attract 150,000 fans from all over the eastern bloc. And they came not for Formula 1 but for

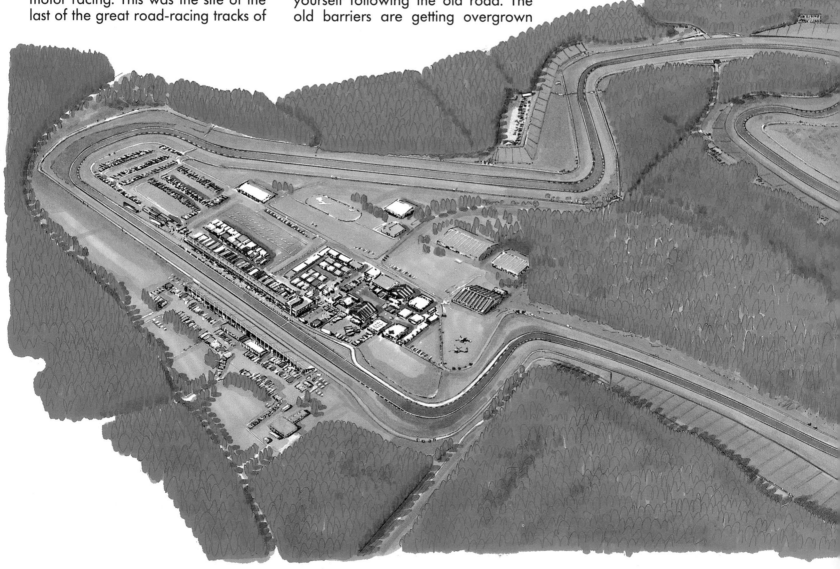

touring cars. Yet this was not the oldest of the Brno tracks. The original was 18 miles in length, including a formidable section of track called the Serpentines of Ostrovacice. It was on this longer track that the Grand Prix men of the 1930s raced in their Mercedes and Auto Unions.

Racing at Brno dates back to the earliest days of the sport. In 1903 the town was a staging post on the Vienna–Breslau race and two years later it was included on the route of the Vienna–Berlin event. With the demise of city-to-city races and the Great War, Brno dropped from the racing scene but in 1923 the locals

introduced 'The Brno Kilometre', a sprint race for cars and bikes, which drew competitors from all over eastern Europe.

In 1930 it was decided to lay out a more permanent road course and with the patronage of Jan Masaryk, son of the country's Liberator and first president, new link roads were built and the circuit was born. The Masaryk ring, as it was then known, quickly gained an international reputation for derring-do and throughout the 1930s was the venue for the Czechoslovakian GP. Many of the great names of the era raced at the track: Nuvolari, Stuck, Varzi, Farina, Seaman, Rosemeyer and Caracciola. In the early years, though, it was Louis Chiron who emerged as the star, winning in 1931-3. After that the big German firms took over. In 1935 the great Bernd Rosemeyer won for Auto Union, his first Grand Prix victory. And in the last pre-war race, in 1937, Caracciola triumphed for Mercedes. But

then came the Second World War and, as it drew to a close, the Soviet army swept through the country, driving out the retreating Germans and by 1945 Czechoslovakia was behind the Iron Curtain.

Competitions went on, but it was not until the 1960s that international racers began to return to Brno. The track had changed, but it was still a daunting place. Initially the young stars of Formula Junior went to entertain the crowds, but it was touring cars which were the biggest draw and, from 1968, Brno became a regular fixture in the European Touring Championship. The speeds achieved were incredible, and changes had to be made, but by 1975 a final layout had been established.

Tom Walkinshaw, like Chiron before him, was the master of Brno, and the car that suited the track best was the Jaguar XJS. Walkinshaw and Chuck Nicholson arrived in 1982 and defeated the massed BMWs to score

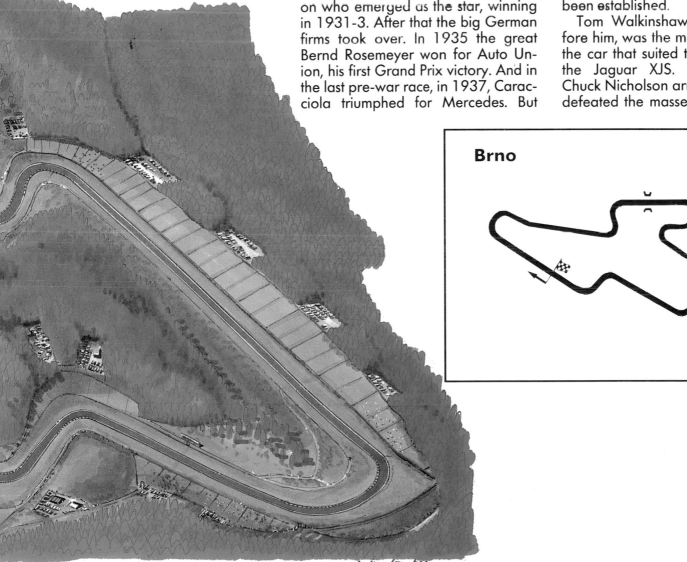

Brno

Left Three XJS Jaguars lead the field in the 1984 Touring Car Championship race at Brno. Just over three and a half hours later this trio came in 1-2-3.

Jaguar's first major international victory of the modern racing era. Twelve months later Tom did it again, and in 1984 he scored his hat-trick with the Big Cats. This time, his team collected a 1-2-3 finish.

Win Percy was a member of the team. 'In the Jaguar XJS,' he remembers, 'that track was just beautiful. Down from the pits on the long bumpy blast to the fast sweepers which led through the village. We used to do them in fourth, scanning the sky as we went in to see if there was any debris flying up there, indicating a crash in the village. Flick into fourth and flat out through left-right, then a tighter left-right. We used to actually rub the front of the cars gently against the barriers. On the way out of the village you couldn't cross the road because the surface was so bad. You had to stay on your line.'

The cars would emerge into open fields, pulling slightly uphill on a piece of road which fell away on either side. Get off line here and the road would take the car from you and deposit you in the corn. A straight brought the cars screaming flat out into the collection of houses — too small to be a village — at Veselka. Here the escape road disappeared straight on for 850

yards, most of which were needed if the cars left the track here. Those who got their braking right had to turn sharply right between two houses. 'That was a tight right and the road was almost banked,' remembers Percy, 'and you would run right out to the house at the exit and then off uphill through these long open sweepers — a ditch on either side.'

A tight righthander into the forest led you through a series of climbing curves which were identical to parts of the old Nürburgring. Then the track burst into a housing estate at Kohoutovice and under the trolley-bus wires into a series of fast downhill sweepers which would not have been out of place at the old Spa. Down the hill the saloon men used to clang the barriers as they dived towards the valley floor and the tight right-handed hairpin leading past the pits. Over $8\frac{1}{2}$ miles in under four minutes!

By the end of 1986, unable to hold back the calls for improved safety, the Czechs had begun work building a new track not far from the famous Serpentines and within the boundaries of the original 1930s circuit. It was designed on a grand scale and was an enormous task: cutting through the forests and moving mountains of earth

Below Old Brno circuit was a throwback to an earlier age of racing, but many of the drivers in the European Touring Car championship races loved the place.

to create a circuit in the hope of retaining the flavour of the old track. But there was more to it than that, because Czechoslovakia wanted a Formula 1 Grand Prix again. Opened in 1987, Brno had one of the best equipped facilities in the world. The drivers, of course, complained that it wasn't like the old Brno. 'Brno,' remembers Gerhard Berger, who raced BMW touring cars there: 'Yeah, that was something else!'

Hungaroring

Hungaroring

current circuit

The only other topline circuit currently in action in the eastern bloc is the Hungaroring, which held its first Formula 1 Grand Prix in 1986. Motor racing in Hungary dates back to the 1936 Budapest GP held on a figure-of-eight circuit, 5 km long, in a park in the centre of the city. It was won by the Alfa Romeo of Tazio Nuvolari. After the war racing was slow to recover and it was only in the early 1960s that Formula Junior races took place at Ferihegy, Budapest's airport. These continued for three years but thereafter racing moved back to a modified version of the 1936 track, where European Touring Car Championship events took place in the mid-1960s.

It was not until 1984 that Hungary had another international race, but this was on a brand new track, built in a natural bowl just off the M3 motorway to the east of Budapest. Designed to give spectators the maximum view-

Below Vast crowds were attracted in 1986 to the first world-championship Grand Prix in an East European country, and most of them enjoyed excellent viewing in the natural bowl of the Hungaroring.

Hungaroring Formula 1
1986   N. Piquet (Williams)
1987   N. Piquet (Williams)
1988   A. Senna (McLaren)

The Hungaroring is a little too sinuous to be genuinely quick, although in 1989 modifications made it faster. Here a Williams-Honda heads a quintet in the 1987 Hungarian Grand Prix.

ing, the Hungaroring has the capacity for enormous crowds and, indeed, the Hungarian GP of 1986 — the first F1 World Championship event to be held behind the Iron Curtain — attracted almost 200,000 people. Though the facilities are good, the track itself offers very few overtaking spots for the modern F1 cars apart from at the first corner, where spectacular braking action can be seen. The original design might have been better, but during construction the workers discovered an underground spring and had to divert the track through the downhill wriggles away from the pits.

There are, however, plans to make the circuit appreciably faster.

In the Eastern bloc there is only one other circuit visited by international racing, at **Most** in Czechoslovakia, where the German Interserie has held races in recent years. There is continued talk of a Soviet Grand Prix in either Moscow or at Tallinn in Estonia. Local races tend to be for saloon cars or for Formula Easter, although in the early 1960s there was a Formula 3 Peace Cup instituted between the Eastern bloc countries which visited such circuits as the East German Sachsenring, Schleizer Dreieck, Halle-

The first European Touring Car championship in 1963 included a street circuit race at Budapest, where tyres were used to mark its line across a city square. The cars seen here are the Mk 2 Jaguars driven by Peter Nocker (that year's champion) and Peter Lindner.

Saale-Schliefe, and Dessau.

Both Poland and Romania held international races in the 1930s, with Hans Stuck Sr and Caracciola winning at the Polish circuit of **Lwów** in 1931 and 1932, while **Bucharest** held a similar event in 1937 and 1939, Stuck winning the latter. Other smaller races have taken place at Poznań and Kraców in Poland, but there has been very little in the modern era.

Elsewhere there are no permanent circuits for car racing. Neither Yugoslavia nor Bulgaria has any real tradition in the sport, although on 3 September 1939, just after the

Second World War broke out, there was a Yugoslav GP on a street circuit in **Belgrade** won by Tazio Nuvolari and in the mid-1960s the European Touring Car Championship made a number of visits to the same city. An international Formula Junior race took place in 1961 at the seaside resort of **Porteroza** with F3 cars returning there five years later, while a similar street track for Formula Juniors was laid out in **Zagreb** in 1962.

In the USSR, racing interest is strong in Estonia, where many of the Formula Easter chassis are built, with races regularly held at Tallinn and Riga.

FRANCE

France was the cradle of motor racing. It was here that the sport was born and nurtured through its early years. Paris was the centre where all the great events of that first era began and it remains the home of the Fédération Internationale du Sport Automobile (FISA), which is housed in offices on the Place de la Concorde.

The very first motor race — or, to be precise, 'reliability trial' — was run from Paris to Rouen in 1894, sponsored by a Paris magazine. In these days of political in-fighting in motor sport, it is nice to be able to report that controversy over the result of a race dates back to the very first. A year later the Automobile Club de France (ACF) was established and in 1895 it organised a trial from Paris to Bordeaux and back again. The era of the great city-to-city races had begun. The Paris races headed off in all directions in the following years, to Marseilles, Amsterdam, Toulouse, Berlin and Vienna. There were countless smaller regional races in the closing years of the century, running from Paris to points around the country: Dieppe, Trouville, St Malo, Arras, Ostend. Increasingly, too, the sport spread to regional events, the Marseilles–Nice and Bordeaux–Biarritz races being the most celebrated.

These were exciting times for the new sport, but with the turn of the century and the increase in international competition a more determined and professional attitude was evident. In this era, it was the French who were the great car builders: Lorraine-Diétrich, Mors, Richard-Brasier, Darracq, Renault, Peugeot, Panhard-Levassor, Turcat-Méry, Gobron-Brillié, Grégoire and Clémont-Bayard all built powerful racing cars. Many of

Left Ferenc Szisz waits in his 12.9-litre Renault at the start line at Pont-de-Gennes, east of Le Mans, before the first-ever Grand Prix in 1906.

Below Public roads were the basis for most French circuits for many years, one of the classics being the Lyon-Givors course used for the 1914 and 1924 French GPs. Here, in 1924, an Alfa Romeo P2 heads a Bugatti T35 down through the series of bends known as the Piège de la Mort (Death Trap).

the top drivers in the 1890s were Frenchmen: Léon Théry, Victor Hémery, Fernand Gabriel, Henri Farman and Fernard Charron were among the most outstanding, and there were numerous others. This was also a time when racing was on a grand scale, with the Tour de France of 1899 and the Circuit de Sud-Ouest and Circuit du Nord taking in huge routes.

Dreaming of a more formalised international competiton, an expatriate American newspaper owner, James Gordon Bennett, introduced the Coupe Internationale in 1900. It

soon became known as the Gordon Bennett Cup, the most sought after prize in Europe. The first Gordon Bennett race was from Paris to Lyons, and Paris–Bordeaux followed. In the 1902 Paris–Vienna race the French were finally toppled, the event being won by Englishman S.F. Edge in a Napier.

City-to-city racing, however, was doomed and the 1903 Paris–Madrid race brought the era to a dramatic close; the event was cancelled by the French government after more than a dozen people — onlookers as well as drivers, of whom most notable was one of the Renault brothers, Marcel — had been killed before the race had even reached Bordeaux. The great city-to-city races were over.

Racing moved to circuits, but now nationalism began to cause problems. The Gordon Bennett rules restricted each national entry to three cars and, not unnaturally, the French — strongest by far in the industry and the sport — wanted greater participation. In 1905 the ACF announced it would not host the Gordon Bennett races again unless the rules were changed. Thus was born the Grand Prix de l'ACF, the first international race using the title 'Grand Prix'. It would become the grandfather of the modern Grand Prix races, in which teams represent manufacturers, not nations. And it killed the Gordon Bennett races. It was fitting that the French should mount the first Grand Prix, but, strangely, to this day the French event has never had a permanent home: it has always been a moveable feast.

Le Mans

The town of Le Mans to the west of Paris was host for the first Grand Prix. This was nothing to do with the Le Mans circuit of today, but an enormous course to the east of the city, laid out on public roads in a triangular shape linking Le Mans with St-Calais and La Ferté-Bernard — 65 miles (105 km) in length. The race was held over two days and 12 laps of the course and was won by Ferenc Szisz, a Franco-Hungarian test engineer at the Renault factory.

Thereafter the Grand Prix was held on similar road courses in Dieppe, Amiens and Lyons-Givors before returning to Le Mans and a new track which had been laid out to the south

of the city. In the period 1921-9 the Le Sarthe course ran into the Pontlieue suburb of Le Mans. And it was on this new circuit that in 1921 Jimmy Murphy became the first American to win a European Grand Prix, overcoming terrible pain from an accident in practice to guide his Duesenberg to victory. In 1929 the French GP returned to Le Mans, with this time the spoils going to William Grover Williams in a Bugatti.

But the international fame of Le Mans was to rest not on the French Grand Prix, but on the Vingt-Quatre Heures du Mans — the Le Mans 24

Above Pontlieue corner at Le Mans in the mid-1920s, with one of the legendary Bentleys. In 1929 this section of the circuit was abandoned, bringing Dunlop Curve, the Esses and Tertre-Rouge into play.

Left Jimmy Murphy in a 3-litre Duesenberg on his way to an all-American victory in the 1921 French GP at Le Mans. The atrocious road surface led to his team-mate Joe Boyer's famous remark that the race had been 'a damn' rock-hewing contest'.

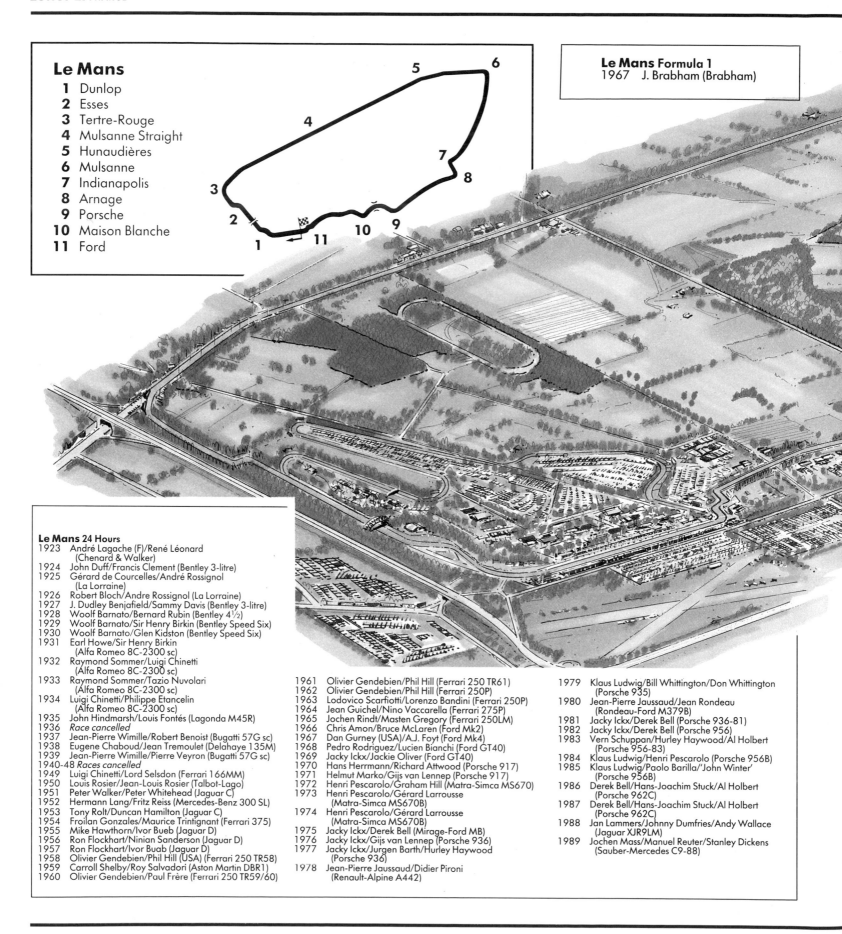

Le Mans

1 Dunlop
2 Esses
3 Tertre-Rouge
4 Mulsanne Straight
5 Hunaudières
6 Mulsanne
7 Indianapolis
8 Arnage
9 Porsche
10 Maison Blanche
11 Ford

Le Mans Formula 1
1967   J. Brabham (Brabham)

Le Mans 24 Hours

1923   André Lagache (F)/René Léonard
            (Chenard & Walker)
1924   John Duff/Francis Clement (Bentley 3-litre)
1925   Gérard de Courcelles/André Rossignol
            (La Lorraine)
1926   Robert Bloch/Andre Rossignol (La Lorraine)
1927   J. Dudley Benjafield/Sammy Davis (Bentley 3-litre)
1928   Woolf Barnato/Bernard Rubin (Bentley 4½)
1929   Woolf Barnato/Sir Henry Birkin (Bentley Speed Six)
1930   Woolf Barnato/Glen Kidston (Bentley Speed Six)
1931   Earl Howe/Sir Henry Birkin
            (Alfa Romeo 8C-2300 sc)
1932   Raymond Sommer/Luigi Chinetti
            (Alfa Romeo 8C-2300 sc)
1933   Raymond Sommer/Tazio Nuvolari
            (Alfa Romeo 8C-2300 sc)
1934   Luigi Chinetti/Philippe Etancelin
            (Alfa Romeo 8C-2300 sc)
1935   John Hindmarsh/Louis Fontés (Lagonda M45R)
1936   *Race cancelled*
1937   Jean-Pierre Wimille/Robert Benoist (Bugatti 57G sc)
1938   Eugene Chaboud/Jean Tremoulet (Delahaye 135M)
1939   Jean-Pierre Wimille/Pierre Veyron (Bugatti 57G sc)
1940-48 *Races cancelled*
1949   Luigi Chinetti/Lord Selsdon (Ferrari 166MM)
1950   Louis Rosier/Jean-Louis Rosier (Talbot-Lago)
1951   Peter Walker/Peter Whitehead (Jaguar C)
1952   Hermann Lang/Fritz Reiss (Mercedes-Benz 300 SL)
1953   Tony Rolt/Duncan Hamilton (Jaguar C)
1954   Froilan Gonzales/Maurice Trintignant (Ferrari 375)
1955   Mike Hawthorn/Ivor Bueb (Jaguar D)
1956   Ron Flockhart/Ninian Sanderson (Jaguar D)
1957   Ron Flockhart/Ivor Buab (Jaguar D)
1958   Olivier Gendebien/Phil Hill (USA) (Ferrari 250 TR58)
1959   Carroll Shelby/Roy Salvadori (Aston Martin DBR1)
1960   Olivier Gendebien/Paul Frère (Ferrari 250 TR59/60)

1961   Olivier Gendebien/Phil Hill (Ferrari 250 TR61)
1962   Olivier Gendebien/Phil Hill (Ferrari 250P)
1963   Lodovico Scarfiotti/Lorenzo Bandini (Ferrari 250P)
1964   Jean Guichel/Nino Vaccarella (Ferrari 275P)
1965   Jochen Rindt/Masten Gregory (Ferrari 250LM)
1966   Chris Amon/Bruce McLaren (Ford Mk2)
1967   Dan Gurney (USA)/A.J. Foyt (Ford Mk4)
1968   Pedro Rodriguez/Lucien Bianchi (Ford GT40)
1969   Jacky Ickx/Jackie Oliver (Ford GT40)
1970   Hans Herrmann/Richard Attwood (Porsche 917)
1971   Helmut Marko/Gijs van Lennep (Porsche 917)
1972   Henri Pescarolo/Graham Hill (Matra-Simca MS670)
1973   Henri Pescarolo/Gérard Larrousse
            (Matra-Simca MS670B)
1974   Henri Pescarolo/Gérard Larrousse
            (Matra-Simca MS670B)
1975   Jacky Ickx/Derek Bell (Mirage-Ford MB)
1976   Jacky Ickx/Gijs van Lennep (Porsche 936)
1977   Jacky Ickx/Jurgen Barth/Hurley Haywood
            (Porsche 936)
1978   Jean-Pierre Jaussaud/Didier Pironi
            (Renault-Alpine A442)

1979   Klaus Ludwig/Bill Whittington/Don Whittington
            (Porsche 935)
1980   Jean-Pierre Jaussaud/Jean Rondeau
            (Rondeau-Ford M379B)
1981   Jacky Ickx/Derek Bell (Porsche 936-81)
1982   Jacky Ickx/Derek Bell (Porsche 956)
1983   Vern Schuppan/Hurley Haywood/Al Holbert
            (Porsche 956-83)
1984   Klaus Ludwig/Henri Pescarolo (Porsche 956B)
1985   Klaus Ludwig/Paolo Barilla/'John Winter'
            (Porsche 956B)
1986   Derek Bell/Hans-Joachim Stuck/Al Holbert
            (Porsche 962C)
1987   Derek Bell/Hans-Joachim Stuck/Al Holbert
            (Porsche 962C)
1988   Jan Lammers/Johnny Dumfries/Andy Wallace
            (Jaguar XJR9LM)
1989   Jochen Mass/Manuel Reuter/Stanley Dickens
            (Sauber-Mercedes C9-88)

Hours — first held in 1923. The Le Mans circuit did not take on its modern shape until 1929, and small changes have been made over the years as, for the most part, these are still public roads. Today, there is a chicane in the Dunlop Curve, the sweeper that leads away from the pit straight. This new section is a minefield of hidden apexes, particularly tricky in the dark. Under the Dunlop Bridge the track rushes downhill to the Esses and on to the sharp right-hander at Tertre Rouge, where the drivers drift their cars right out to the barriers to get maximum speed on to the long Mulsanne Straight. Flashing past houses and the famous café, the cars reach speeds of up to 250mph as they rush between the pine trees. The Mulsanne was resurfaced for 1988 because the bumps caused by everyday traffic on Route Nationale 138 had made it dangerous to switch from one 'groove' to another. Here the faster cars have to be wary of backmarkers,

for the differences in speed between the cars is startling.

Ahead is the infamous Kink — a flat out corner taken at 200mph! Then it's over the brow and braking like mad for Mulsanne Corner. Passing the signalling pits the cars accelerate again through the three kinks up to the tight lefthander at Indianapolis and the swiftly following righthander at Arnage before the sweeping Porsche Curves to Maison Blanche. Ahead lie the Ford Curves and the pits once again — a lap of eight and a half miles in three and a half minutes — which is repeated for 24 long hours.

The Vingt-Quatre Heures has a unique atmosphere. Like many of the world's great races it is much more than a competition between cars, having become a week-long carnival attended by thousands of spectators from all across Europe. Race day, when finally you get there, seems to drag on forever. Most people have spent the day wandering around wait-

The pits straight at Le Mans looks ridiculously narrow as drivers line up for the first post-war race, in 1949. Five French cars head the line-up, which was in capacity order; the Hay-Wisdom streamlined Bentley is nearest the camera.

ing for the off and the crowds are massed along the pit straight, every available viewing spot taken up. At these moments, Le Mans is magical: the constant noise, and jostling of the crowds and then, finally, at the traditional start hour of 4pm, the race is on. The traditional Le Mans start, where drivers used to run across the track to their cars, was banned after 1969, but the excitement is still electrifying as the ranks of powerful, streamlined machines roar away in a rolling start towards the first corner.

It isn't long before dusk falls and the drivers have to negotiate the course in the most difficult half-light. Many thousands of visitors choose to camp in the vicinity, to watch the race from the grandstands, pausing to stroll around the fairground or to visit the hair-raising Mulsanne Straight, where the headlights probe the darkness and spectators' faces are momentarily lit up as they strain to identify the cars. Le

Mans at night is a thrilling laser show of lights and noise. In the darkness, the roads all around the track are packed with people wandering from one viewing spot to another. The hot aroma of barbecues mingles with the petrol fumes hanging in the air. By this stage of the race, the fairground is in full swing, with its music, bright lights, fat ladies, snake charmers, walls of death and all the rest.

As the race passes midnight, the paddock clears, many fans disappearing to sleep off the evening's excesses. But on and on the titanic struggle of men and machines continues. Although the race is held in midsummer the night can get cold and dawn is greeted by the enticing scent of warm croissants and strong coffee in the air. Then the crowds begin to drift back; and after lunch, fighting off the fatigue, you enter the final hours, waiting for the exultant scenes as the winning car crosses the line and the

track is promptly invaded by the fans.

Not everyone enjoys Le Mans, and some drivers refuse to indulge in dicing on the Mulsanne Straight, dodging slower cars and sitting on the rev limiter, travelling at maximum speed for too long.... 'If something breaks,' says French sportscar ace Jean-Louis Schlesser, one man who refuses to race there, 'there is nothing you can do about it. You have no control at speeds like that.'

Le Mans has had many victims and it was here in 1955 that the sport suffered its greatest disaster when Pierre Levegh's Mercedes 300SLR hit an Austin-Healey on its 42nd lap and flew into the crowd, killing the driver and 83 spectators, with more than 100 being injured. Across the world races were cancelled and racing was banned in several countries, notably in Switzerland, where the sport has never been re-established. Mercedes withdrew from competition as a result

of this terrible accident, and it was not until 1988 that the company returned in an official capacity.

The race has always had a British flavour to it, dating back to the 1920s when the Bentley Boys won four 24 Hours in a row, Woolf Barnato (who had bought the Bentley company) establishing a record that is unlikely ever to be beaten – three wins in his three starts as a driver. It was at Le Mans in 1933 that Tazio Nuvolari in the superlative Alfa Romeo 8C-2300 won his only start in the race, beating Luigi Chinetti in a similar car by just under a quarter of a mile.

After a break during and immediately following the war, the race returned in 1949 and has run uninterrupted ever since. In the 1952 race there was heartbreak for Pierre Levegh who, having driven single-handed, had a four-lap lead, only to see his car break down just two hours from the flag. The 1950s saw the emergence of the Jaguar C-Type (winner in 1951-3). Victory in the 1954 race went to the Ferrari 375 of Froilan Gonzalez and Maurice Trintignant by a mere 90 seconds over the chasing Jaguar D-Type of Tony Rolt and Duncan Hamilton. Jaguar's success continued until 1957, but the following year Phil Hill and Olivier Gendebien signalled the beginning of a Ferrari era, scoring the first of three victories together.

By 1964 the Ford GT40 had arrived to take on Ferrari and two years later Henry Ford II was present to see Chris Amon and Bruce McLaren head a stage-managed finish for the company, with team-mates Ken Miles and Denny Hulme in the winning car's slipstream. First home in 1967 was the all-American pairing of Indy ace A.J. Foyt and Dan Gurney. Two years later Jacky Ickx won his first race (sharing his GT40 with Jackie Oliver), with a winning margin of just 230 yards. The 1971 race was the fastest ever, before alterations to the circuit at Arnage slowed the lap times, with Gijs Van Lennep and Helmut Marko averaging 138mph in their Porsche 917.

The French came on song in the 1970s with Matra, Renault and (in 1980) Rondeau winning the race, but after that there was total Porsche domination until the return of Jaguar as a serious threat in 1985. This was the era of Jacky Ickx and Derek Bell, the Belgian gaining six victories and the Englishman five. Perhaps the greatest race of the modern era was in 1988 with Porsche and Jaguar head to head for the full 24 hours, and emotional scenes when Jaguar returned to the victory podium. 'I couldn't bear to watch,' commented Jaguar boss Sir John Egan after the 1988 race. 'I had to go away for a while, the tension was so great.' Like it or not, Le Mans remains one of the great road races to this day.

Far Left Daunting conditions for really high-speed motoring: spray from the rainy track hangs in the air as the cars brake hard at Mulsanne Corner. The high safety barriers became mandatory after shortcomings had been tragically demonstrated.

Near Left Headlights bleach the trees at Tertre-Rouge, where the circuit curves right onto the Mulsanne straight.

Above The towering main grandstand before the Dunlop Curve is a Le Mans landmark. The spectator enclosures are packed through the first phase of the 24-hour race.

Montlhéry

Road racing has been the backbone of the sport in France and there have been tracks laid out all over the country. In the 1920s there were major events at **Boulogne**, which held a Speedweek annually in 1921-8; **St-Germain**, home of the Bol d'Or, in 1922-37 and **Lille**, organised the Circuit des Routes Pavées throughout the 1920s until an accident in 1931 killed a spectator and the race faded away. In the mid-1920s, however, came the first purpose-built autodromes, ushering in the next chapter in French motor racing.

By the mid-1920s, following the trend set by Brooklands and Indianapolis, the French had embarked on the construction of permanent circuits with the great speedways of Montlhéry in the north and Miramas in the south. Situated beside the N20 on the south-

Above The start of the Bol d'Or at St-Germain, Paris, in 1931. For small-capacity cars only, it was inaugurated in 1922 – the first 24-hour race in Europe.

ern outskirts of Paris, Montlhéry autodrome was built in 1924 on land purchased specifically for the purpose by Alexandre Lamblin. The track, designed by Raymond Jamin, featured a banked oval *piste de vitesse* attached to an L-shaped road course running westward into the surrounding wooded countryside. There were six possible circuit layouts, the longest being 7.7 in length. Montlhéry soon became an important venue and was

Montlhéry

1 Piste-de-Vitesse
2 Deux Ponts
3 Quatre Bornes
4 Lacets de Couard
5 Bruyères
6 Le Biscornes
7 V. de la Forêt
8 V. du Gendarme
9 Faye

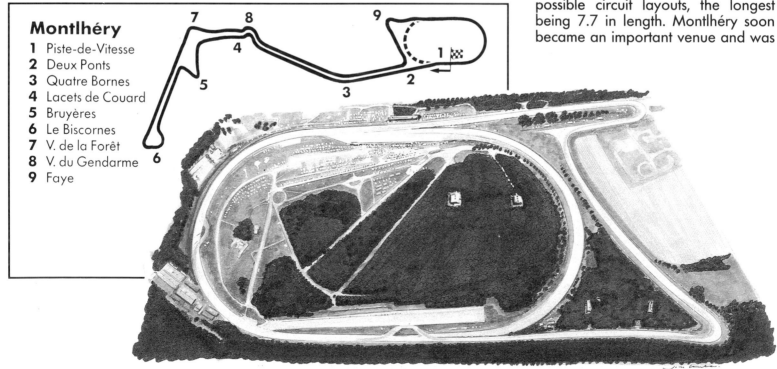

host to the French Grand Prix of 1925 won by Robert Benoist and Alberto Divo in a Delage. Interestingly the accompanying 1500cc event, won by George Duller in a Talbot, saw the unusual situation of the second-placed driver, Conelli, crossing the line upside down!

Throughout the 1930s Montlhéry was the centre of French racing, the site of numerous speed-record attempts and major races of all forms, including the French Grand Prix in 1931 and from 1933-7. After the war the circuit retained its importance and although the French Grand Prix did not return, Montlhéry became the home of the Paris GP Formula 1 races, the Bol d'Or, the Coupe de Paris and the Coupe de Salon, not to mention major sportscar events such as the Paris 12 Hours and the Paris 1000.

Unfortunately a serious accident in 1964, which left two drivers and three officials dead, sent the track into decline at a time when new permanent facilities were being built elsewhere. Despite decaying badly in the late-1960s, however, Montlhéry is used to this day as a venue for national championship meetings. And the old banking was still in use in the late 1980s, giving the Formula 3 youngsters an insight into what their predecessors had to handle.

Above Faye corner at Montlhéry during the 1933 GP with Alfa Romeo Type B drivers Etancelin and Taruffi heading towards the banked Piste de Vitesse.

Left End of an era. The stands at Montlhéry are packed as Louis Chiron leads the 1934 French GP in an Alfa-Type B; but the Mercedes Benz W25 behind him is a forerunner of a new order in racing.

Miramas

Built on the flat plains in the northwest of Marseilles in the same year as Montlhéry, Miramas was the dream of former racer Paul Bablot. The history of Miramas is less celebrated than its northern counterpart; yet it too was the site of a French GP, in 1926, when just two cars finished,

veteran Jules Goux winning for Bugatti.

Although the French GP never returned to Miramas, the Grand Prix de Provence, which started in 1925, was held there four times, victory twice going to Henry Segrave in a Talbot. Later still, the Marseilles Grand Prix of 1932 saw Raymond Sommer defeat Tazio Nuvolari, with a talented Algerian, Guy Moll, third in his first European event. Chicanes were added to the track to slow the racing and the autodrome at Miramas quietly declined, although it continued to be

used for record attempts and, still standing today, is now a major test facility.

While the two autodromes were in their heyday, other public road courses continued to come and go. Most are now long gone: **Péronne**, the home of the Grand Prix of Picardy; the **St-Gaudens** circuit at Comminges in the Garonne valley, close to the Spanish border; **La Baule** in Britanny, **Dieppe, Boulogne, Troyes, Nimes** and many other names evoking echoes of the old days.

Reims

The most famous of the road tracks of the 1920s — and one of the most enduring — was built near Gueux, about 6 miles (9.5 km) west of Reims in the Champagne region. First used in 1925, the circuit was initially the home of the Grand Prix de la Marne. It boasted a straight to rival the Mulsanne, where slipstreaming was all-important. In 1932 Reims was chosen to host the French Grand Prix, which turned out to be an Alfa Romeo benefit won by Nuvolari, chased home by Baconin Borzacchini and Rudolf Caracciola.

The race was held at Montlhéry until 1938, when Reims once again took over, Manfred von Brauchitsch winning for Mercedes. 1939 was to see an Auto Union victory at Riems before war broke out and once more racing ceased. After the war Reims returned to play host to French Grands Prix throughout the 1950s and 1960s until financial and political difficulties and competition from other circuits finally closed the track in 1970.

The Grand Circuit de Compétition de Reims, just to the west of the city, was one of the classic circuits of Europe, and often the fastest. **Right** Three Ferrari 156s lead the 1961 French GP field away, with the long straight from Thillois behind them. **Below** Out of Muizon and onto N31, this 1966 Grand Prix pair heads south-east towards the slight kink at Garenne and the straight drop down towards Thillois — and there is not a spectator in sight!

Monaco

At the same time as Reims was becoming established in the late 1920s, a cigarette manufacturer, Antony Noghes, who lived in Monte Carlo, came up with the idea of staging a race on the streets of the principality. As President of the Automobile Club de Monaco and a personal friend of Prince Louis II, Noghes had enough influence to realise his dream, and in 1929 the first Monaco Grand Prix took place

Overlooked by the Grimaldi castle, the race around the harbour of Monaco has become the epitome of motor racing glamour, situated as it is in a summer playground of Europe's mega rich. It's a crazy, round-the-houses affair, a unique survivor of racing from another era and — today few of the drivers relish the event. It is dangerous — the cars are too fast for the track and the pits are crude and cramped — but for the sport and its sponsors, this is the big one. Monaco is about being seen with the right people — that is, the aristocrats or the seriously rich — on the right yacht with the right sunglasses or with the right royal princess in tow. Everything is ridiculously overpriced to cater for the heavy wallets who have flown or sailed in. The pits are crammed with people who should not be there.

It was not always like that. The first event was won by the French-based Bugatti-driving Englishman William Grover Williams who would die a resistance hero in the Second World War. Since then Monaco has changed almost beyond recognition and every year sees yet more cranes against the skyline as yet more hotels and apartment blocks spring up. The track, too, has changed, and now retains only parts of the original. The entire waterfront section from Tabac

Left Monaco, 1931: four Bugattis approach Tabac corner along the Quai des Etats-Unis, with the chicane in the background.

Above Monaco, 1933: one of the great duels of racing history. Varzi (Bugatti) leads Nuvolari (Alfa Romeo) through Station (now Loews) hairpin.

Below Monaco, 1988: the climb up to Casino Square, as a marshal warns back-marker Yannick Dalmas of a faster car (Benetton) behind him.

Corner to Gasworks was altered with the construction of the Swimming Pool; the tunnel has changed; and, in an effort to slow the cars, the corner at Ste-Dévote was turned into a chicane. More recently, along the waterfront the chicane grew to be too fast for the modern machines. In these safety-conscious times it is alarming to see the terrifying potential for speed in the F1 car being smothered as it crawls round the hairpins. But somehow Monaco survives each passing year without the long-forecast disaster. It is unlikely that it can continue forever, but no one seems to heed the warning signs.

Monaco has seen any number of great races, for it is a track that will occasionally submit to genius. Achille Varzi and Nuvolari fought two of Monaco's greatest ever duels in 1932 and 1933. On both occasions the two switched positions with almost every lap. In 1932 Varzi suffered engine failure just after half-way. The following year they diced to the bitter end until Nuvolari's Alfa blew up and he was disqualified trying to push the smoking wreck to the finish. A year later the meteoric career of Guy Moll reached its zenith with victory on the streets of the principality; yet within a few months he was dead, leaving Alfa team boss Enzo Ferrari to mourn the loss of the man who might have been the greatest, had he lived.

Monaco has seen tragedy. Louis Fagioli died from injuries he received in a crash in the tunnel in 1952. He was 54 years old. Lorenzo Bandini died from dreadful burns after a crash at the chicane in 1967. Others were luckier. Both Alberto Ascari in 1955 and 10 years later Paul Hawkins ended up driving off the road and into the harbour, but were able to swim to safety. Derek Daly found his Tyrrell launched skyward, above the field, at Ste-Dévote in 1980, then crashing down on to his team-mate Jean-Pierre Jarier's car. Neither was hurt. In the Formula 3 race of 1984 John Nielsen was lucky to survive a huge accident in the chicane which left him with a shattered hip.

Monaco is a track where a little luck does not come amiss. Yet is is also a track where the 'impossible' can happen. Stirling Moss achieved that in 1961, outpacing the mighty Ferrari in his ageing Lotus 18. Jean-Pierre Beltoise was untouchable in the wet in 1972 — yet he never won another Grand Prix. A decade later Riccardo Patrese scored his first Grand Prix victory in a race that no one seemed able to win: Prost crashed, Patrese spun, Pironi and De Cesaris ran out of fuel, Daly crashed. Patrese, cursing his spin, was given a push start and crossed the line without even knowing that he had won. Those who saw the race in 1984 will never forget Prost, Senna and particularly the young Stefan Bellof in the pouring rain.

Some drivers seem to have an affinity for the circuit. Graham Hill won five times in seven starts (and came second and third in the other

two), Alain Prost has four victories, Stirling Moss and Jackie Stewart three apiece, and Juan-Manuel Fangio and Niki Lauda two each. But what of Jim Clark? That great driver had the artistry but had no luck here.

Today Monaco is not really a race. Qualify badly and you have no chance, for overtaking is practically impossible. But, in the best tradition of show business, the show must go on.

Above There's little room for error in the tight 1967 version of the chicane. Down the years this has been located at different points, and recently has been eased. Only two GP cars have ever plunged into the harbour.

Monaco

1 Virage Ste-Dévote
2 Virage Massenet
3 Virage Casino
4 Virage Mirabeau
5 Virage Anc. Gare
6 Virage du Portier
7 Tunnel
8 Chicane
9 Virage du Tabac
10 Virage la Rascasse
11 Virage Antony Noghes

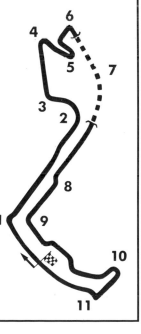

Monaco Formula 1

1950	J.M. Fangio (Alfa Romeo)	1973	J. Stewart (Tyrrell)
1955	M. Trintignant (Ferrari)	1974	R. Peterson (Lotus)
1956	S. Moss (Maserati)	1975	N. Lauda (Ferrari)
1957	J.M. Fangio (Maserati)	1976	N. Lauda (Ferrari)
1958	M. Trintignant (Cooper)	1977	J. Scheckter (Wolf)
1959	J. Brabham (Cooper)	1978	P. Depailler (Tyrrell)
1960	S. Moss (Lotus)	1979	J. Scheckter (Ferrari)
1961	S. Moss (Lotus)	1980	C. Reutemann (Williams)
1962	B. McLaren (Cooper)	1981	G. Villeneuve (Ferrari)
1963	G. Hill (BRM)	1982	R. Patrese (Brabham)
1964	G. Hill (BRM)	1983	K. Rosberg (Williams)
1965	G. Hill (BRM)	1984	A. Prost (McLaren)
1966	J. Stewart (BRM)	1985	A. Prost (McLaren)
1967	D. Hulme (Brabham)	1986	A. Prost (McLaren)
1968	G. Hill (Lotus)	1987	A. Senna (Lotus)
1969	G. Hill (Lotus)	1988	A. Prost (McLaren)
1970	J. Rindt (Lotus)	1989	A. Senna (McLaren)
1971	J. Stewart (Tyrrell)		
1972	J.P. Beltoise (BRM)		

Pau

Pau was the second of the classic French street tracks of the modern era. Hidden away in the foothills of the Pyrenees, west of Lourdes and Tarbes, Pau was the home of the first ever race to bear the name 'Grand Prix', a local affair in 1901 won by Maurice Farman in a Panhard. It was not until 1930 that Pau emerged as an international event, hosting the French Grand Prix on a 9.86-mile triangle on public roads to the east of the town.

Three years later the first of the true Pau GPs took place, on the streets of the charming Gascon town itself. The race quickly became a regular feature in the international calendar, traditionally being held a week after Monaco. The first Pau GP proved to be an extraordinary affair won in a snow storm by Algerian Marcel Lehoux ahead of his North African compatriot Guy Moll, neither entirely familiar with such conditions.

Today the hay bales have been replaced by safety barriers, but little has changed since its earliest days and it remains an awe-inspiring spectacle. Pau is now the blue riband of Formula 3000, an event where instinct and raw skill count for much, as the drivers thread their cars between the walls at alarming speeds,

Right Fast downhill curves leading to the station at the lowest point on the Pau circuit.

Below The ever-enthusiastic Gascon crowd watches F3000 drivers start on the climb up from the station in a 1988 race.

Below right Stefano Modena swings an F3000 Reynard round a familiar feature at Pau.

watched by a large and enthusiastic Gascon crowd. The venue is splendid, offering the finest foods and wines, and the atmosphere is relaxed. This is a driver's circuit, make no mistake, and the list of past winners is indeed impressive: four victories for Jim Clark; three apiece for Jean Behra, Maurice Trintignant and Jochen Rindt; with two each for Juan-Manuel Fangio, Alberto Ascari and Jack Brabham.

Past the pits is a fast downhill section into the station hairpin, from where the track winds uphill, under the Pont Oscar and up to the hairpin at Virage du Lycée. Ahead is the sweeping Park Beaumont section, a series of high-speed lefts and rights which provide spectators with the most hair-raising action, and the drivers with the oppor-

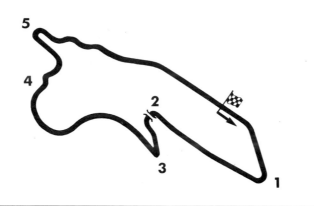

Pau

1 Station
2 Pont-Oscar
3 School
4 Foch
5 Buisson

Albi

tunity to scare themselves stupid. Then comes the helter-skelter downhill section, through the hairpin at Virage du Buisson and back to the pits.

There have been some ferocious accidents and some amazing races, not least a terrific battle in the rain in 1983 when Alain Ferté and Jo Gart-

Below Pau 1988: street racing in the traditional manner, with old tyres and armco at the edge of the narrow thoroughfare.

ner disputed the lead right to the line, Ferté minus the nosebox of his Maurer. Behind them Stefan Bellof charged through to finish third despite three pit stops! Ferté and Bellof were both later disqualified but it mattered little for each had proved his talent for all to see.

Pau survives as a spectacular reminder of racing of days long gone and it is popular with everyone who visits. Undoubtedly, there will come a time when racing can no longer use the streets but until that day Pau will remain one of the greatest tests for man and machine.

Another survivor from the pre-war era, albeit in name only, is Albi, about 50 miles north-east of Toulouse, held its first race in 1934 on the fast tree-lined Les Planques circuit beside the River Tarn. The triangular 5.52-mile track staged voiturette races throughout the 1930s and, revived after the war, was a regular location for non-championsip Formula 1 races until 1955.

After the Le Mans disaster there was a backlash against motor racing; tracks were scrutinised for safety and Albi did not past muster. It had to change and in 1959 the Albi Grand Prix was run again on a narrow track around an airstrip on the western outskirts of the town. Formula Junior was a regular visitor in 1959-63, when Formula 3 took over. The track was suggested as a possible venue for the 1970 French GP, but it never happened; and after a series of European F2 races in the early 1970s, the track returned to Formula 3, staging an annual round of the French national championship.

The facilities are basic, but the track features a superb fast sweeping corner on to the back straight. It seems, however, that Albi will never regain its former status.

If Albi was the last of the surviving tracks from the 1930s, the immediately post-war era — as had happened after the First World War — provided a host of new venues as racing re-established itself wherever it could. The first major post-war race took place on 9 September 1945 in the Bois-de-Boulogne in **Paris** where Jean-Pierre Wimille triumphed in a Bugatti. There seemed to be a thirst for the excitement of racing, and there were street races in **Strasbourg, Marseilles, St-Germain,** and

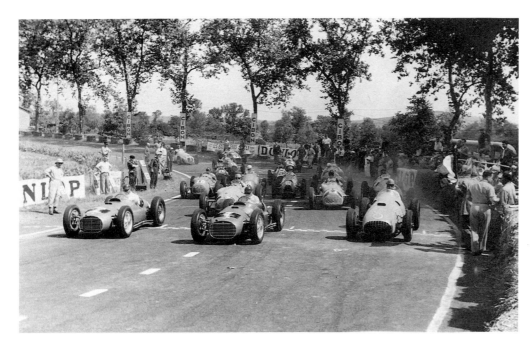

Left Tree-lined roads made up the fast Albi circuit, and Argentinians Fangio and Gonzalez were brave men to race V-16 BRMs on this circuit — but here they head the grid for the 1952 Grand Prix.

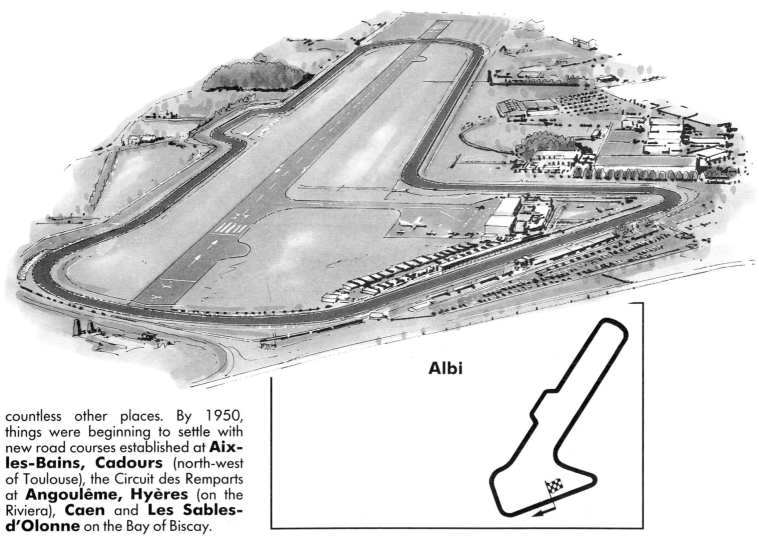

Albi

countless other places. By 1950, things were beginning to settle with new road courses established at **Aix-les-Bains, Cadours** (north-west of Toulouse), the Circuit des Remparts at **Angoulême, Hyères** (on the Riviera), **Caen** and **Les Sables-d'Olonne** on the Bay of Biscay.

Rouen

The outcry after the 1955 Le Mans disaster put paid to many circuits in France, but a few survived, notably Rouen-Les Essarts in Normandy. Les Essarts, which dives through wooded hillsides to the west of the city on the Seine, was devised in 1950 by the AC Normand and staged an F1 race in 1951 and the French Grand Prix the following year. The circuit featured a cobbled hairpin called Nouveau Monde at the bottom of its hair-raising downhill sweeping section.

'Jeez, that was fast,' recalls Denny Hulme. 'We used to listen to the Formula 1 guns going down there to see if they could hold it flat down the hill.'

After the initial French Grand Prix, the race was staged at Reims until 1957, by which time the Rouen circuit had been altered and extended from its original 3.16 miles to 4.06 miles.

Rouen Formula 1		
1952	A. Ascari	(Ferrari)
1957	J.M. Fangio	(Maserati)
1962	D. Gurney	(Porsche)
1964	D. Gurney	(Brabham)
1968	J. Ickx	(Ferrari)

Above Main grandstand facing the pits at Rouen, where banks on the edge of the woods around the circuit made natural spectator areas.

Rouen

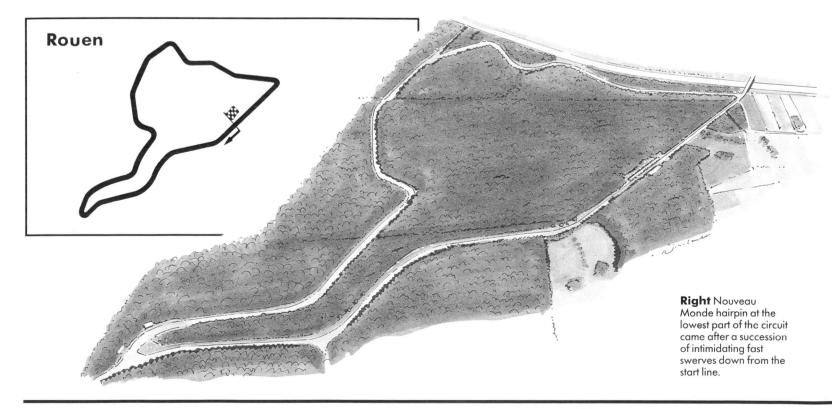

Right Nouveau Monde hairpin at the lowest part of the circuit came after a succession of intimidating fast swerves down from the start line.

That day in 1957 saw one of Juan-Manuel Fangio's greatest victories, and his four-wheel drifts through the downhill sweepers are still talked about with awe by those who saw it.

Reims, however, was still the dominant circuit and the Grand Prix did not return to Rouen until 1962, when Dan Gurney scored his first Grand Prix victory in the air-cooled Porsche. Two years later Gurney proved himself a Rouen specialist when he did it again in a Brabham, scoring his second GP win!

Although Reims' star was now waning, Rouen's claim to the national Grand Prix was challenged in the next few years by both the new Clermont-Ferrand and Le Mans (on the new purpose-built Bugatti circuit, which included sections of the famous Sarthe

track). Thus is was not until 1968 that the French GP returned to Rouen. It was to prove disastrous. In pouring rain, Jo Schlesser crashed his brand-new Honda on the sweepers and perished in the fire that followed. The F1 teams packed up that night, never to return to Rouen.

After a Formula 3 race in 1970 claimed two lives, chicanes were installed — but Rouen was living on borrowed time. Major changes were made when a new motorway was built through the area, but the F2 races continued and inevitably there was more tragedy, Gerry Birrell being killed in the sweepers in 1973. A new chicane was installed at the spot and F2 visits continued until 1978, before this track for the bravest of the brave slipped to national Formula 3 status.

Charade

Rouen suffered in that it emerged at the same time as another track in the same mould – the Louis Rosier circuit at Charade, Clermont-Ferrand. Incredibly the idea of a circuit in the hills of the Auvergne had been looked at as early as 1908, but it wasn't until July 1958 that this became a reality. The result was an up and down track, winding without a discernible piece of straight, twisting around the volcanic outcrops of the Puy de Charade and Puy de Gravenoire on the town's western outskirts.

It was a particular favourite of Denny Hulme. 'I loved that place,' he remembers, 'and it was always very kind to me. A lot of people used to wear open-faced helmets there so they could throw up as they went down the hills, left-right-left-right. I found that the best way was to hold your breath!'

The annual Trophées d'Auvergne event was run for a variety of formulae before the circuit was awarded the French GP in 1965, when Clark won in a Lotus. Four years later the race was back in the Auvergne. Charade had arrived at the wrong time, for in 1971 the most complete racing facility in the world at the time was opened at the Paul Ricard circuit near Toulon, and another new track at Dijon was also demanding the Grand Prix. Charade lost the Grand Prix, but continued to host races for the Trophées d'Auvergne. It closed finally in 1988, with plans to build a shortened version. Ironically, away to the north at Rouen, similar plans for a new circuit at Mauquenchy were being laid.

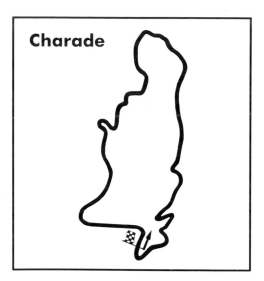

Charade Formula 1
1965   J. Clark (Lotus)
1969   J. Stewart (Matra)
1970   J. Rindt (Lotus)
1972   J. Stewart (Tyrrell)

Charade

The Charade circuit was made up of local roads and linking stretches around two Auvergne hills, and the only straight of any length was a one-kilometre climb just after the start.

Other French Circuits

The new generation of French circuits in the 1960s included all the tracks which are today the regular venues for the thriving French national racing scene. There are Albi, Magny-Cours, Nogaro, the Bugatti track at Le Mans, and the tiny La Châtre circuit near Châteauroux.

The Circuit Jean Behra at **Magny-Cours** is perhaps most famous as the home of the Winfield Racing School, the kindergarten for an entire generation of French Formula 1 stars of the 1970s. Near Nevers, on the Loire, Magny-Cours was for years a ramshackle place which held occasional races and used as a base by several top teams and manufacturers (notably Automobiles Martini). It was a working circuit. In 1988, however, in the hope of wresting the French GP away from Paul Ricard, major rebuilding work was completed, with a new industrial park built beside the track into which the Ligier F1 team quickly moved. The sinuous new track at Magny-Cours with a variety of layouts will probably be the the home of the French Grand Prix in the 1990s.

Nogaro lies deep in the Armagnac region, about 50 miles north of Lourdes; the track is on the northern outskirts of the small, sleepy Gascon town. Circuit Paul Armagnac, as it is known, is a curious mish-mash of tight corners and high-speed straights, a mixture which forces compromise in the set-up of cars. As an international venue it staged European Formula 2 events in the mid-1970s before slipping to European F3. When that series was cancelled in 1984, the circuit's major event became a round of the European Touring Car Championship. As at Magny-Cours, Nogaro has a celebrated racing school — the École Motul Nogaro.

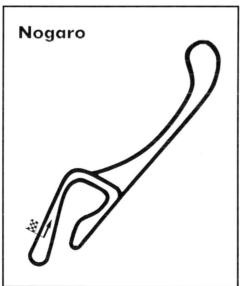

Nogaro

Le Mans Bugatti is the home of the École ACO/Gitanes and, after its unsuccessful French Grand Prix of 1967, there was little international racing at the track until Formula 3000 first visited in 1987. **La Châtre** was and still is a semi-road track, incorpor-ating a highway (D940) as its main straight. There are no pits and no paddock, the cars being driven from the village square a mile away! Despite the basic facilities La Châtre hosted a regular round of the European Formula 3 Championship until that series was cancelled in 1984. Today, La Châtre is used only for national racing although, like most of the French tracks, it has a racing school on the site that is operational for much of the year.

In addition to these, there are working tracks at **La Croix-en-Ternois**, near Arras, which briefly staged European F3 races and is occasionally used for testing brakes (the track being extremely tight and twisty) by Formula 1 teams en route to Monaco; **Ledenon**, near Nîmes in the south; **Le Luc**, not far from Paul Ricard; and **Pau-Arnos**, to the west of Pau itself. None of these circuits, however, is an international-standard venue.

Paul Ricard

The Circuit Paul Ricard overshadowed all the new French tracks of the 1960s. Situated at Le Castellet, on a flat and arid plateau above the coast near Bandol in the south of France, it has long been the dominant permanent circuit of the country. It was built in 1969, the brainchild of the drinks magnate and inventor of pastis, Paul Ricard. The track arrived on the scene when Reims was fading and quickly usurped the great Rouen and Clermont circuits.

Aside from its fabulous facilities it is in a splendid location. You approach Ricard through impressive gorges on the road from Toulon, passing along the tree-lined avenues of Le Beausset, and up into the sandy, pine country, from where you can look across to the sea. Not far away are the little coastal villages of Bandol, Cassis and La Ciotat, where the wine is rough and wholesome and the food distinctively Provençal.

Ricard has three possible layouts, a large area of industrial park and an airstrip. For many years it was considered to be the safest facility in Europe and with this in mind — not to mention the pleasant locality — it soon became a major winter-testing location. Although the layout is fairly uninspiring, the facilities are splendid, with the comfortable, air-conditioned, three-storey pit buildings and an extensive tree-fringed paddock.

The track itself is dominated by the aptly-named Mistral Straight (when the Mistral wind in this region blows, you certainly know about it), a mile long and feeding into the flat-out Signes corner. — This is a real test. Have an accident at Signes and it will be a serious one — there have been many, but fortunately few injuries. Ricard, however, blotted its copybook in 1985 when Elio de Angelis died after a testing accident in his Brabham. In the furore that followed the track was shortened to 2.4 miles, cutting the Mistral Straight by half.

Opened with a 2-litre sportscar race in 1970 (won by Brian Redman), the track played host to the French GP the following year, Jackie Stewart dominating. Two years later the race returned, Ronnie Peterson picking up the pieces after Emerson Fittipaldi and

Left The start/finish line and impressive facilities of the Paul Ricard circuit at Le Castellet.

wane. While the races at Ricard are seldom thrilling, the track remains dominant in France, though the frantic work being carried out at other tracks indicates the belief today that Ricard can be toppled.

new boy Jody Scheckter had taken each other out.

Dijon-Prenois had now opened for business and a pattern of alternation emerged between the two, continuing until 1985 when Dijon's star began to

Right Cars in the complex of corners which link the Mistral and pits straights.

Paul Ricard
1 La Bretelle
2 Verrérie
3 Mistral
4 Signes
5 Beausset
6 Le Village
7 L'Épingle
8 Pont

Paul Ricard Formula 1
1971	J. Stewart	(Tyrrell)
1973	R. Peterson	(Lotus)
1975	N. Lauda	(Ferrari)
1976	J. Hunt	(McLaren)
1978	M. Andretti	(Lotus)
1980	A. Jones	(Williams)
1982	R. Arnoux	(Renault)
1983	A. Prost	(Renault)
1985	N. Piquet	(Brabham)
1986	N. Mansell	(Williams)
1987	N. Mansell	(Williams)
1988	A. Prost	(McLaren)

Dijon-Prenois

Dijon has already been toppled after a brief interlude as a major racing circuit. Built in the early 1970s on an escarpment to the west of Dijon overlooking the city, Dijon-Prenois, as it is known, is delightfully located in the wine country of Burgundy. A few miles to the south are Nuits-St-Georges, Beaune and Meursault: in short, heaven for many racing followers!

As a track Dijon has always been too short. A plunging extension was added in 1976, but it remains too short. It is full of interest, though, with strange cambers, different types of slow and fast corners, some rising, some falling — a track which demands full concentration.

The first French Grand Prix at Dijon took place in 1974, but it was immediately clear that changes had to be made to lengthen the track. The following year it organised a qualifying race under the title of Swiss Grand Prix (this would be accorded

Right This view of the main straight gives the misleading impression that Dijon is just another flat autodrome circuit.

the status of a World Championship event in 1982). By 1977 the principle of alternation with Paul Ricard had been established and for the next few years Dijon was to provide some great events. The battle between John Watson's Brabham and Mario Andretti's Lotus in 1977 is remembered as a classic duel settled on the last lap as the American sneaked into the lead, crossing the line just 1.55 seconds ahead. Two years later there was another classic remembered by everyone who saw it. This race was

Dijon-Prenois: Formula 1
1974   R. Peterson (Lotus)
1977   M. Andretti (Lotus)
1979   J.P. Jabouille (Renault)
1981   A. Prost (Renault)
1982   K. Rosberg (Williams)
1984   N. Lauda (McLaren)

the first victory for a turbocharged engine, so in itself it was historically significant, but no one remembers Jean-Pierre Jabouille disappearing off at the front. What leaps to mind is the last lap duel between the Renault of René Arnoux and the Ferrari of Gilles Villeneuve — the wildest piece of Grand Prix action in the modern era. In 1981 Dijon witnessed another landmark and another Renault triumph — the first victory for a young man called Alain Prost, who would go on to become the greatest Grand Prix driver in French history.

Dijon has since faded considerably and memories of the place are bitter-sweet. The fine races were always counterbalanced by the overzealous stewards imported by the management for crowd control, who had none of the charm of the region. France continues to search for a permanent home for its great race. New circuits are planned at Rouen, Charade and a new facility not far from Dijon in Burgundy. Magny-Cours is bidding for the race as well. The French Grand Prix will probably continue on its merry way from region to region.

Dijon-Prenois
1 Grand Ligne
2 S.de Sablières
3 La Combe
4 Petite Combe
5 Droit

Above Away from the main straight the circuit is hilly and sinuous, and, as these ETC saloons show, the cambers are not always favourable.

Right A McLaren leads a Williams out onto the extension loop during the last GP run at Dijon in 1984.

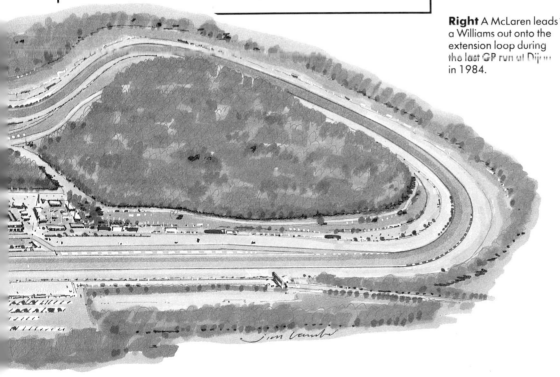

GERMANY

Avus

Given the strength of its automotive industry — with such illustrious marques as Mercedes, Auto Union, Porsche and BMW — it is strange that there are very few permanent racing circuits in Germany. The history of German racing is dominated by the Nürburgring and more recently Hockenheim; but apart from these two venues, Germany has no other regular racing facilities. The German national championships of today in Formula 3, sports and touring cars visit a string of airfield tracks or one or two of the surviving street circuits; beyond these the German racers have been forced to go abroad to Austria, Belgium and even further afield to Hungary and Czechoslovakia to find racing venues.

German racing dates back to the 1904 Gordon Bennett race held in the Taunus mountains above Frankfurt, in the wake of Belgian Camille Jenatzy's victory for Mercedes the previous year at Athy in Ireland. Three years later Kaiser Wilhelm II, eager in his nationalist pride not to be outdone by France, introduced the Kaiserpreis, offering considerable financial reward to attract an international field. The event, held just two weeks before the second Grand Prix de l'ACF at Dieppe, took place on a course in the Taunus mountains which overlapped that of the 1904 Gordon Bennett Cup. Won by Italian Felice Nazzaro's Fiat, the race was not repeated. Plans were already being laid for a permanent racing facility outside Berlin — AVUS.

The Automobil Verkehrs und Ubungs-Strasse (AVUS) was conceived in 1907 as a test track for the motor industry as well as for motorsport. It was the idea of the Automobilklub von Deutschland (AvD) but there was little money for the project and it was six years before work began. The track took the form of a section of dual carriageway on the south-west outskirts of Berlin from Charlottenburg to Nikolassee, with banked loops at each end. By 1913 the enormous undertaking had run out of money, and with the war, work stopped. Later, Russian prisoners were employed to continue construction, although the track was still only half built when the 1918 armistice came.

Post-war Germany was virtually

Left Felice Nazzaro on his way to victory in the 1907 Kaiserpreis aboard an 8-litre FIAT.

bankrupt, but the remainder of the track was financed by Huge Stinnes and AVUS opened at last in September 1921. This was the site of the first German Grand Prix (for sportscars) in 1926, won by the Mercedes of Rudolf Caracciola. The following year, with competition from the new Nürburgring, it was decided to increase the banking in the north curve to 43 degrees. Throughout the 1930s racing continued in Berlin but AVUS was overshadowed by the infinitely more entertaining Nürburgring.

Then came the Second World War and the collapse of Germany. When Berlin fell, among the first to visit AVUS were American GIs and one of

Right Berlin Grand Prix, 1954: the simple south curve at Avus, introduced to link the two straight stretches of motorway when racing resumed after the Second World War.

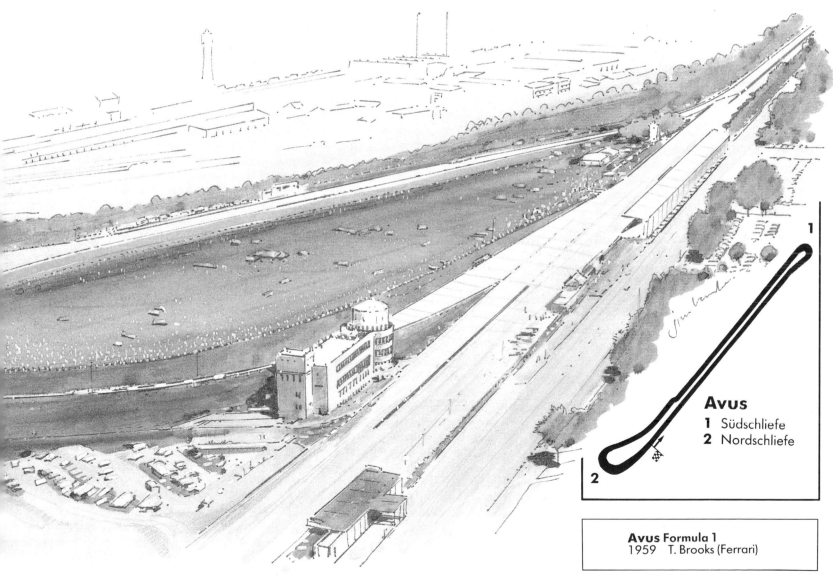

Avus
1 Südschliefe
2 Nordschliefe

Avus Formula 1
1959   T. Brooks (Ferrari)

Right The brick-surfaced 43-degree banked Nordkurve was built in time for the 1937 Avusrennen, when Rosemeyer in an Auto Union lapped at 171.6mph.

blockade of Berlin during the Cold War, it was a long time before racing returned to Berlin. In 1954, with a new unbanked south loop cutting the track to 5.15 miles, AVUS returned with the non-championship F1 grand Prix of Berlin — a Mercedes 1-2-3, with local hero Karl Kling leading home Juan-Manuel Fangio and Hans Herrmann.

In 1959 the German GP paid a final visit to AVUS — the only World Championship GP held there, won by Tony Brooks — at a meeting now chiefly remembered for the death of Jean Behra on the banking. Thereafter the track held little more than international Formula Junior races, although German national events have continued to visit each year. The north bend was dismantled in 1967, but the character of AVUS remains as it always was — fast up, fast back and an absurd corner at each end.

their number, Chris Economaki, remembers lapping the track in a Jeep and having the alarming experience of finding a wooden staircase built across one of the loops! It was here too that President Harry Truman inspected the U.S. troops during the Potsdam conference. But AVUS had a problem: the south loop (at the Nikolassee end) was on the wrong side of the city, in the Soviet sector!

With Germany in ruins, and the

Left The only races spectators in the Avus grandstands see nowadays are minor national events.

Nürburgring

'Nothing gave me more satisfaction than to win at the Nürburgring,' said Jackie Stewart years ago, 'and yet, I was always afraid. When I left home before the German GP I always used to pause at the end of the driveway and take a long look back. I was never sure I'd come home again.'

Of all the racing circuits of the world, the Nürburgring ranks as the greatest in its spectacle and in its challenge. Today there is a new and clinical circuit of constant-radius corners and enormous run-off areas. Even the magnificent wooden grandstand and the old Sporthotel have gone to make way for functional space-age buildings. Much of the romance of the Ring went with the bulldozers.

For those who competed on the old Ring, a visit to the new track always involves a sideways glance, down the valley towards Hatzenbach, out where the old track heads off into the hills through the trees. The drivers are getting used to the new track but when it first opened, it was greeted with contempt. It was certainly grand, expensive beyond doubt, but it wasn't the same. 'This isn't the Nürburgring,' said Pierre Dieudonne at the time, 'the Nürburgring is out there in the hills.'

It is still there today, used occasionally by hairy-chested locals in big saloons, who care little for their safety. But when it is in use, the crowds come pouring in to put up their tents, park their camper vans, have a barbecue and drink beer. There is an atmosphere which is as unforgettable as it is unique — woodsmoke, the pungent smell of pine and scorched rubber.

Originally there were two loops: the Nordschleife (14.2 miles) and the Sudschleife (4.8 miles). The smaller southern loop has gone but the Nordschleife remains, bouncing along between the trees, a ribbon of twisting, rising and falling tarmac. For most of the year, this is open for tourists to potter around in their road cars. Centred on Nürburg village (hence its name) with its weatherbeaten 12th-century castle, the Ring is a legend now.

Out in the hills are famous names carved into the history of the sport

The broad Startplatz in the nationalistic 1930s, when German cars were dominant in Grand Prix racing and uniforms abounded.

Left Jackie Stewart at the aptly-named Flugplatz in 1966, with all wheels of his BRM well clear of the road.

Below Perhaps the most famous corner at the old 'Ring was the Karussell. It seemed to turn through almost a full circle, and the one-time ditch on the inside came to be used as banking by the fastest drivers.

and a lap of the old Ring is still an experience. There is the Flugplatz — where the cars 'flew' — along the ridge to the long curling Aremberg and under the bridge, fast downhill to Fuchsröhre (Fox Throat), bottoming out before the sweep uphill again to Adenauer Forst, and on to Kallenhard, before the road sweeps downhill again towards Adenau Bridge. It was at the righthander before the descent that Onofre Marimon flew off the track during practice for the 1954 GP, crashing to his death below.

Across the bridge the road curls uphill and round behind the hillside towards Bergwerk, and on to the high-speed run along the valley floor towards Karussell. This fast stretch was where Niki Lauda's Ferrari crashed in 1976, bringing an end to Grand Prix racing at the Ring — and almost to the Austrian's life as he was trapped in the burning wreckage.

At the end of the valley the road curls around to the left and climbs steeply to the Karussell; the tree which the drivers used to line up their approach to the corner is still there, as is the mini-banking in a dip in the road — the fastest way through. From here the road rises still more to Hohe Acht,

before the descent through Wippermann and Brünnchen to the two famous and fearsome jumps at Pflanzgarten (Nurseries) where many a driver cartwheeled. Ahead is the curling Schwalbenschwanz (Swallowtail), the little Karussell, and the fast downhill out of the trees close to Dottinger-Hohe and on to the 1.5-mile-long straight which used to run between hedges, rather than the modern barriers. Here, Ernst von Delius tangled with Dick Seaman in 1937, when the German's car cartwheeled off the track and across the main road that runs parallel to the track. The sweeping high-speed swerves at the Tiergarten (Zoo) lead you back to the new track.

Mere words can never capture the grandeur of the Ring, nor its thrill. From the grandstand at the start/finish

Above In the first corner after the start of the 1937 GP, Lang and Caracciola (Mercedes) lead Rosemeyer and Müller in Auto Unions through the sweep of the South Curve.

Right A mixed bunch of mid-1960s cars — Fords, Porsches and Ferraris — enter the same bend the 1937 GP cars are leaving. Schloss Nürburg is in the background.

line, the cars would roar off towards the South Curve and disappear; there would be silence for seven or eight minutes before they returned, flashing by for another lap. This was the scene of so many great moments in the sport and the inevitable loss of life: Marimon, Collins, von Delius, John Taylor, Gerhard Mitter, Herbie Muller, Carel de Beaufort and many more. Many argue that the alterations of 1970 ruined the track, but to the modern racing fan, starved of great tracks, even the revised Ring seems truly unbelievable.

This was no road circuit, closed a couple of times a year; this was a permanent track, built in the 1920s as a means of alleviating unemployment in the area. The first stone was laid in September 1925 and the first German GP to be held here took place the following year. The Ring was ready — the greatest arena for the immortals of motor sport. It was the venue for the immortal Nuvolari's conquest in 1935 of the full might of the German Mercedes and Auto Union teams in his outdated Alfa Romeo P3. It was the site in 1957 of Fangio's greatest drive, fighting back after a delayed refuelling and finally destroying the challenge of Hawthorn and Collins; and of Jackie Stewart's incredible victory — by four minutes! — in the wet in 1968. And what of Rudolf Caracciola, who won four Grands Prix here and five Eifelrennen races in all manner of machinery? Alberto Ascari won three consecutive GP victories here, while Stirling Moss won the Nürburgring 1000 sportscar classic four times.

Nürburgring was much more than simply a Grand Prix venue, for it staged major international events such as the 1000 km, the traditional F2 Eifelrennen race, the 12-Hour and later 24-Hour events, and the Nürburgring 500 km. The track was resurfaced in 1957 and all but rebuilt in 1970, when the German GP had to be moved for a year to Hockenheim. By 1976 the drivers were growing anxious about safety once again and the race that year was to prove them right, for Lauda nearly perished in the wreckage and flames of his Ferrari.

Once Formula 1 departed it was really just a matter of time before the old Ring faded away. Formula 2, the World Sportscar and European Touring Car Championships continued to visit until the last international motor race in 1983. It was the end of the greatest racing track ever built.

Left The unloved new Nürburgring is a clinical, safe and unspectacular autodrome: the 'Ring is no longer ranked among the world's great circuits . . . .

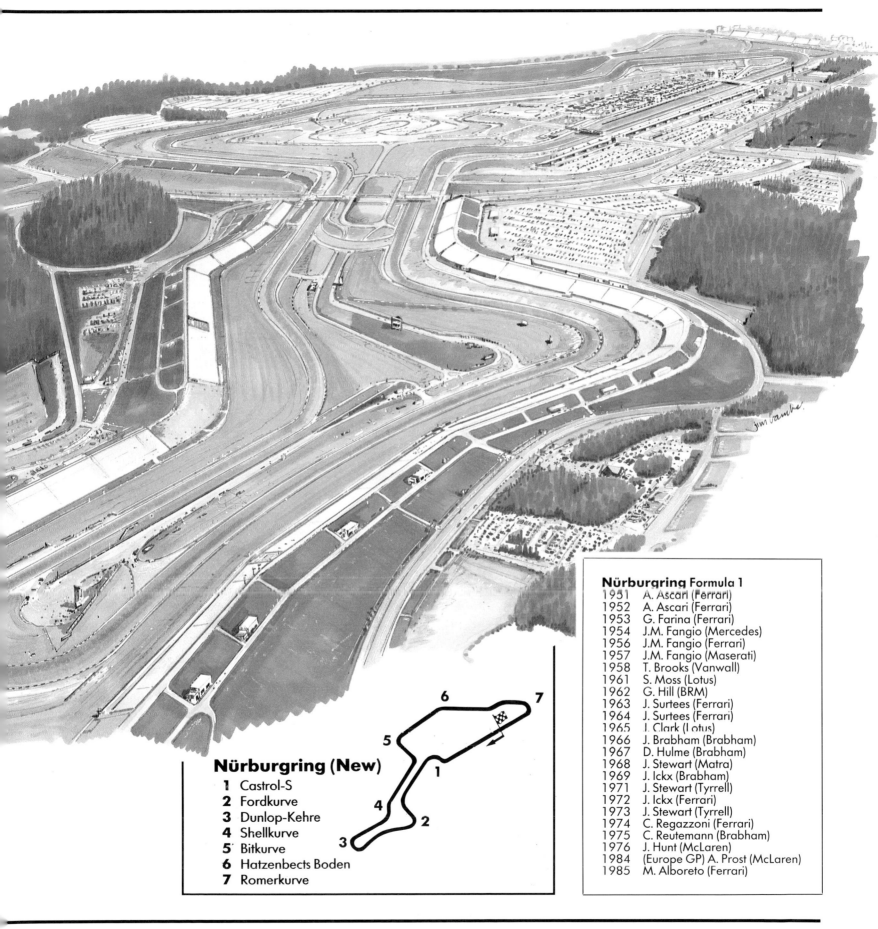

Nürburgring (New)

1 Castrol-S
2 Fordkurve
3 Dunlop-Kehre
4 Shellkurve
5 Bitkurve
6 Hatzenbects Boden
7 Romerkurve

Nürburgring Formula 1

1951	A. Ascari	(Ferrari)
1952	A. Ascari	(Ferrari)
1953	G. Farina	(Ferrari)
1954	J.M. Fangio	(Mercedes)
1956	J.M. Fangio	(Ferrari)
1957	J.M. Fangio	(Maserati)
1958	T. Brooks	(Vanwall)
1961	S. Moss	(Lotus)
1962	G. Hill	(BRM)
1963	J. Surtees	(Ferrari)
1964	J. Surtees	(Ferrari)
1965	J. Clark	(Lotus)
1966	J. Brabham	(Brabham)
1967	D. Hulme	(Brabham)
1968	J. Stewart	(Matra)
1969	J. Ickx	(Brabham)
1971	J. Stewart	(Tyrrell)
1972	J. Ickx	(Ferrari)
1973	J. Stewart	(Tyrrell)
1974	C. Regazzoni	(Ferrari)
1975	C. Reutemann	(Brabham)
1976	J. Hunt	(McLaren)
1984	(Europe GP) A. Prost	(McLaren)
1985	M. Alboreto	(Ferrari)

Hockenheim

When the name Hockenheim is mentioned in racing circles, it means one thing above all – the track where Jim Clark died. Out in the woods beside the circuit, on the run out into the forests from the amphitheatre section, there is a simple stone memorial to the great Scottish driver, the victim of a still-unexplained accident in an unimportant F2 event in the spring of 1968.

The original circuit at Hockenheim was built in 1929, 4.8 miles long, consisting of two high-speed straights and a fast curve, through the flat woodland of the Rhine valley a few miles to the south-west of the ancient university city of Heidelberg. Mercedes used the track for testing before the war but, overshadowed by the great Nürburgring in the post-war

era, Hockenheim organised only minor events throughout the 1950s. The construction of a major new Autobahn saw the old track cut in two in the early 1960s, but a shortened 4.2-mile course was used when racing resumed in 1966. Regarded as very fast but safe, Hockenheim didn't hit the headlines until Clark's death.

It's a weird place, with much of the track out in the pines inaccessible to spectators. The fast, curling straights are like a tunnel for the drivers, who arrive in the twisty amphitheatre to be greeted by the huge crowds crammed into the immense concrete grand-

Hockenheim Formula 1	
1970	J. Rindt (Lotus)
1977	N. Lauda (Ferrari)
1978	M. Andretti (Lotus)
1979	A. Jones (Williams)
1980	J. Laffite (Ligier)
1981	N. Piquet (Brabham)
1982	P. Tambay (Ferrari)
1983	R. Arnoux (Ferrari)
1984	A. Prost (McLaren)
1986	N. Piquet (Williams)
1987	N. Piquet (Williams)
1988	A. Senna (McLaren)

stands that ring the tight stadium section. Once this was a slipstreaming track but the addition of chicanes on each straight in the wake of Clark's death has made that impossible.

While the Nürburgring was a joyful place, Hockenheim has no soul. That

When the Grand Prix returned to the Ring in 1971, Formula 2 racing continued at Hockenheim, as it had since the start of the European Championship in 1967. Then, after Niki Lauda's accident at the Ring in 1976, the German Grand Prix returned to Hockenheim. Lauda, amazingly recovered from his horrifying injuries, and won in 1977 at Hockenheim to the delight of the locals. Two years later the Australian driver Alan Jones took his Williams FW07 to the first of many victories leading ultimately to his World Championship triumph the following year.

Hockenheim 1980 was a miserable affair, coming a few days after the death of Patrick Depailler while testing his Alfa. His death at the Ostkurve led to the introduction of yet another chicane, destroying the one decent corner Hockenheim had left to offer. Two years later Didier Pironi, the World Championship leader for Ferrari, was grievously injured as his car cartwheeled down the track after running into another car in a wet practice session. This ended the Frenchman's career. Coming just a few months after the death of Villeneuve it was a dreadful blow to Ferrari; but Patrick Tambay, under immense pressure, raised the team's spirits the following day by winning his first Grand Prix in only his fourth race with the Maranello outfit.

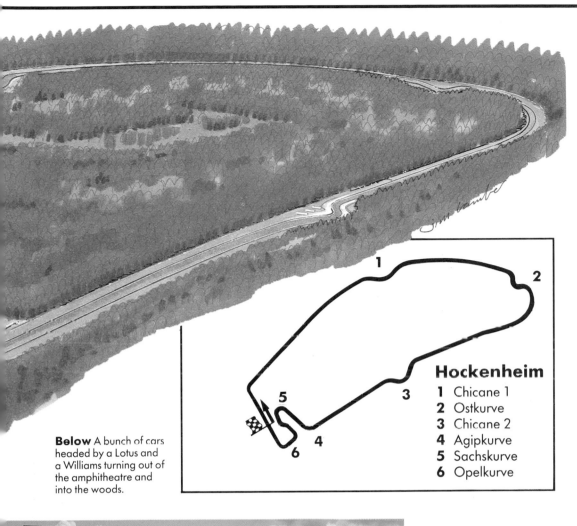

Hockenheim
1 Chicane 1
2 Ostkurve
3 Chicane 2
4 Agipkurve
5 Sachskurve
6 Opelkurve

Below A bunch of cars headed by a Lotus and a Williams turning out of the amphitheatre and into the woods.

Below The huge stands overlooking the twisting infield are sometimes filled for the German Grand Prix.

this unpopular track stages the German GP is testament to the dangers of the Ring rather than to any merit in Hockenheim. Formula 1 arrived at Hockenheim for the first time in 1970, while the 'Ring was being updated, Jochen Rindt winning for Lotus.

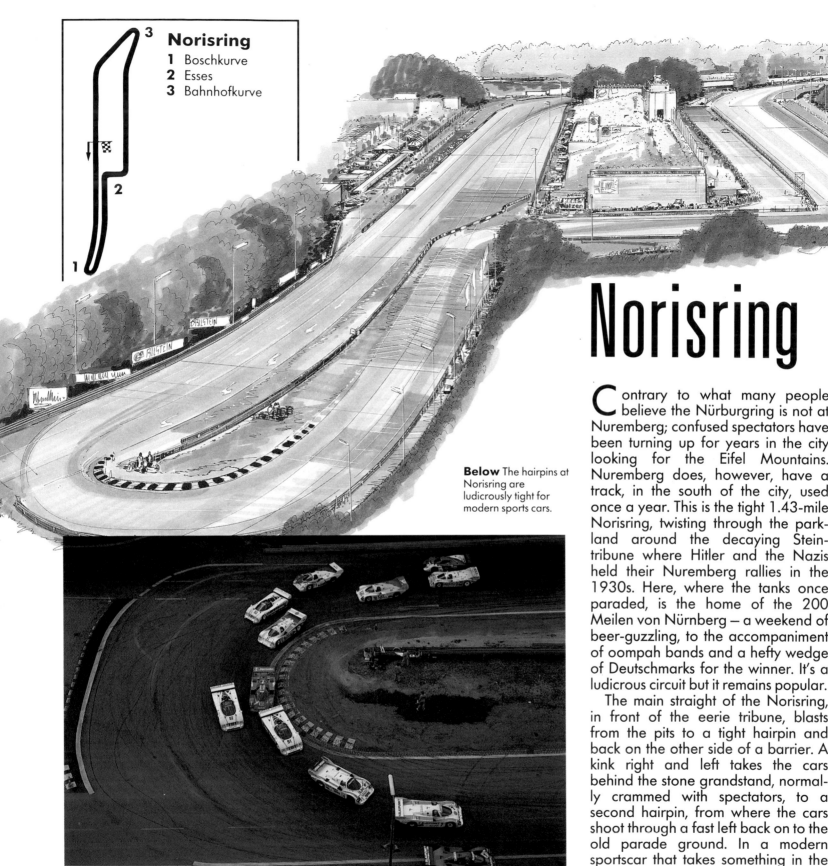

Norisring
1 Boschkurve
2 Esses
3 Bahnhofkurve

Below The hairpins at Norisring are ludicrously tight for modern sports cars.

Norisring

Contrary to what many people believe the Nürburgring is not at Nuremberg; confused spectators have been turning up for years in the city looking for the Eifel Mountains. Nuremberg does, however, have a track, in the south of the city, used once a year. This is the tight 1.43-mile Norisring, twisting through the parkland around the decaying Steintribune where Hitler and the Nazis held their Nuremberg rallies in the 1930s. Here, where the tanks once paraded, is the home of the 200 Meilen von Nürnberg — a weekend of beer-guzzling, to the accompaniment of oompah bands and a hefty wedge of Deutschmarks for the winner. It's a ludicrous circuit but it remains popular.

The main straight of the Norisring, in front of the eerie tribune, blasts from the pits to a tight hairpin and back on the other side of a barrier. A kink right and left takes the cars behind the stone grandstand, normally crammed with spectators, to a second hairpin, from where the cars shoot through a fast left back on to the old parade ground. In a modern sportscar that takes something in the region of 46 seconds! There is a

Right The Steintribune makes an unusual backdrop to the end of the back straight at the Norisring.

surreal atmosphere to the place, with more than a hint of *Ben Hur*. But plenty of fraught action is on view, not least at the end of the straight under brakes where the field tries to file through the absurdly tight hairpin.

Other German Circuits

Apart from the airfield tracks, past and present, at such places as Trier, Neubiberg, Mainz-Finthen, Erding, Kassel-Calden, Diepholz and **Ulm-Mengen**, Germany has no other circuits, though two street tracks, now long gone, are worthy of mention: Solitude and the Grenzlandring. Laid out on closed public roads, in wooded countryside around the Schloss Solitude, near Stuttgart, the **Solitude** track was in its day considered to be a mini-Nürburgring. Its narrow 7.1-mile circuit was the venue of major international events sporadically between 1925 and 1965. The Solitude Grand Prix was run to F1 regulations on four occasions, the first being in 1961 when Innes Ireland gave Lotus one of its earliest victories after a thrilling battle with Jo Bonnier's Porsche. A year later Dan Gurney led Bonnier in a Porsche 1-2, while wins by Jack Brabham and Jim Clark rounded off the track's F1 history in

1963 and 1964. A year later the race was held for Formula 2 cars and Chris Amon triumphed for Lola. Solitude, however, ran into difficulties and was closed down soon afterwards.

Grenzlandring in the north was an F2 venue from 1948. An extremely fast track, it disappeared after several spectators were killed in an accident in 1951.

Left Solitude was an attractive circuit, largely in woods, and the German crowd loved this 1960 F1 Porsche procession (Herrmann leading Bonnier and Graham Hill), and perhaps even Wolfgang von Trips' victory in a Ferrari.

IRELAND

Odd though it may seem, Ireland was the birthplace of racing in the British Isles. With road racing banned on mainland Britain, the first major international motor-racing event in the British Isles took place at Athy, to the south-west of Dublin, just a few weeks after the tragic Paris–Madrid race in 1903. This was a Gordon Bennett Trophy race, the previous year's event, won by S.F. Edge, giving Britain the right to mount the 1903 race.

The tradition started at Athy continued, both north and south of the border, with major races run on spectacular road circuits. Once permanent circuits had begun to emerge on mainland Britain after the Second World War, Ireland's importance in international racing faded. Today even national racing struggles to survive. Recent years have seen the best drivers from the Emerald Isle move to mainland Britain to make their names:

John Watson, Derek Daly, David Kennedy, Kenny Acheson, Tommy Byrne, Martin Donnelly and Michael Roe were among this wave of talent seeking glory over the water.

Of the great Irish tracks, few survive: Skerries, The Curragh (the home of the O'Boyle and Wakefield Trophies), Wicklow, Tallaght and Dunboyne have all long gone. There remains **Phoenix Park**, home of the Irish Grand Prix, the only survivor of the early years. This public park in Dublin staged major international races in the 1920s and 1930s when such celebrated names as Rudolf Caracciola and Sir Henry ('Tim') Birkin won. Although it was revived after the war its history has been chequered with financial troubles and more re-

cently by major drainage works.

The only permanent circuit in Ireland dates from 1968. **Mondello Park**, near Naas, on the road from Dublin to Athy, in County Kildare staged a F5000 meeting the following year. It is a twisty, narrow and bumpy 1.24 miles and since 1969 has struggled to survive. Recently, after a period of acute financial difficulty it was bought by Martin Birrane who has plans for bigger and better things. The occasional street circuit still pops up from time to time, the most recent being at **Ballyjamesduff** in County Cavan: scarcely half a mile long, it was a throwback to the old days of street racing.

North of the border in Ulster the story is much the same. The world's

Below The roads in Pheonix Park were — and are — narrow, and crowd protection in the 1930s would have been unthinkable for modern officials, especially when cars like these thunderous Mercedes SSKs driven by Lord Howe and Caracciola were racing . . . .

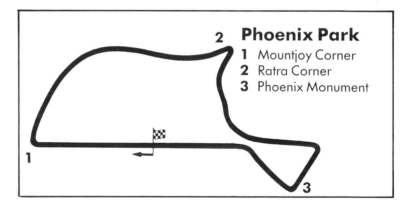

Phoenix Park
1 Mountjoy Corner
2 Ratra Corner
3 Phoenix Monument

oldest surviving motor race, the RAC Tourist Trophy, which began in 1905 on the Isle of Man, arrived at the **Ards** circuit in 1923. It attracted some great names in its day, notably Caracciola, Nuvolari and Varzi; but in 1936 eight spectators were killed in an accident and Ards fell victim to the official axe. In the post-war era **Dundrod** took on a similar role, with the Tourist Trophy returning to Ireland in 1950. That first event was won by a youngster called Stirling Moss, his first major victory. He won again in 1951 and 1955 but that year a dreadful accident at Deer's Leap claimed several more lives. The RAC dictated that the track could not continue.

Other tracks have come and gone in Ulster: Long Kesh, Cluntoe,

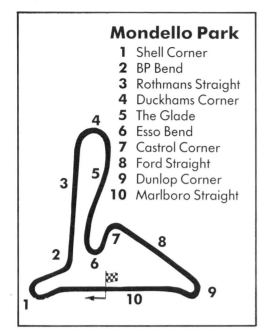

Mondello Park
1 Shell Corner
2 BP Bend
3 Rothmans Straight
4 Duckhams Corner
5 The Glade
6 Esso Bend
7 Castrol Corner
8 Ford Straight
9 Dunlop Corner
10 Marlboro Straight

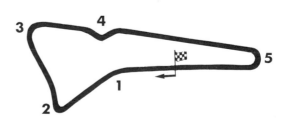

Above Mondello Park has always been narrow, with facilities that are no more than basic. It is acceptable for small cars such as these F. Ford 1600s — but it seems extraordinary that F5000 cars once raced here.

Left Tazio Nuvolari in an MG Magnette lifts a wheel as he leaves the square at Newtonards, on his way to a dramatic victory in the 1933 Tourist Trophy on the Ards circuit.

Donaghadee, Bangor, Bishopscourt and Ballyclare. Today, Ulster has one permanent track at **Kirkiston**, first used in 1953. The old airfield a few miles south of Ards has never staged international races of note but remains the only venue left to the modern generation of racers in Northern Ireland.

Kirkiston
1 Debtors Dip
2 Colonial
3 Fishermans
4 Chicane
5 Hairpin

ITALY

Racing began in Italy at the turn of the century with the first race, the Coppa Florio, taking place in 1900 at Brescia. This was to be the forerunner of the great Italian road races, the Targa Florio, Mille Miglia, Giro di Sicilia, Circuito del Mugello and numerous others. You can still drive on the roads over which the Mille Miglia was run, marvelling at the routes, fraught with danger at the Futa and Raticosa passes high up in the Appennini. There you may stumble upon the Carlo Biondetti Memorial, honouring the man who won four Mille Miglias (no one else won more than two).

The Mille Miglia continued despite spectator deaths in 1938 but in 1957, so soon after the Le Mans disaster, the deaths of Alfonso, Marquess de Portago, his co-driver and 11 spectators could not be ignored. A couple of truncated versions around Brescia

Right Unencumbered by any protective barriers, spectators in Campofelice watch the Porsche 908/3 Spyder driven into second place in the 1970 Targa Florio by Rodriguez and Kinnunen.

Below The Mille Miglia was one of the greatest road races, and one of the last to survive. The final race, in 1957, was won by Taruffi; here he is, 25 years earlier, descending from the Futa pass in an Alfa Romeo 6C-1750.

were mounted; but to all intents and purposes the Mille Miglia died in 1957.

The Targa Florio in the mountains of Sicily was the oldest (first run in 1906) and, for the aficionado, the greatest road race of all. But in 1973 the cars — especially the ferociously powerful Ferraris and Porsches — had become too fast for the tortuous route, and its closure ended the classic era of Italian road races. At some stage or other, almost every major town and city in Italy has held some form of street races. Some have had outstanding international histories. There was Circuito del Garda at **Salò**, dating from 1921, which was still being used for Formula 3 in the 1960s; **Caserta**, one of the centres of Imperial Rome, held its first race in 1928 and also survived until the 1960s; **Pescara**, the home of the longest circuit ever to host a World Championship Grand Prix (in 1957), dated back to 1924. With its mad rush through the Abruzzi mountains and the four-mile straight beside the sea, Pescara was over 15 miles in length, and dangerously encumbered with level crossings, bridges and hill villages. The track was always crammed with crowds of people, not to mention chickens and dogs. This was the home of the Coppa Acerbo and also a 12-hour sportscar race in the early 1950s. Although unaffected by the Le Mans disaster when countless other races were being stopped, it too faded away in the 1960s.

Another of the famous Italian tracks was at **Modena**, in the centre of Ferrari country. This held pre-war street races (Enzo Ferrari won two) which after the war were switched to a military airfield, the Aeroautodromo Modena, which was used for F2 in the late 1950s and for F1 in 1961. It was here during testing in 1957 that Eugenio Castellotti was killed.

Many other circuits did not survive as long: **Alessandria**, which held a major annual event in 1924-34; **Avellion**, which ran major sportscar events from 1928–33; and another sportscar venue in the post-war period at **Belluno**. There was the **Montenero** circuit at Livorno, home of the Coppa Ciano from 1921-39, an event dominated by Nuvolari, Varzi and Materassi. It ceased with the war. **Posillipo**, near Naples, hosted the Naples Grand Prix in the late 1930s and was revived after the war, staging F1 races into the mid-1950s; it closed in 1962. And there was **Bari** and its post-war **Lungomare** circuit, 8.93 miles in length, which was used for F1 and F2 events. It could not, however be modified to safety standards introduced after the Le Mans disaster in 1955. The arrival of Formula Junior in the late 1950s gave many street tracks a new lease of life and indeed created new venues: **Messina**, **Cesenatico**, **Salerno**, **Syracuse**, and **Teramo**. All have long since vanished.

Below A Cooper-Climax passes the protective hay bales at a corner during the 1959 Syracuse Grand Prix.

Monza

The Italians love motor racing. To the *tifosi* — the fervent Ferrari fans — it is not a sport, it is a religion. The cathedral of Italian motor racing is the Autodromo Nazionale at Monza. This is hallowed ground, as Cardiff Arms Park is to a Welshman or Lord's is to the English. Monza was reputedly built in 110 days in the magnificent grounds of the Monza royal palace, to the north-east of Milan. Vincenzo Lancia and Felice Nazzaro laid the first stone on February 1922 but two days later conservationists interrupted the project. Work was finally started on 3 May, finished on 15 August and

Left The tifosi always invade the track at the end of a race. If, as here at Monza in 1988, Ferrari have taken the first two places, it's carnival time.

Right Monza 1955, when the combined circuit was first used for the Grand Prix. A Ferrari leads a streamlined Mercedes off the South banking; another streamlined Mercedes leads one of its open-wheel team-mates out of the south curve of the road circuit.

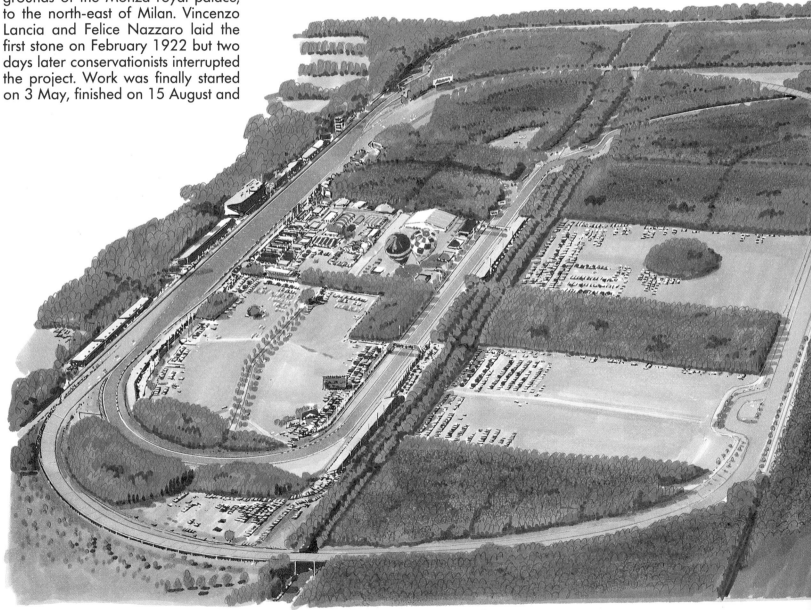

the track opened on 28 August. It was an amazing feat — 6.25 miles of tarmac with two huge banked curves, interlinked with the road course. Monza has changed several times since then but the spirit of the original has survived everything.

Today the Autodromo is decaying, as it has been for years. The fearsome banking put up in 1955 is locked up to keep the *tifosi* out. The pits were chipped at the edges until demolished in 1989. But the atmosphere is pure Monza. Some love it and some hate it but few are unmoved by its splendour.

Monza on a clear day, the mountains visible in the distance and the derelict old banking stark among the trees, is magical — they call it the *pista magica*, and with good reason. 'It's always good to be back in Italy, and especially Monza,' says triple World Champion Nelson Piquet, 'because of the atmosphere and the *tifosi*. Monza is a lucky track for me and brings back good memories of the races I have won in the park.'

But Monza has not always been a happy place, far from it. More than any other circuit in the world, Monza

has ghosts out there among the parkland trees. This was a killing ground: Emilio Materassi and 27 spectators in 1928; Luigi Arcangeli in 1931 and the same year three spectators killed when Philippe Etancelin crashed at Lesmo; Giuseppe Campari, Baconin Borzacchini and Count Stanislas Czaykowski all on the same black September day in 1933. The great Alberto Ascari in May 1955 (he was merely testing his nerve in a sports Ferrari shortly after his car plunged into the harbour at the Monoco GP); Wolfgang von Trips and 10 spectators

Monza

1 Variante del Rettifilo
2 Curva Grande
3 Curva della Roggia
4 Curve di Lesmo
5 Curva del Serraglio
6 Curva del Vialone
7 Curva Parabolica

Monza Formula 1

Year	Winner	Year	Winner
1950	G. Farina (Alfa Romeo)	1969	J. Stewart (Matra)
1951	A. Ascari (Ferrari)	1970	C. Regazzoni (Ferrari)
1952	A. Ascari (Ferrari)	1971	P. Gethin (BRM)
1953	J.M. Fangio (Maserati)	1972	E. Fittipaldi (Lotus)
1954	J.M. Fangio (Mercedes)	1973	R. Peterson (Lotus)
1955	J.M. Fangio (Mercedes)	1974	R. Peterson (Lotus)
1956	S. Moss (Maserati)	1975	C. Regazzoni (Ferrari)
1957	S. Moss (Vanwall)	1976	R. Peterson (March)
1958	T. Brooks (Vanwall)	1977	M. Andretti (Lotus)
1959	S. Moss (Cooper)	1978	N. Lauda (Brabham)
1960	P. Hill (Ferrari)	1979	J. Scheckter (Ferrari)
1961	P. Hill (Ferrari)	1981	A. Prost (Renault)
1962	G. Hill (BRM)	1982	R. Arnoux (Renault)
1963	J. Clark (Lotus)	1983	N. Piquet (Brabham)
1964	J. Surtees (Ferrari)	1984	N. Lauda (McLaren)
1965	J. Stewart (BRM)	1985	A. Proust (McLaren)
1966	L. Scarfiotti (Ferrari)	1986	N. Piquet (Williams)
1967	J. Surtees (Honda)	1987	N. Piquet (Williams)
1968	D. Hulme (McLaren)	1988	G. Berger (Ferrari)

in 1961; the World Champion-elect of 1970, Jochen Rindt; Ronnie Peterson in 1978; and many more besides – Marazza, Count Zobrowski, Giaccone, Pittard. The list is frighteningly long, tragically distinguished.

With the tragedy there have been triumphs. Who can forget Niki Lauda's remarkable comeback so soon after his Nürburgring nightmare in 1976? He was a terrified figure in the pit lane, fighting to overcome his fears and succeeding.

Monza can claim to have held the fastest Grand Prix and the closest finish both in the same event when Peter Gethin took the flag just 0.01 second ahead of Ronnie Peterson after averaging 150.754mph from start to finish in the last of the great Monza slipstreamers before introduction of the chicanes in 1972. This was one of the many changes in Monza's history. The speed bowl was dropped after the cataclysmic happenings of September 1933; a shorter track was run through the woods in the immediate pre-war era. The Italian GP was transferred to Livorno in 1937. What was left of Monza was used as a military dump during the war and a tank parade afterwards put paid to much of the original track. In 1948, however, reconstruction began, with new banking being added in 1955. Monza staged the two Races of Two Worlds, when the Americans brought their roadsters to Europe in 1957 and 1958 but by 1960 drivers were boycotting the great oval.

Monza is still fast but for the modern racers the high speed flow of the curves has been broken up by the chicanes. Past the pits and the magnificent old grandstands, the cars are flat out as they head towards the chicane at the Rettifilo. Once this led into the seemingly never ending Curva Grande but today, as you approach the point where the old banking swings away to the right, it is time to drop anchors to thread through the left-right-left-right complex. All around are sandtraps to catch the

Above On a warm-up lap of a touring-car race at Monza the field fills the straight leading into the Parabolica.

Left Pit scene: Berger's Ferrari is fuelled before the start of the 1988 Grand Prix.

unwary and they are visited often. Swinging out, the drivers floor the throttle and gather speed through the Curva Grande, trees all around. Then it is on with the brakes again for another chicane where once the fast left-hander at the Curva Roggia swung the cars up towards the Lesmos. Today these are still fast, a pair of righthanders with little run-off. Hook a wheel over a kerb here and disaster is not far away. Out of the second Lesmo, the track dives downhill, passing houses hidden in the woods; then it goes under the old

north banking and it starts to rise again. Once the Vialone was a fast lefthander, but today the Ascari chicane interrupts the flow. The exit from the chicane is all important for it dictates the pace on to the back straight, where the cars emerge from the trees and howl towards the Curvetta (nowadays known as the Parabolica) where the brakes go on once more and the teetering corner begins, curling back towards the main straight, deceptive right the way through. To the left the old South Curve feeds on to the straight before the grandstands begin and, feet to the boards, the drivers head off towards Rettifilo again.

A walk in the park jolts the memory, bringing to mind incidents from the countless races that have taken place here. Not merely the Italian Grand Prix but also the famed Lotteria, a race in which the youngsters could make their names; the sportscar classic, the Monza 1000; the Monza 4 Hours, the Autodrome GP, the Inter Europe Cup. Listen to the racing engines here and you get a chill running down your spine. Walk through the crowds — feel the electricity in the air.

Unique it may be, but Monza has problems to this day. Conservationists insist on blocking attempts to build new facilities. Where once they wanted no circuit, now they want the one they have.

To improve safety would mean cutting down more trees. And what would the *tifosi* make of this? For the trees are their grandstands. Out in the woods, each robust tree has nails hammered into it, footholds up which the fans scramble to perch in the branches to catch sight of the Ferraris.

It is difficult to explain, to those who have not seen the *tifosi* in action, the strength of feeling they have for the blood-red cars bearing the yellow shield with its prancing horse. When a Ferrari passes by, the *tifosi* don't cheer, they applaud politely; the cheering is reserved for after victory is won. Only someone who has witnessed a Ferrari victory at Monza can truly understand the meaning of the word chaos. While other tracks have wire fencing around their paddocks Monza is protected by iron bars, lest the *tifosi* invade with wire-cutters....

Imola

Standing atop the Appennini on the route of the old Mille Miglia, you can breathe motor racing. Down below is the great Roman road which runs north-west from Bari, along the coast, passing Pescara and Ancona until, at Rimini, it turns west-north-west, marching inland through Imola, Bologna, Modena (Maranello is nearby), and on to Milan. This is country where Gilles Villeneuve is regarded as a saint and Ferrari red is the only colour that matters.

At Imola is the Autodromo Dino Ferrari, named after Enzo's tragic son and the home of the San Marino Grand Prix. The tiny principality of San Marino is 50-miles away, but it doesn't matter — this is Italy's second Grand Prix and if for political reasons, it must be named after a different country, so be it. Built in 1950 in wooded parkland on the outskirts of the town 20 miles to the south-east of Bologna, Imola is a fabulous track. Being close to the Ferrari base, its name guarantees patronage from Maranello. And in motor racing that means a lot.

It was only comparatively recently that Imola shot to prominence. It had staged the odd international sportscar race in the 1950s and a non-championship F1 race in 1963, won inevitably by Jim Clark. But its ambitions seemed limited. Early in the 1970s, however, Imola was massively updated with a three-storey pit complex, hospitality units, a press centre and even a restaurant. In the autumn of 1979, in a highly charged atmosphere following the death of Ronnie

The start/finish area at Imola, one of the finest of the newer venues on the Formula 1 schedule.

Peterson in the previous year's Italian GP at Monza, Imola hosted a non-championship F1 race, won by the Brabham-Alfa of Niki Lauda.

In September 1980, the Italian Grand Prix arrived. Few will forget

Gilles Villeneuve's lucky escape that year at Tosa, the French-Canadian's Ferrari being ripped apart, the remains coming to rest in the middle of the road. The corner is now called Villeneuve. A year later, with the Italian GP back at Monza, Imola adopted San Marino and landed another full World Championship F1 event.

It was here in 1982 that the Formula One Constructors' Association (FOCA) teams boycotted the event, leaving Ferrari and Renault to put on a show for the fans. And what a show it turned out to be, with the Ferraris of Didier Pironi and Villeneuve fighting tooth and nail in the closing laps, team orders thrown out of the window. After the race Villeneuve swore never to speak to his team-mate again; nor did he, for he died a fortnight later in practice for the Belgian GP at Zolder. It was at Imola a year later that Gilles's greatest friend, Patrick Tambay,

The high-speed Tamburello curve ends the gently curving dash from the pits.

guided Ferrari No. 27 to victory in a symbolic and emotional triumph. It was at Imola in 1985 that Elio de Angelis won his second and last Grand Prix victory when Prost's McLaren was disqualified for being underweight. And here too in 1987 Nelson Piquet survived a brush with death when a tyre blew at high speed as he went through Tamburello.

The drivers used to complain about a lack of run-off, but today it is the chicanes they hate. Unusually for a European track it is anticlockwise and has no real straight to speak of, merely the high-speed sweeper called Tamburello, away from the pits, the corner overlooked by a distant church. Through Villeneuve Corner — really little more than a kink — the track winds into the uphill curling Tosa. From here it is hard uphill to Piratella and along the top of the hill amid the trees into Acque Minerali, spoiled by a tight chicane. Then across the top, through another chicane before the road plunges away downhill to the tricky double lefthander at Rivazza and the run back, through another chicane complex on to the pit straight and Tamburello once again.

At any time of year Imola is a pleasant place to be and as a result it is much used for winter testing. The wine of the region is *frizzante*, and at Grand Prix time the place bubbles as the *tifosi* come to town, filling the huge spectator banks at Tosa and overlooking the final chicane.

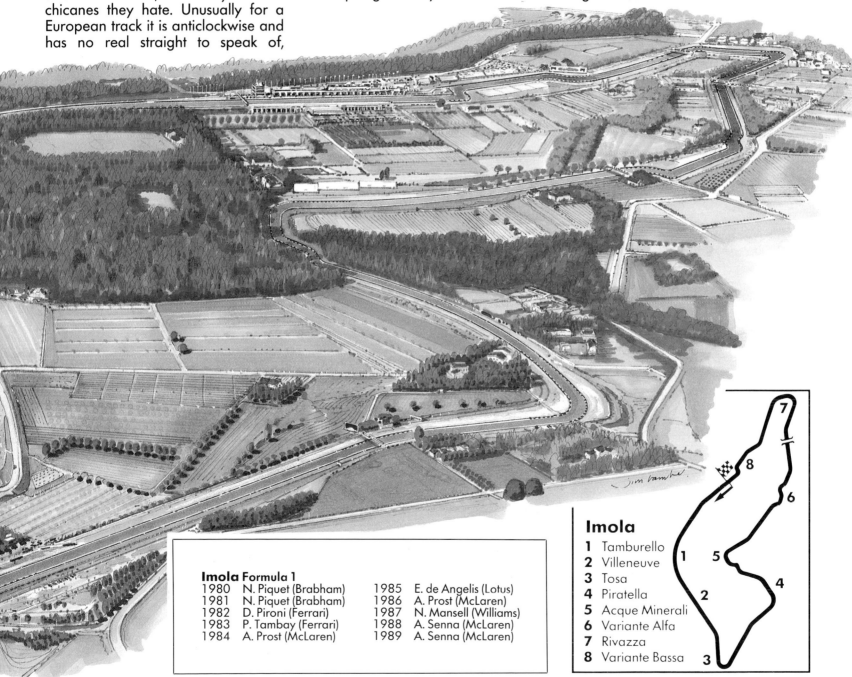

Imola Formula 1

1980	N. Piquet (Brabham)	1985	E. de Angelis (Lotus)
1981	N. Piquet (Brabham)	1986	A. Prost (McLaren)
1982	D. Pironi (Ferrari)	1987	N. Mansell (Williams)
1983	P. Tambay (Ferrari)	1988	A. Senna (McLaren)
1984	A. Prost (McLaren)	1989	A. Senna (McLaren)

Imola

1 Tamburello
2 Villeneuve
3 Tosa
4 Piratella
5 Acque Minerali
6 Variante Alfa
7 Rivazza
8 Variante Bassa

Mugello

If Imola is picturesque, across the Appennini towards Florence there is an even more pleasant track at Mugello, hidden away in the rolling hills of the Chianti region. The name is historic, for the Circuito di Mugello was a famous event in the 1920s when the likes of Giuseppe Campari, Alfieri Maserati and Enzo Ferrari thundered through the Tuscan countryside on a 40 mile road course reaching north towards Bologna and incorporating the great Futa pass.

Though revived in the late 1950s and 1960s, the Circuito, like the other great Italian road races, could not survive and a proper circuit was constructed near Barberino di Mugello. It is a superb, sweeping track ranged across a valley with the main straight feeding into a rising and curling right-hander. Sweeping across the hillside behind the pits, the track then rushes downhill across a bridge and soars uphill through a fast right-hander to the other side of the valley.

This was to become the home of Formula 2 and World Sportscar Championship races in the 1970s, though in the 1980s the circuit ran into increasing financial difficulties and slipped into decay. There was constant talk of the valley being flooded to create a reservoir to serve nearby Florence; but it never happened, and in 1988 the track was bought by Ferrari to be used as a testing facility. If international racing returns to Mugello, the sport as a whole will be the better for it.

Right Tucked away in the hills of Tuscany's Chianti region, Mugello is now used as a Ferrari test track. The absence of spectators at this 1980s F2 event explains the circuit's demise.

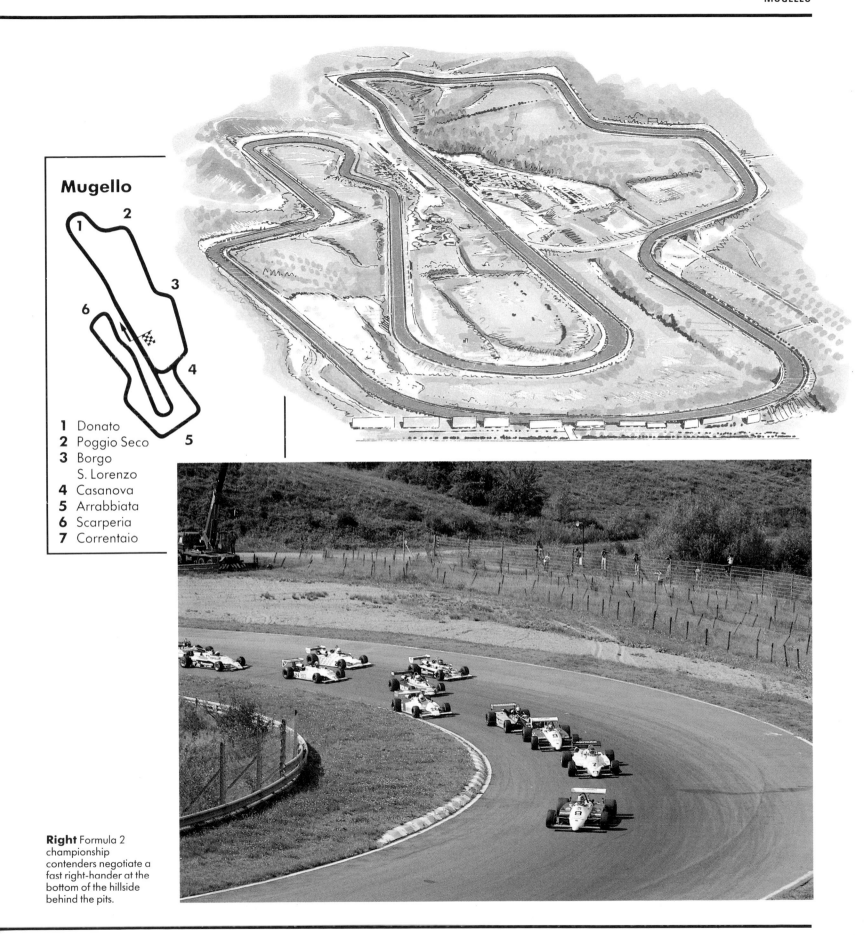

Mugello

1 Donato
2 Poggio Seco
3 Borgo
  S. Lorenzo
4 Casanova
5 Arrabbiata
6 Scarperia
7 Correntaio

Right Formula 2 championship contenders negotiate a fast right-hander at the bottom of the hillside behind the pits.

Misano

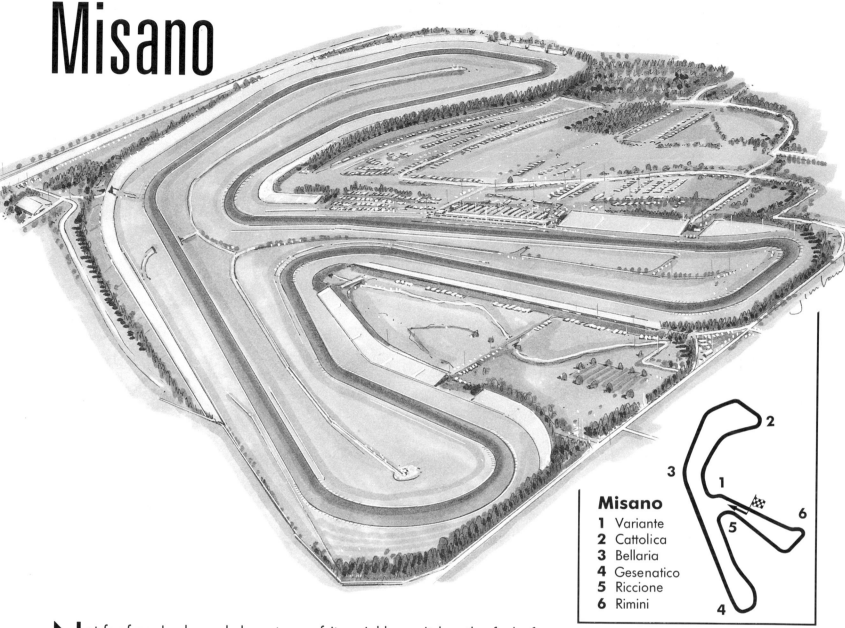

Misano
1 Variante
2 Cattolica
3 Bellaria
4 Gesenatico
5 Riccione
6 Rimini

Not far from Imola, and closer to San Marino than the Autodromo Dino Ferrari, is another of the major modern tracks of Italy, the Autodromo Santamonica at Misano-Adriatico. Just inland from the tourist beaches of the Rimini-Riccione-Cattolica strip, with their neon-encrusted Crazy Horse Saloons, amusement arcades and pedal boats, Misano is a strange, Mickey Mouse circuit, twisting back on itself inside a ring of high concrete fences. Like Imola this track runs anti-clockwise but Misano has none of the flowing curves and elevation changes of its neighbour. It has the feel of a municipal sportsground with flood-lights overhead allowing night racing. Otherwise it is rather uninteresting, being flat and tortuous. For drivers it is always a challenge, with high temperatures a normal occurrence and concentration at a premium. Given the space into which it fits, the 2.16-mile track has a fairly long straight, albeit with a couple of quick kinks, before another hairpin interrupts.

Like Mugello, Misano was a regular Formula 2 track in the 1970s with the occasional visit also from the World Sportscar Championship. Into the 1980s, the track briefly hosted a round of the European Touring Car Championship, witnessing one of the closest finishes in a 500km touring car race in 1986 when Roberto Ravaglia's BMW outran the Volvo 240 Turbo of Johnny Cecotto by just 5 seconds! Recently, however, the track has slipped quietly into the Italian national racing scene, although the occasional Formula 1 team still drops in for a spot of winter testing by the seaside.

Vallelunga

The Grand Prix of Rome has had a long and colourful history dating back to 1925 when the first event to carry the title took place at Monte Mario in the city's north-western suburbs. There followed a succession of other venues — Valle Giulia, Parioli, Tre Fontane, Littorio, Caracalla and Castel Fusano — before the race finally found a permanent home, in 1963, at Vallelunga. The track is hidden away in the hills to the north of Rome, surrounded by vineyards, close to several picturesque lakes where the teams relax by spending their time sailing or merely soaking up the sun, of which there is plenty.

Initially Vallelunga was a tiny oval track, not really suitable for Formula 1, although Bob Anderson won the 1963 event in an F1 Lola. Thereafter Vallelunga became a venue for Formula 2, sports and touring car races. Major reconstruction and extension in 1971 saw racing switch from anti-clockwise to clockwise and the addition of the loop at the back of the track and the twisty infield, in addition to a new paddock, new pits and a huge grandstand.

The Vallelunga of today is very much a compromise kind of circuit with the switch-back infield, offset by the fast blasts away from the natural bowl of the original track. The outstanding corner of the track is a weirdly cambered fast left where the circuit bursts through a rock gorge (blasted out in 1971) and back into the infield. The track drops away as the cars arrive at high speed and many a hero has found himself rolling down the road, having failed to take the corner quite right! Although Formula 2 was cancelled in 1984, Vallelunga is still a venue for rounds of the Formula 3000 Championship, the nature of the track promoting close and spectacular racing.

The hairpin at the back of the circuit. The pits area is visible in the distance.

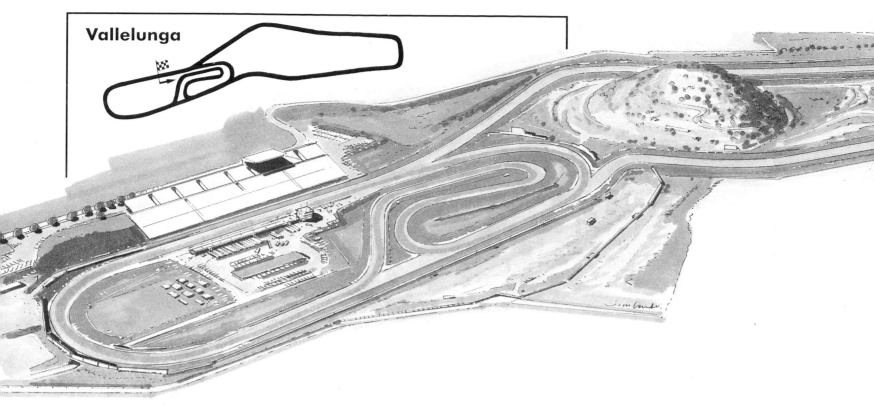

Vallelunga

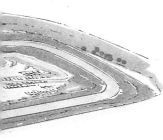

Left The start/finish line and pits at Vallelunga, viewed from the grandstand area.

Right An F3000 field streaming out of the rock gorge that was an essential part of the circuit's 1972 extension.

Enna-Pergusa

The speedbowl at Enna-Pergusa in central Sicily is not a particularly enthralling race track — a fast blast around a stagnant lake far from anywhere. The countryside is rugged but the locals are friendly and the atmosphere slow and relaxed. Before the track was opened in 1964, Enna hosted a road race, the F1 Mediterranean GP, from 1962 as part of a Sicilian Speed fortnight. Lorenzo Bandini won the first event and John Surtees the second but when the race moved to Pergusa, Jo Siffert proved to be unbeatable, triumphing in both 1964 and 1965. Thereafter Formula 1 quickly departed from Sicily, leaving Enna to the boys in Formula 3. They amused the locals with frightening slipstreamer battles around the lake.

Pergusa then became an important round of the European Formula 2 Championship and when that was cancelled in 1984, the replacement Formula 3000. At the same time, the circuit became a regular stopping point for the European F3 and European Touring Car Championships and even the World Sportscar series was an occasional visitor. The addition of chicanes, however, has turned the track into a point-and-squirt circuit, with a first corner almost guaranteed to cause an accident as the cars accelerate away from the line.

In the early days of Pergusa, when drivers were of a different ilk to those of today, the lake was used as a swimming pool, the snakes scared away with a handful of stones thrown into the water. Today's visitors prefer swimming in pools at the local hotels . . . .

Enna

Right The top F3000 drivers complete the 3-mile tour around Enna's lake in about one and a half minutes.

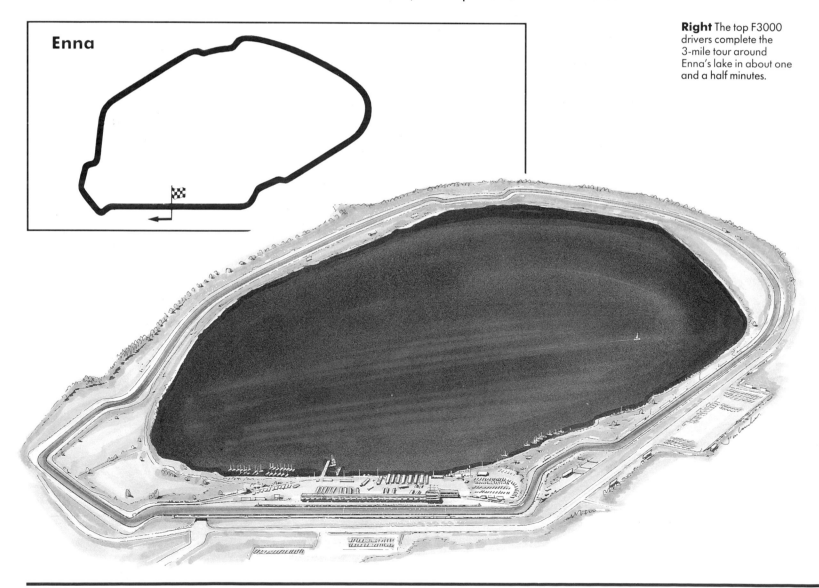

Other Italian Circuits

Italy has a couple of other tracks in regular use; both are tight and tiny. **Magione**, between Lake Trasimeno and the city of Perugia in Umbria, is just over a mile in length and is shaped like a paper clip, twisting back on itself. International racing has not been near the track but it is used regularly by national competitors as a test track and the Italian F3 series visits once a year. The Autodromo Riccardo Paletti at **Varano**, named after the young Italian killed in the Canadian GP of 1982, is scarcely larger than Magione, with the Formula 3 cars lapping in the 45-second region. Close to Parma in the hills of Romagna, Varano is the home of Dallara Automobili, the hugely successful Formula 3 constructor.

Aside from the active racing tracks already mentioned, Italy boasts three important testing facilities at Fiorano, Balocco and Nardo. Built in the early 1970s, **Fiorano** is the Ferrari test track, a figure-of-eight layout with a little bit of everything thrown in to enable performance on all kinds of tracks to be gauged with an advanced electronic monitoring system. **Balocco** is Alfa's test track, near Turin, while **Nardò** is a spectacular circular banked test track to the south of Brindisi on the heel of Italy looking towards the Gulf of Taranto — out of sight of prying eyes.

NETHERLANDS Zandvoort

Motor racing in the Netherlands means only one thing — Zandvoort, the country's only permanent racing facility and for many years home of the Dutch Grand Prix. A fast track among the sand dunes along the North Sea coast just south of Haarlem, Zandvoort was based on a link road built through the dunes by the Germans in the Second World War to connect their shore batteries, although this was refined somewhat by the man who is rightly credited with the superb design of the track, John Hugenholz.

Zandvoort is an extremely varied circuit with numerous different cambers and angles of corner, and with a couple of elevation changes, notably the superb Scheivlak corner which dives downhill, turning right as it does so. Bos Uit, the corner on to the main straight, is testing; and Tarzan, at the end of the straight, is very much a corner for the brave late-brakers. Not only is the circuit tricky by nature, but when the wind gets up sand may be blown on to the track, so that the drivers never know where they will find grip on the tarmac.

The first event at Zandvoort took place in 1949 under the title Zandvoort Grand Prix, a Formula Libre event won by the Maserati of Prince Bira. The following year, being run to F1 regulations, the race was won by Gigi Villoresi's Ferrari, followed home by Baron de Graffenried. There were to be two further non-championship F1 races (by this stage called the Dutch Grand Prix), both won by Louis Rosier, before the first World Championship event in 1952, which was won by Alberto Ascari's Ferrari, a result which was repeated a year later. Reading through the list of Dutch Grand Prix winners leaves one in little

doubt that this is a driver's circuit: Jim Clark won four GPs at Zandvoort and Jackie Stewart and Niki Lauda three times each.

Zandvoort witnessed the desperate last laps of the 1985 race as team mates Niki Lauda and Alain Prost battled for victory all the way to the flag. Here, Gilles Villeneuve three-wheeled at vast speed for a lap in 1979, tearing his suspension apart in frustration after a puncture. There was Derek Daly's frightening air display in his Tyrrell at Tarzan. Countless other memories remain of this place, includ-

Left An early 1960s field in the loop behind the cramped paddock, which allowed grandstand spectators to see the cars twice during a lap. Leading this 1961 Dutch GP group up Hunze Rug is Jim Clark in a Lotus, followed by Gurney (Porsche), Moss (Lotus) and von Trips (Ferrari).

ing the bad ones: the death of Piers Courage in 1970 and the awful accident which claimed the life of Roger Williamson three years later and saw David Purley's heart-rending attempts to rescue his fellow countryman from the blaze, while the marshals hung back; and there was Hans-Georg Burger, killed in an F2 race at Scheivlak, just as he was making his mark in international racing.

The overriding memories of Zandvoort, however, are happy ones: of

standing on the tallest dune in the centre of the track and being able to see much of the circuit; of brisk North Sea winds; and of chips with mayonnaise! Noise pollution was the reason they gave for taking away its licence, but thankfully plans to build a much modified new facility are well advanced. A huge man-made sand dune will shield the town from the noise — and will shield Zandvoort from those who don't appreciate something good when they see it.

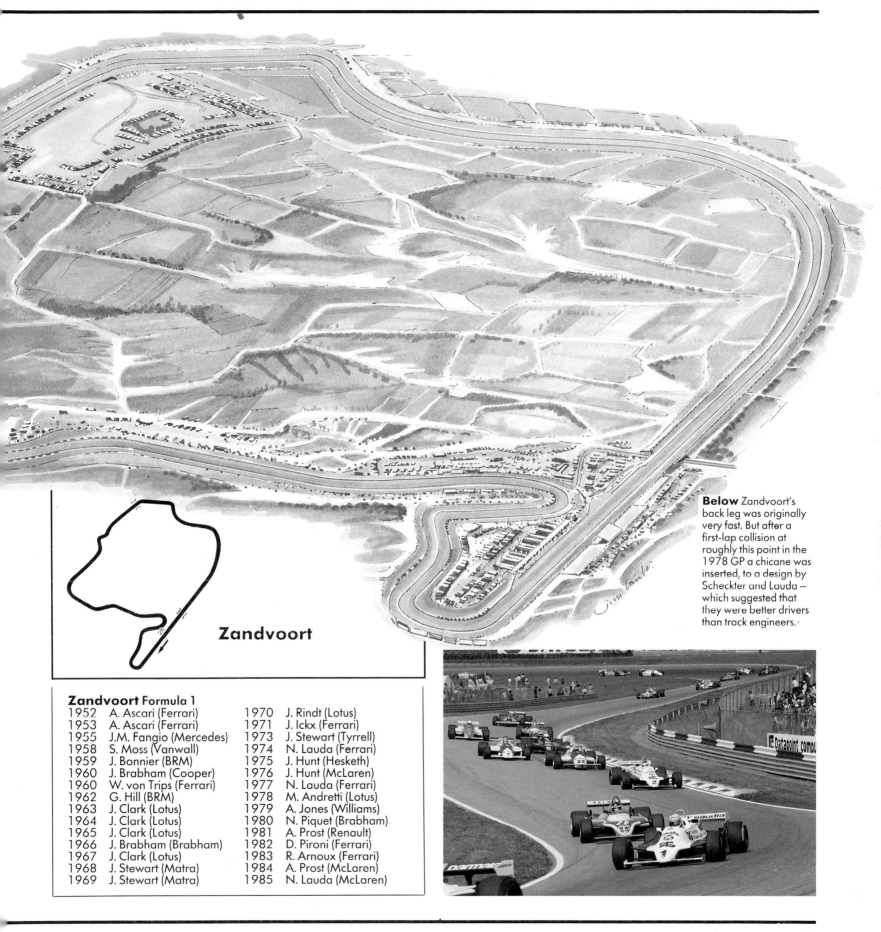

Zandvoort

Below Zandvoort's back leg was originally very fast. But after a first-lap collision at roughly this point in the 1978 GP a chicane was inserted, to a design by Scheckter and Lauda — which suggested that they were better drivers than track engineers.

Zandvoort Formula 1

1952	A. Ascari (Ferrari)	1970	J. Rindt (Lotus)
1953	A. Ascari (Ferrari)	1971	J. Ickx (Ferrari)
1955	J.M. Fangio (Mercedes)	1973	J. Stewart (Tyrrell)
1958	S. Moss (Vanwall)	1974	N. Lauda (Ferrari)
1959	J. Bonnier (BRM)	1975	J. Hunt (Hesketh)
1960	J. Brabham (Cooper)	1976	J. Hunt (McLaren)
1960	W. von Trips (Ferrari)	1977	N. Lauda (Ferrari)
1962	G. Hill (BRM)	1978	M. Andretti (Lotus)
1963	J. Clark (Lotus)	1979	A. Jones (Williams)
1964	J. Clark (Lotus)	1980	N. Piquet (Brabham)
1965	J. Clark (Lotus)	1981	A. Prost (Renault)
1966	J. Brabham (Brabham)	1982	D. Pironi (Ferrari)
1967	J. Clark (Lotus)	1983	R. Arnoux (Ferrari)
1968	J. Stewart (Matra)	1984	A. Prost (McLaren)
1969	J. Stewart (Matra)	1985	N. Lauda (McLaren)

PORTUGAL Estoril

If you happen to find yourself in Lisbon, heading along the coast road of the Tagus estuary – they call it 'La Linea' and the locals claim it is the most dangerous stretch of public road in Europe – you are not far from Estoril, a town bristling with grand hotels which haven't been quite the same since the 1930s when deposed monarchs found exile there in the sunshine. Today Estoril claims the biggest casino in Europe, catering for a better class of package tours, and a racing circuit.

A few miles inland from the coast, up in the barren rocky plateau overlooked by a coastal range, is the circuit with its long main straight and towering white grandstand. The track switches back on itself continually and there are several changes of elevation, although the most interesting features for the drivers are the long curling corner on to the main straight (negotiate this quickly and you get the extra revs to carry you quicker down the main straight past the pits) and the fast kink behind the paddock.

Built in 1972, the track has had a chequered history. Its early progress was hampered by the fuel crisis of 1973 and the Portuguese revolution of the following year. In 1975, however, Estoril staged a round of the European Formula 2 championship, won by Jacques Laffite, and the F2 men returned for two more visits, the French dominating with René Arnoux winning in 1976 and Didier Pironi the following year. After this brief interlude Estoril dropped from the international racing scene and fell into disrepair. It was not until the early 1980s that it began to re-emerge, being used as a special stage for the Portuguese Rally, which is run through the machis-

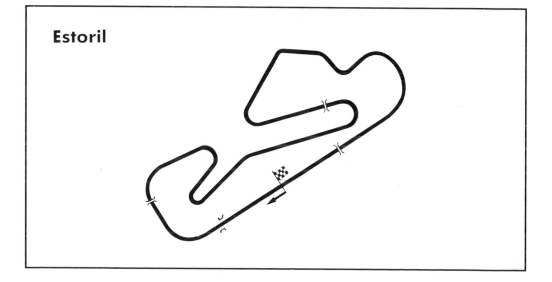

Estoril

Estoril Formula 1
1984   A. Prost (McLaren)
1985   A. Senna (Lotus)
1986   N Mansell (Williams)
1987   A. Prost (McLaren)
1988   A. Prost (McLaren)

Right A long telephoto lens greatly foreshortens the entry to the first right-hander after the start-finish area at Estoril.

Below Nelson Piquet in a Lotus followed by Michele Alboreto (Ferrari), blasts up the highest point on the circuit in the 1988 Grand Prix, past some convenient viewing points.

Right Heavy traffic as a line of cars sweeps through the left-hander to begin the fast section behind the paddock.

mo-testing roads in the hills overlooking the track.

With the Grand Prix teams needing a place for winter testing and now being unable to visit South Africa for political reasons, Estoril returned to favour and major redevelopment work was completed. Thus, by October 1984, Portugal was ready to organize its first full World Championship Formula 1 Grand Prix. Not only that, it was lucky enough to be the title decider between McLaren team-mates Niki Lauda and Alain Prost. Prost won the race, but he could do nothing to stop Lauda finishing second and taking the title by just half a point. Only a few months later, Estoril relocated in the F1 calendar, and the teams returned in April 1985 for a wet race which saw the first victory of a young man called Ayrton Senna, the latest Brazilian prodigy.

In 1987 the race was dominated by another youngster, Ferrari driver Gerhard Berger, who had led throughout but in the closing stages

Other Circuits

Prost was remorselessly inching ever closer. With just two laps to go Berger spun off and Prost swept through to win his 28th Grand Prix victory, thus passing Jackie Stewart's long-standing record of F1 wins in a career. In recent years, Estoril has also been the venue for a regular round of the European Touring Car Championship, while a national Formula Ford 1600 series was instituted in the mid-1980s. Being just a few miles from the westernmost point of Europe and close to the Atlantic shoreline, the weather at Estoril can be temperamental with stiff breezes and sharp rain squalls sometimes disrupting activities.

Right Oporto 1958: Street furniture could be protected with straw bales, while cobbles and tram tracks were accepted hazards in F1 street circuits even towards the end of the 1950s. Here a BRM is chased by a Vanwall and a Maserati in the Portuguese Grand Prix.

Before the construction of Estoril, racing was held at a number of street tracks around the country, notably **Oporto** in the north and at **Monsanto** in Lisbon. The first Portuguese Grand Prix was actually held at **Oporto** in 1950 and was for sportscars. The track was in the centre of the town and was flat out between the buildings and lamp-posts; an added difficulty were the tramlines which had to be negotiated! It was totally unsafe and after several major accidents it faded away. The Portuguese Grand Prix switched between Oporto and Monsanto, although both circuits continued also to hold their own races: the Oporto Grand Prix and the Governor of Lisbon's Cup respectively, both of which were for sportscars in the mid-1950s.

Two other street tracks of note are used annually, the more important being at **Vila Real**, inland from Oporto in Mateus country. Each year in July, dating back to 1931, the roads of the area have been closed off to form a 4.3-mile track, bordered by houses, lamp-posts, trees and stone walls. A grandstand and pits are situated just outside the town from where the track disappears off into the countryside, downhill across a narrow bridge and then sweeping through a series of fast uphill corners, across a level-crossing, to its highest point. After this it is downhill, through a series of extremely fast sweepers back towards the town, diving between the houses, across a second level-crossing and across a second bridge, this one over a deep ravine. Revived after the war, the track hosted major international sportscar races in the 1950s and later Formula 3. The last of the international races came in 1974, although the circuit is still used to this day for the national touring car championship. The other street circuit at **Vila da Conde** runs along the seafront of the resort to the north of Oporto.

SCANDINAVIA

The Scandinavian landscape of vast lakes and forests has nurtured off-road driving, and Swedish and Finnish rally-drivers have excelled for many years. Racing on tracks in Scandinavia is dominated nowadays by events in Sweden, although the first in the region took place in Finland, beginning in 1932 with a Finnish GP on a road course at Munkkiniemi. In the same era there were races on frozen lakes in Norway (Lakes Bogstad and Gjerson) and Sweden (the Winter Grand Prix at Lake Ramen), but it was not until after the Second World War that any serious competition got under way in Scandinavia.

As in many other countries without permanent circuits, the first races took place on airfields. The earliest example was in 1947 at Rommehed, which was another Winter GP won by the ERA of Reg Parnell and a year later at Skarpnack, near Stockholm. There followed sportscar races in the 1950s on the streets of Kristianstad, the first Swedish Grand Prix being won there in 1955 by Fangio.

At around the same time, racing at Karlskoga (about 150 miles due west of Stockholm) was gaining importance with the Kanonloppet sportscar races. Moss had won three consecutive races before the circuit decided to switch to a non-championship F1 meeting. Moss won that too! Formula 1 lasted until 1963 after which Karlskoga turned to Formula 2. By the mid-1970s the track staged a round of the European F2 Championship. It was also the local track of Ronnie Peterson, who won there in 1974.

Anderstorp

The Scandinavian Raceway at Anderstorp was the dream of Sven 'Smokey' Asberg. Anderstorp lies deep in the forests of central Sweden to the south-east of Göteborg, and was ready for action by 1973. A young generation of Swedish drivers, inspired by the exploits of

Swedes to the fore at the Scandinavian Raceway. **Above** Ronnie Peterson leads the 1973 Swedish Grand Prix in a Lotus 72. **Left** Sparser crowds for a European Touring Car race a dozen years later: a Volvo leads a Rover in this shot.

Jo Bonnier, had made their presence felt in Formula 1, notably Ronnie Peterson and Reine Wisell (to be followed later by Gunnar Nilsson), and Anderstorp was intended to be the place where they could win in front of their home crowd.

Anderstorp was built in the middle of a flat marsh and, as time passed, of all the tracks it proved to be the joker in the pack. It was unusual in many ways: the pits were separated from the start-finish line; the twisty infield was offset by a runway forming the back straight, making compromise in set-up vital; the corners seemed to go on forever with slight bankings so that finding the right tyre combination was a nightmare; and the results were seldom as expected.

When the Grand Prix circus first arrived in June 1973, Peterson had yet to win a race for Lotus, although he had been knocking on the door all year. He was leading in the closing laps to the obvious delight of the locals, when a tyre deflated and Denny Hulme swept past to win. Ronnie was to take his first win in the next race, (the French Grand Prix) and went on to add three more victories by the end of 1973. But he would never win at home. A year later Jody Scheckter secured his debut victory and he repeated that success in 1976, making history by guiding the six-wheeled Tyrrell to victory. Jacques Laffite surprised everyone 12 months later with a victory for Ligier and next we had Niki Lauda (the 1975 victor) in the infamous — and subsequently banned — Brabham fan car.

A few months later, the Swedes Peterson and Gunnar Nilsson were both dead. The Swedish Grand Prix did not outlive them and Anderstrop was badly run down by 1985 when international racing returned in the form of the European Car Championship. At the time Volvo was achieving startling results with its 240 Turbo and the locals turned out to see a home victory for Thomas Lindstrom. A year later they were treated to one of the great ETC races in what was a great era for the series — Ulf Granberg crossing the line just 0.37 second ahead of the Rover of Armin Hahne after more than 310 miles of red-blooded racing.

Anderstorp

1 Start Kurvan
2 Opel Kurvan
3 Karusell
4 Gislaved
5 Sodra
6 Norra
7 Loktor

Anderstorp	Formula 1	
1973	D. Hulme	(McLaren)
1974	J. Scheckter	(Tyrrell)
1975	N. Lauda	(Ferrari)
1976	J. Scheckter	(Tyrrell)
1977	J. Laffite	(Ligier)
1978	N. Lauda	(Brabham)

Mantorp Park

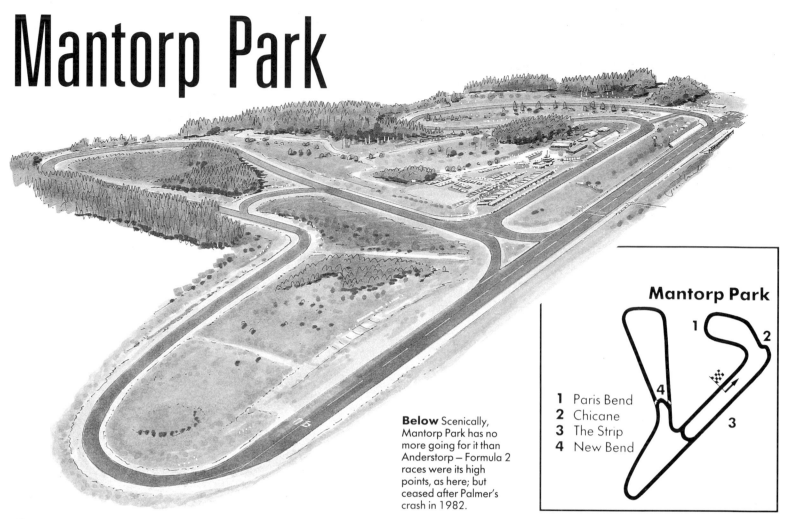

Mantorp Park

1 Paris Bend
2 Chicane
3 The Strip
4 New Bend

Below Scenically, Mantorp Park has no more going for it than Anderstorp — Formula 2 races were its high points, as here; but ceased after Palmer's crash in 1982.

Even before Anderstorp was built, Mantorp Park had staged international events. On the E4 motorway between Linköping and Jönköping in Östergötland, Mantorp was better positioned than other Swedish tracks to attract crowds. First used in 1969, it started out well as an international venue, when Ronnie Peterson won the Formula 2 race of 1971. Formula 2 was to continue until 1974, when the Swedish leg of the European Championship was transferred to Karlskoga.

Featuring three different track layouts and incorporating a drag strip, Mantorp was under-used until extensive modifications were made and Formula 2 returned in 1981. Once again it was a perfect result with Sweden's new rising star Stefan Johansson winning in a Toleman. A year later the F2 circus returned, but local heroes Johansson and Eje Elgh were quickly out of the running. The race was dominated by the works March cars (as were many that year) and Johnny Cecotto triumphed. In the same event Jonathan Palmer's Ralt flipped dramatically, breaking its roll hoop and trapping the Englishman unconscious beneath his car. Though unscathed, Palmer took an age to be extricated from the wreck. Formula 2 did not return.

Mantorp survives today, but in common with all Sweden's circuits it no longer hosts international races. Stefan Johansson, though talented, could not deliver a Formula 1 victory and a younger generation of drivers found it hard to find the money to compete on the international scene. Without local entries, the Swedes had little interest in paying to see the foreign drivers in action.

Knutstorp

For a time after the disappearance of the Swedish Grand Prix and the Mantorp F2 race, the tiny, twisty track at Knutstorp was the venue for Sweden's only international motor race, a round of the European Formula 3 Championship. Buried in the countryside to the south-east of the southern port of Helsingborg, Knutstorp is scarcely above club-racing level, with no pits to speak of and a track which is only 1.3 miles in length. The Formula 3 cars of the 1980s could lap the track in around 58 seconds! Squeezed into a valley, the track is overlooked by a huge bank that surprisingly is quickly filled with people. Their view of the track is spectacular.

Though small, Knutstorp is quite an

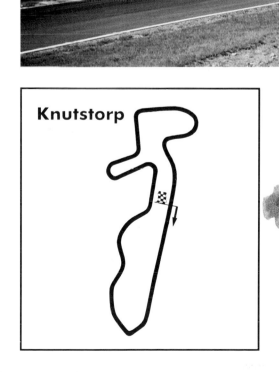

Left Hondas in a club race at Knutstorp. The leader is turning on to the pit straight.

Knutstorp

interesting track, with a double-apex first corner curling behind the paddock and through a section of esses to a difficult climbing lefthander where the track leaves the view of the pits and rushes up to a hairpin. Coming back into view there is a wild dropping righthander, followed by a tight left on to the pit straight. The local heroes were always hard to beat at home: Conny Adersson and Anders Olofsson dominating the early European F3 visits, until a curly-haired youngster called Prost came along in 1979. And in the following years almost all the major F1 drivers of the modern era rattled their way around Knutstorp. Today the likes of Nelson Piquet and Gerhard Berger will have forgotten the place, although a few national Swedish racers still drop in for the Kvallsposten races in August.

Finland

Having inaugurated international competition in Scandinavia, Finland was somewhat left behind by the growth of international racing. The severe weather and remoteness of the huge country does not help and although Finnish national racing is relatively strong, the lure of rallying and rallycross has tended to attract drivers who might make their names on the international racing scene. After its initial Grand Prix at Munkkiniemi in 1932, the Finns held a

second event in 1937 on the **Elaintarha** road course near Helsinki, an exercise repeated in 1939. Neither attracted any big international names, and further progress was interrupted by the war.

The post-war recovery was slow, but in 1960 Formula Junior visited Elaintarha. In the mid-1960s a number of new tracks began to appear. Outstanding among these was **Hämeenlinna**, also known as Ahvenisto, a twisty and undulating 1.88-mile figure-of-eight track, which has been the country's premier circuit since it opened in 1967. A spectacular place, fringed with pines, Hämeenlinna is 52 miles north of Helsinki on the road to Tampere. It staged a non-championship Formula 2 race in

1967, won by Jochen Rindt, since when no international races of note have been run.

At the same time as Hämeenlinna opened, Keimola and Artukainen began to operate. **Keimola**, on the northern outskirts of Helsinki, opened in September 1967 with the Finnish F2 GP, a non-championship race won by Jim Clark. **Artukainen** is a short airfield track near the seaside town of Turku to the west of Helsinki. More recently the short and undulating **Kemora** circuit appeared. Situated 100 miles south of the Arctic Circle, it has in recent years hosted a Midnight Sun race. Finland also boasts its own street circuit at **Seinäjoki** (southeast of the port of Vaasa), a rising and falling series of twists and turns 1.3 miles in length.

Despite having had a World Champion in Keke Rosberg, Finnish racing remains on a relatively small scale, its brightest stars whisked away to race in England on their way to Formula 1. Meanwhile, the rally stars crash on through the forests and wilderness.

Other Scandinavian Circuits

Of the remaining Scandinavian circuits Sweden's **Kinekullering** has been used since 1969. Near Lidköping, on Lake Vänern, the track sweeps around a valley, and is a fine spectator track, though too remote to draw large crowds. The European F2 championship visited only once in 1973, Jochen Mass recording a lap record of 49.5 seconds in a Surtees. On the west coast south of Göteborg is **Falkenberg**, lapped in 1981 by a Formula 3 car in 38.2 seconds! Almost circular with a couple of kinks, it is too small to be used for international competition, though the Swedish national F3 championship visits intermittently.

Across the Kattegat, the Danes have had a number of circuits, though today none is regularly used for international competitions. As in the other Scandinavian countries, the top drivers quickly move south to West Germany and they have had notable successes there, John Nielsen, Kurt Thiim and Kris Nissen all winning the German F3 title and Thiim also winning the national touring car crown. The most famous of the Danish tracks is the **Roskildering**, west of Copenhagen, a very short anticlockwise circuit crammed into a natural bowl. Now closed, Roskilde opened in 1956 and held sportscar races (the 1959 event being won by Stirling Moss). In 1961-2 it even went so far as to stage a non-championship F1 event, the Copenhagen Grand Prix. The first was won by Moss, the second by Jack Brabham. Thereafter Formula Juniors and Formula 3s came and went. With modern safety requirements, however, the Roskildering disappeared.

The **Jyllandring**, close to Denmark's second city Århus, is another tiny track, though it switches back on itself dramatically; while further east the **Djurslandring** is equally small and suitable only for Formula Ford competitions. Finally Norway has few permanent racing facilities, although there has been talk of constructing an international facility at Halden, to the south of Oslo.

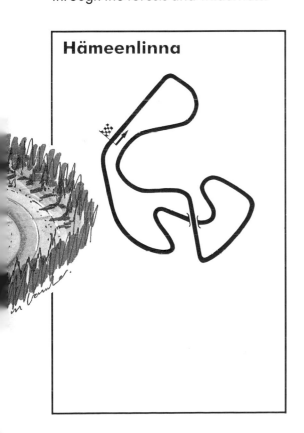

Hämeenlinna

Roskildering: a suitably small field of sports-racing cars negotiate a fast right-hander on this short Danish circuit in the late 1950s.

SPAIN Jarama and Montjuich

The Spanish Grand Prix has a long if intermittent history dating back to the first such event at **Guadarrama**, to the north-west of Madrid, in 1913 — a race won by a Rolls-Royce! Even before that, there had been racing in Spain with the Catalan Cup at Sitges on the coast south of Barcelona, in 1909 and 1910, both of which were won by Jules Goux of Peugeot. Racing was to return to Sitges and the banked circuit of **Sitges-Terramar**, completed in 1922. The second Spanish GP was held there the following year, won by Alberto Divo's Sunbeam, before the race moved to San Sebastian in 1926. Sitges-Terramar was used very little but survives to this day, overgrown and forgotten. Before the great banked circuit, however, there was the Penya Rhin GP, held for three years at Villafranca.

The first of Barcelona's three circuits, **Villafranca de Panades**, was a triangular 9.1-mile track laid out on public roads on which races were held in 1921–3. The Spanish GP, however, would not take place in Barcelona until years later; until its home was the **Lasarte** circuit at San Sebastian on the Bay of Biscay. This was another road course, 11.03 miles long, and the venue for the race until 1935. The European Grand Prix of 1926 was won at San Sebastian by Jules Goux in a Bugatti, while Louis Chiron won three times; other triumphs went to Achille Varzi in 1930 and Rudolf Carraciola in 1935.

The Penya Rhin GP was revived in 1933 and held on a new track laid out in Montjuich Park, Barcelona. With the outbreak of the Spanish Civil War in 1936, it was to be 10 years before racing returned to Spain, back in

Barcelona on the street track known as **Pedralbes** on the city's western outskirts. The 1946 Penya Rhin GP was one of the first European races after the war, held on a 2.77-mile course on the avenues of downtown Barcelona. This was a regular feature until 1954, also staging the Spanish GPs of 1951 (won by Fangio in an Alfa) and 1954 (Mike Hawthorn's Ferrari). Thereafter Spain disappeared from the international calendar.

It was to be a long time before international drivers returned to Spain. In 1964 the Royal Automobile Club of Spain (RACE) contacted John Hugeholz (the designer of Zandvoort in Holland and Suzuka in Japan) to build a permanent racing circuit near Madrid. The club owned an area of sun-scorched scrubland 18 miles north of Madrid alongside the main N1 road to Burgos, and Hugenholz was given a small part of it — much less

than he wanted — to construct a Grand Prix track. (The RACE used the rest for golf courses and a country club.)

The Circuito Permanente del Jarama was not as Hugenholz had originally intended. His eight-food-wide grass verges became loose granite chips and were used by all drivers. The Dutchman had wanted a long straight continuing from the present Ascari corner with a fast return leg. As a result, Jarama became a track where the premium was on low speed pickup and traction. At the time it opened, it was a modern facility with a multi-storey control tower dominating the area and a large grandstand opposite the pits.

As work on Jarama was being finished in 1966, Montjuich suddenly re-emerged, Barcelona not wanting Madrid to steal the Grand Prix. Situated in the largest park in Barcelona, close to the harbour, the Montjuich

Right Barcelona's Montjuich Park circuit was beautiful, but fated. Bumps led to aerofoil failures on both Lotus 49 cars in the 1969 GP, and they crashed within yards of each other: Hill's is in the background, Rindt's in the foreground; and Colin Chapman sprints from the first as the second comes to rest.

Left Pedralbes, in Barcelona's suburbs, comprised a wide avenue and a return leg through residential streets. Here Fangio winds his Alfa Romeo 159 up for the flat-out blast along the avenue, on the way to a last victory for this magnificent old car in the 1951 Spanish GP.

Right One of the shortcomings of Jarama resulted from the attempt to pack too much track into too small an area. But as this shot indicates, it meant that the handful of spectators opposite the pits could also see cars on the return leg as they completed the warm-up lap in the 1987 Touring Car Championship race.

circuit was a tortuous and undulating 2.35 miles. 'It was a nice circuit,' remembers Denny Hulme. 'It dropped downhill through the park and had that terrifying jump at the top of the hill. What I remember best were the fights we had with the police every year. About five minutes before the race they seemed to take over the administration. Of course the mechanics always wanted to go on to the grid to sort out something or other and there was a big fisticuffs. The race was always delayed for 15 minutes because everyone was fighting!'

The first event at the revived Montjuich was in 1966 for Formula 2 cars. It was won by Jack Brabham and the following year by Jim Clark: the top international stars liked Montjuich. It was Clark, too, who won the first race at Jarama in July 1967, the F2 Madrid GP, and before the end of the year he had also won the non-championship Formula 1 Spanish GP at the Madrid track. As pressure for a World Championship Spanish Grand Prix increased, a compromise between Jarama and Monjuich, Madrid and Barcelona, was sought. The race would alternate between the two, with Jarama hosting the first in 1968, when Graham Hill won for Lotus.

Hill was to figure prominently in 1969 as well with the first race at Montjuich. This was the era of the high wings and Hill had a huge accident when his wing collapsed, followed moments later by his team-mate Jochen Rindt's wing doing the same. Both were fortunate to emerge unhurt. Amon's Ferrari led but seized up as expected, and Jackie Stewart found himself the winner, the first of three consecutive Spanish victories for the Scot. Emerson Fittipaldi won the next two; but in 1975, back at Montjuich, the then reigning World Champion packed his bags on the morning of the race and left. There had been little practice, the drivers almost to a man complaining of unsafe barriers, but a threat to impound the cars forced the teams to race. It was to be a disaster.

Two drivers withdrew after a couple of laps and there was carnage as suspensions and driveshafts broke, leaving Rolf Stommelen's Hill in the lead. Then the German's car shed a rear aerofoil and he crashed heavily, the car careering off the track, killing four bystanders. Jochen Mass was awarded the race and half points but Montjuich was finished.

Thereafter the Spanish GP was held at Jarama. There was a fine victory by Patrick Depailler in 1979 in a Ligier — the Frenchman's last GP win. And in

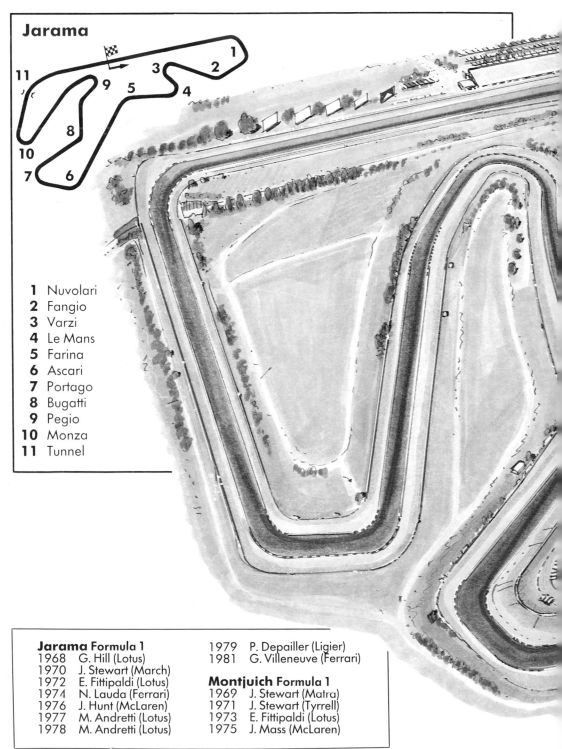

Jarama

1	Nuvolari
2	Fangio
3	Varzi
4	Le Mans
5	Farina
6	Ascari
7	Portago
8	Bugatti
9	Pegio
10	Monza
11	Tunnel

Jarama Formula 1		1979	P. Depailler (Ligier)
1968	G. Hill (Lotus)	1981	G. Villeneuve (Ferrari)
1970	J. Stewart (March)		
1972	E. Fittipaldi (Lotus)	**Montjuich** Formula 1	
1974	N. Lauda (Ferrari)	1969	J. Stewart (Matra)
1976	J. Hunt (McLaren)	1971	J. Stewart (Tyrrell)
1977	M. Andretti (Lotus)	1973	E. Fittipaldi (Lotus)
1978	M. Andretti (Lotus)	1975	J. Mass (McLaren)

Below Jarama: World Sportscar Championship 1987. The Sigala/Brancatelli Brun-Torno-Porsche 962 chased by the Wiedler/Nissen Kremer-Porsche 962, which came fourth.

the midsummer of 1980, at the height of the FISA-FOCA civil war in Formula 1, an 'illegal' FOCA Grand Prix was won by Alan Jones. A year later saw the last Grand Prix at Jarama and perhaps one of the greatest, for on a scorchingly hot afternoon, Gilles Villeneuve's cumbersome but powerful Ferrari held off four other cars, the five blanketed by just 1.24 seconds.

Jarama, however, was becoming dilapidated and dangerous for Formula 1; and for the next few years, as it continued its slide, there were only occasional Formula 2, touring car and European Formula 3 meetings. A lick or two of paint in recent years and a rebuilt pitlane has seen several World Sportscar Championship races and a round of the one-off World Touring Car Championship in 1987, but Jarama is finished as a major circuit. The RACE is apparently now more interested in golf.

Jerez

Montjuich and Jarama seemed to evolve together, thrive and decline together, as local and regional rivalries dictated. Grand Prix racing, however, was not finished in Spain. In 1985 the Mayor of Jerez decided to build a circuit close to his town in an effort to promote the famous sherry region on the international scene. The track, finished just in time for the Grand Prix of 1986, nestles in a natural amphitheatre in the dry and underpopulated region where life is slow, relaxed and *mañana* is never too late. Seville and Cádiz are the nearest cities, but Jerez has been unable to draw anything resembling a crowd.

As a winter testing facility for grand prix cars, however, it has been welcomed by European racing teams impressed by its state-of-the-art facilities. As a race venue it is without soul, lost in the wilds of nowhere, devoid of atmosphere. Grand Prix racing has done its best for Jerez, Nigel Mansell and Ayrton Senna recording one of the closest Grand Prix finishes ever in

Jerez
1 Expo-92
2 Michelin
3 Chicane
4 Dry Sack
5 Nieto
6 Peluqui
7 Ducodos

Left Pit-stop action at Jerez, venue of an FIA Sports-Prototype World Championship race since 1986.

Jerez Formula 1
1986   A. Senna (Lotus)
1987   N. Mansell (Williams)
1988   A. Prost (McLaren)

Above Jerez has everything racing's controlling body thinks a circuit should have — except crowds. This is the start of the 1987 Grand Prix.

the first race, crossing the line side-by-side separated by 0.014 second. But it is hard to see Jerez surviving.

In recent years plans have been laid for a new circuit at **Montmelo** to the north of Barcelona and it is likely that Formula 1 will be greeted with open arms in the great Catalan city which has always considered itself the home of Spanish racing.

SWITZERLAND

Switzerland does not have any motor racing – and that's official. True, there was a Swiss Formula 1 Grand Prix in 1982, but this was held at Dijon in France and was really little more than an excuse to let the French have another Formula 1 race on their territory. Motor racing in Switzerland has been banned since the disaster at Le Mans in 1955. There have been occasional attempts to get the sport re-established, but none have been successful. Yet there is plenty of Swiss interest in racing: Jo Siffert, Clay Regazzoni and Marc Surer all made it into the highest echelons of the sport despite having no home tracks on which to race.

Today, Switzerland has a handful of famous hill climbs: the celebrated Ollon-Villars run and the Sierra-Montana-Crans, scene of the Swiss Mountain GPs where Jim Clark and others would take to the hills in the 1960s. That is all. On the western outskirts of the capital city, Berne, however, is **Bremgarten**, the site of one of the great racing circuits of the 1930s. A true road course, Bremgarten was very fast and dangerous. Set in beautiful countryside, the 4.52-mile route blasted through forests. There

were no real straights, merely a succession of fast sweeping corners with no run-off and, to add to the challenge, various changes of surface.

The track was first used in 1931 for motorcycle racing but cars soon followed with the inaugural Swiss Grand Prix taking place in 1934. Victory went to German ace Hans Stuck in an Auto Union and, until the outbreak of the Second World War, the Swiss Grand Prix, held annually at Bremgarten, was dominated by the German Auto Unions and Mercedes. The list of winners includes such great aces of the era as Caracciola, Rosemeyer and Lang. Bremgarten was the site of three of Caracciola's Grand Prix victories; but in 1952 the track ended his career, when he was seriously hurt in an accident while at the wheel of a Mercedes 300SL sportscar. There were deaths too, for this was a dangerous place, the saddest victim being the great veteran Italian Achille Varzi in 1948.

Bremgarten was active as a Formula 1 venue after the war. The German success was replaced by a flood of Italian victories from Alfa Romeos and Ferraris until 1954, when Juan-Manual Fangio gave Mercedes its first

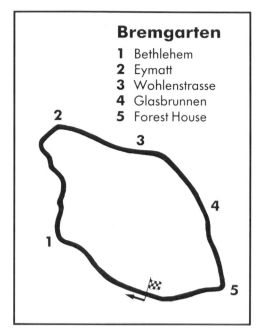

Bremgarten
1 Bethlehem
2 Eymatt
3 Wohlenstrasse
4 Glasbrunnen
5 Forest House

Swiss GP triumph since Lang's in 1939. A year later, in the highly-charged political atmosphere in the wake of the Le Mans disaster, the Swiss Grand Prix was cancelled and motor racing in the country was banned.

A variety of other events had been held throughout Switzerland before the ban, with street races being the favoured format. **Geneva** had a couple of different tracks: the first, a triangular circuit at Meyrin, was used initially in 1924; the second, a tighter street version, was used for the Grand Prix des Nations in 1946, one of the first events after war ended. That survived only until 1950.

Montreux had staged a number of pre-war events, while Formula 1 races were held in **Lausanne** in the immediately post-war period. In 1947 victory went to Gigi Villoresi in a Maserati, and Dr Nino Farina repeated the Maserati success in 1949. In recent years Baron Tullo de Graffenried has organised an Historic GP of Lausanne, although this is more of a parade than an actual race. **Erlen**, in the east of the country, held Formula 2 races in 1950 and 1951, which succeeded in attracting top international competitors.

Left Sunlight and shadow at Bremgarten. The year is 1949, when the Grands Prix were largely fought by Maserati and Ferrari, first and second here.

Above Geneva 1946: Grand Prix des Nations. Tuzio Nuvolari (Maserati 4CL) heads an Alfa Romeo 158, which began its period of domination in this race.

UNITED KINGDOM

Below Until the
Birmingham Superprix
in the 1980s, the only
racing on British public
roads was in Jersey and
the Isle of Man. Here
C.S. Rolls (Rolls-Royce) is
on his way to victory in
the 1906 RAC Tourist
Trophy on Man.

Today Britain is the centre of the
world's racing-car industry. The
majority of the Formula 1 Grand Prix
teams are based there while companies such as Cosworth, March, Ralt,
Reynard, Van Diemen and Lola supply
the bulk of the cars destined for
competition across the world. The
demand for testing facilities is great,
while the thriving national racing
scene keeps the existing circuits busy
on most weekends of the year with a
varied menu of events.

However, there were incredible difficulties in establishing racing tracks in
the early years of the sport in Britain.
Brooklands may have been the
world's first purpose-built racing facility back in 1906; but whereas the
Europeans thought nothing of getting
local authorities to close a road and
having a race, such a thing was
banned by law in Britain. The earliest
British races therefore were held
'offshore' — in Northern Ireland or the
Isle of Man.

The only alternative was to construct circuits on private land. Few
people were in a position to do so,
even fewer were willing. Thus began
the tradition of hillclimbs and sprints
which developed between the wars at
Prescott and Shelsley Walsh. Brooklands was the notable exception. A
huge banked speedway which was to
be the model for many others across
the world, it would be the home of
British racing until the outbreak of the
Second World War; but it was unsuitable for Grand Prix racing.

Also in existence when the war
broke out were Crystal Palace in south
London and Donington Park in Leicestershire. With the war, however, it all
ended. Brooklands was sold and racing ceased. With the coming of peace

in 1945, Donington and Crystal
Palace were unfit for use. At the time
there was little money available to
build new tracks, so racing enthusiasts
did what they could. The 'make do
and mend' improvisatory skills prevalent in the 1940s were put to good
use in motor racing. All over the
country wartime airfields, no longer
required by the RAF, were pressed
into service, and many of these duly
became racing tracks.

The first, as early as June 1946, was
Gransden Lodge, but there followed
many more, most now long forgotten:
Gamston, Brough, Marston Moor, Crimond, Davidstow, Ibsley, Turnberry,
Fairwood, Boreham, Charterhall, Rufforth, Croft and, of course, the modern
survivors: Goodwood, Silverstone,
Snetterton, Thruxton and Castle

Combe. There were even tracks laid
out around army camps such as
Blandford and Oulton Park and street
races in Jersey, on the Isle of Man and
in Northern Ireland.

In 1955, in the wake of the accidents at Le Mans and Dundrod, many
of the airfields were abandoned and,
as more money became available, so
the modern British circuits began to
emerge. Brands Hatch was surfaced in
1949, a year after Silverstone had
staged the first post-war British Grand
Prix. The others followed. Today there
are plenty of tracks serving the sport
at club, national and international
level. And, finally, in 1986 mainland
Britain had a street race in Birmingham, although it took almost 40 years
before Parliament could be persuaded to allow such a thing.

Donington

B ritain's oldest track currently in use is at Donington Park in Leicestershire, atop a windswept hill above the village of Castle Donington, close to the East Midlands Airport and within a couple of miles of the M1 motorway. More than any other track, this is the spiritual home of the British Grand Prix for it was here that the titans of the 1930s raced their Auto Unions and Mercedes: Rosemeyer and Nuvolari both won at Donington.

Today the circuit is a shortened version of the classic pre-war track. Opened in March 1933 for motorcycle races, the original Donington was 2.19 miles in length. It was lengthened twice and the undergrowth thinned out before the great years of 1937-8, but when the war broke out the land was requisitioned by the military and became a stores dump. It remained closed until bought in the 1970s by the rose magnate Tom Wheatcroft. Major rebuilding took place, for it was Wheatcroft's intention to bring the British Grand Prix back from Silverstone and Brands Hatch.

This is a challenging track with the curling Redgate Corner and the fast downhill sweep through the Craner Curves to the treacherous Old Hairpin. Then comes the climb uphill to Mcleans and the short straight to Coppice with its deceptive brow and the high-speed straight back towards the paddock. In 1985 a new section of track was built behind the paddock, restoring the famous Melbourne Hairpin name but most drivers insist that the loop is too artificial compared with the rest of the flowing parkland circuit.

The reopened Donington was soon involved in the international scene with a European Formula 2 round in October 1977. In the 1979 race the

Left The GP Mercedes and Auto Unions first came to Britain in 1937, when they pulverized local opposition in the Donington Grand Prix.

Below The first corner on the modern Donington circuit often sees frantic jostling immediately after the start of a race. Here Sierras and Golf GTIs are involved in a skirmish.

crowds were treated to a dramatic championship showdown between Marc Surer and local hero Brian Henton; but political troubles meant that F2 did not return until 1981, when Geoff Lees won the day. The circuit remained an integral part of F2 and F3000; the first F3000 title was settled at the first corner in 1985 when Emanuele Pirro and Mike Thackwell collided, leaving Christian Danner to take the race and the title. The championship returned in 1987, but the arrival of the Birmingham street circuit and the increasingly complicated battle over the siting of the British Grand Prix meant that Doning-

ton was always living for a tomorrow that might never appear.

Donington has also played an important part in both the European Formula 3 and the European Touring Car (ETC) Championships, while also being the arena for a healthy portion of domestic competitions. The Donington 500 of 1981 marked the first long-distance race for the rebuilt circuit, but the fixture became a major ETC event — though sometimes the April weather made the race rather less than wonderful. ETC was beginning to boom in 1983, when the Jaguars and BMW 635CSis turned up to do battle. It marked the first major

Above Donington in Formula 2 days, with a Ralt leading into Redgate Corner. Later in the 1980s a large grandstand and other buildings went up beyond the tower at the end of the pits lane.

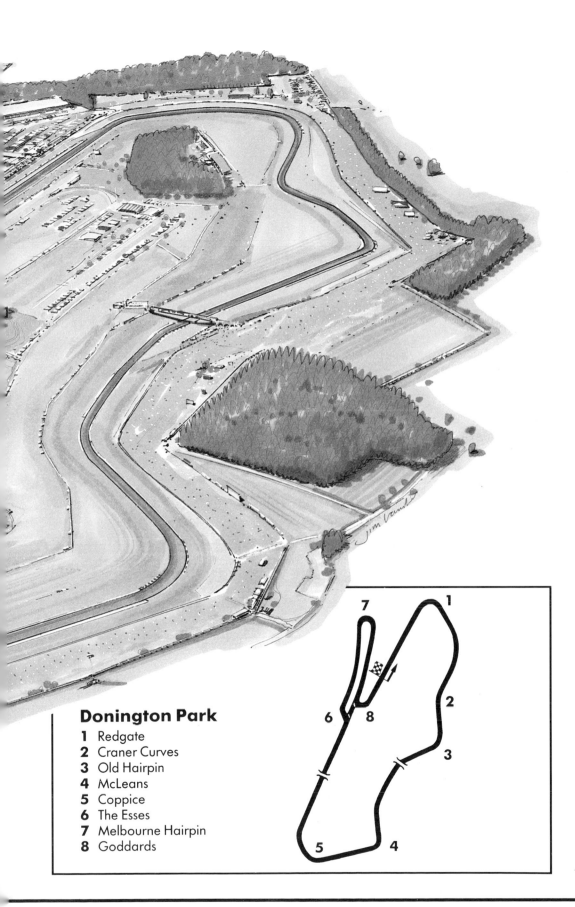

Donington Park

1 Redgate
2 Craner Curves
3 Old Hairpin
4 McLeans
5 Coppice
6 The Esses
7 Melbourne Hairpin
8 Goddards

international victory of Tom Walkinshaw's protégé Martin Brundle, who would go on to become World Sportscar Champion of 1988. Donington was the exclusive property of the TWR team, for with Jaguars or Rovers the team won every race between 1983 and 1986, giving Win Percy a hat-trick of victories. In European F3 local knowledge clearly helped too. British-based New Zealander Brett Riley twice outpaced all the visiting continentals, while Derek Warwick, James Weaver, Brundle and Johnny Dumfries continued the home wins until the series was cancelled at the end of 1984.

Donington may be windswept, fogbound or soaking wet; it even produced snow for the ETC race of 1986! But on a fine day it is a wonderful place to watch motor racing. Britain, however, has a problem. With three circuits in the late 1980s up to Grand Prix standard and regulations meaning that a country may have only one Formula 1 Grand Prix a year, Brands Hatch, Silverstone and Donington seem perpetually at each other's throats. The principle of alternation has given way to five-year contracts for one track, a situation currently enjoyed by Silverstone (and consequently disliked by Brands Hatch and Donington Park).

Certainly Donington deserves more than it is allowed at present. Massive investment improves the track with each passing year and the circuit has pioneered many innovations such as staging rock concerts and attracting spectators with a Sunday market. Today it looks ahead once more, planning a major shopping and office complex in the area bounded by the track! It is a radical move, but perhaps a necessary one at a time when financial survival against the competition is harder than ever. Donington also houses one of the best-known motor racing museums in the world. If it was down to enterprise and innovation, this track would probably succeed. If there is any justice, it will.

Silverstone

Silverstone was the child of an austere age. This was no planned or landscaped venue: it just happened. It has none of the manicure of Paul Ricard, the atmosphere of Monza, or the grandeur of Spa. What it does have is speed — high speed. Some love Silverstone and some hate it but no matter what your opinion of the place it is hard to argue against the track's claim to be the 'Home of British Motor Racing'. Donington, realising this, claims to be the 'Heart of British Motor Sport'; which is also probably true. No Rosemeyer ever graced Silverstone's sweeps.

Less of the brash new kid in town than Brands Hatch but a new boy nonetheless, Silverstone dates only from 1948. With the war over and

Left 'Second-generation' Silverstone pits faced onto an elevated pits lane. A wide lane has since been introduced, and the pits rebuilt twice; they extend beyond the footbridge, and a large press facility has been built above them.

reconstruction under way the RAC, unable to finance the building of a new track and barred from road racing by the laws of the land, went in search of a venue to hold its first post-war Grand Prix. It was a problem: Donington was still a military stores dump, Brooklands had been sold off, Crystal Palace was in disrepair and Brands Hatch was still a dirt track!

All over the country racing enthusiasts had come up with the same idea. The war had seen airfields built everywhere to house the British and

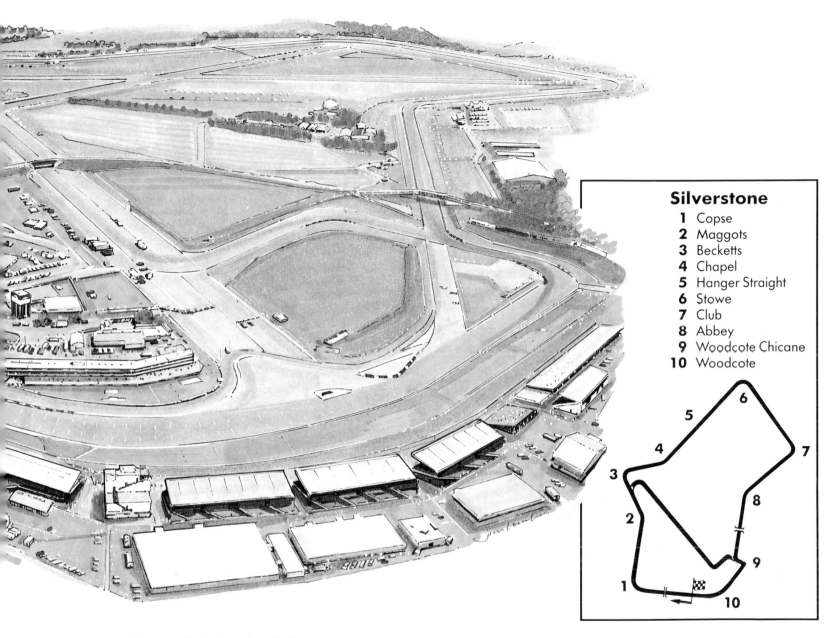

Silverstone

1 Copse
2 Maggots
3 Becketts
4 Chapel
5 Hanger Straight
6 Stowe
7 Club
8 Abbey
9 Woodcote Chicane
10 Woodcote

American planes which bombarded Europe. With the conflict over these were falling into disuse.

Silverstone was just such a place, an old airfield ranged over a gentle bump in the Northamptonshire countryside. The RAC approached the Air Ministry and in the summer of 1948 a lease was arranged. That first track, laid out on the runways and perimeter roads, was very different from the layout of today but all that mattered at the time was to get the place fit for a race. Jimmy Brown was appointed the track manager. Makeshift pits were

Silverstone Formula 1

1950	G. Farina (Alfa Romeo)
1951	F. Gonzalez (Ferrari)
1952	A. Ascari (Ferrari)
1953	A. Ascari (Ferrari)
1954	F. Gonzalez (Ferrari)
1956	J.M. Fangio (Ferrari)
1958	P. Collins (Ferrari)
1960	J. Brabham (Cooper)
1963	J. Clark (Lotus)
1965	J. Clark (Lotus)
1967	J. Clark (Lotus)
1969	J. Stewart (Matra)
1971	J. Stewart (Tyrrell)
1973	P. Revson (McLaren)
1975	E. Fittipaldi (McLaren)
1977	J. Hunt (McLaren)
1979	C. Regazzoni (Williams)
1981	J. Watson (McLaren)
1983	A. Prost (McLaren)
1985	A. Prost (McLaren)

1987	N. Mansell (Williams)
1988	A. Senna (McLaren)

RAC Tourist Trophy

1970	Muir (Chevrolet)
1972	Mass/Glemser (Ford)
1973	Ertl/Bell (BMW)
1974	Graham (Chevrolet)
1975	Graham (Chevrolet)
1976	Xhenceval/Dieudonne/ de Fierlant (BMW)
1977	Quester/Walkinshaw (BMW)
1978	Joosen/van Hove (BMW)
1979	Finotto/Facetti (BMW)
1980	Grano/Werginz/Neger (BMW)
1981	Walkinshaw/Nicholson (Mazda)
1982	Walkinshaw/Nicholson (Jaguar)
1983	Soper/Metge (Rover)
1984	Kelleners/Brancatelli (BMW)

1985	Walkinshaw/Percy (Rover)
1986	Allam/Hulme (Rover)
1987	Calderari/Mancini (BMW)
1988	Rouse/Ferte (Ford)

1000 km

1976	Fitzpatrick/Walkinshaw (BMW)
1977	Mass/Ickx (Porsche)
1978	Ickx/Mass (Porsche)
1979	Heyer/Wollek/Fitzpatrick (Porsche)
1980	De Cadenet/Wilson (De Cadenet)
1981	Schornstein/Grohs/Rohrl (Porsche)
1982	Patrese/Alboreto (Lancia)
1983	Bell/Bellof (Porsche)
1984	Ickx/Mass (Porsche)
1985	Ickx/Mass (Porsche)
1986	Warwick/Cheever (Jaguar)
1987	Cheever/Boesel (Jaguar)
1988	Cheever/Brundle (Jaguar)

put up at the farm and hay bales marked the 3.7-mile hour-glass-shaped track. It was to be a very basic affair but people, used to austerity, flocked in their thousands, eager in October 1948 to see something exciting, something different. They were treated to Gigi Villoresi in a Maserati outpacing fellow Italian Alberto Ascari.

The dominant feature of Silverstone is the immense canopy of the sky, clouds ponderously scudding by often laden with rain. If you stand out in the rain here, with the wind whipping through your clothes, you will swear a solemn oath never to return; but somehow you always do. Why does it

have this draw on you? Because it's fast. Runways and perimeter roads were built straight and thus Silverstone's dominant characteristic is high-speed motoring. The track of today is much like that used for the second event, in the spring of 1949. There was a chicane at Club Corner, but the basic shape was set. Later that summer Silverstone started its second major event, the non-championship Formula 1 *Daily Express* International Trophy (without the Club chicane).

In the following year, with the launching of the new Formula 1 World Championship, Silverstone was granted the very first World Championship *grande épreuve*. King

George IV was present for the Grand Prix of Europe (as was its title) and watched with thousands of others as the dominant Alfa Romeos outpaced everyone, with Nino Farina (who would become World Champion that year) being followed home by Luigi Fagioli and Reg Parnell.

Changes to the track came thick and fast in the 1950s. The Grand Prix and International Trophy (which continued to flourish) exchanged dates, establishing the British Grand Prix in its traditional mid-July slot. A year later the RAC gave up the lease, handing over the track to the British Racing Drivers' Club (BRDC). The pits were moved from the farm to the straight between Woodcote and Copse Corners, thus introducing a Club circuit peeling off the Grand Prix circuit just before Becketts and blasting up a central runway to Woodcote.

The year 1951 was significant, for it marked the first victory of a Ferrari in Grand Prix racing, Froilan Gonzalez emerging victorious after an early

Left Saloons turn into Stowe, at the furthest point from the start/finish area, in the days before a bridge was built roughly where the last cars are in the picture.

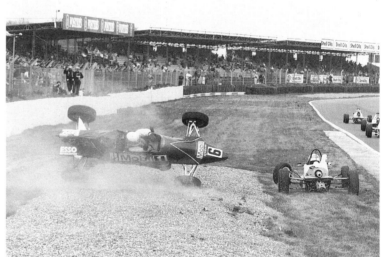

Above Formula Ford racing has often been close .... Gravel traps have taken the place of catch fences, and effectively slow cars still on their wheels. The National Circuit now joins the Grand Prix circuit near this point.

battle with the Alfa of fellow countryman Juan-Manuel Fangio. Two Ascari victories followed, but in 1954 'Pampas Bull' Gonzalez did it again. His career total of World Championship victories was achieved solely at Silverstone! In 1955 the British GP moved to Aintree for the first time and for the

Below The championship sports-prototype race at Silverstone was once a prelude to Le Mans, and attracted a great entry; and — as the background to this Jaguar-Sauber pair shows — a good crowd to watch them.

Right The end of the pits straight, with Alboreto's Ferrari heading a McLaren in the 1988 Grand Prix.

next few years the race would alternate between Northants and Liverpool. In 1961 the BRDC took the decision to buy the track and push ahead with improvements to facilities.

There have been many great races at Silverstone, indeed the 'Silverstone Finish' is something of a cliché, bawled out by commentators whenever cars cross the line in close formation. Before 1973 such finishes were indeed common. The British Grand Prix of 1973 changed that considerably, for at the end of the first lap an impulsive Jody Scheckter triggered a monumental pile-up at Woodcote Corner. Seven cars were eliminated (including the entire Surtees team) and Andrea de Adamich suffered leg injuries. After the race was restarted Peter Revson crossed the line for his

first F1 Championship victory, just clear of a gaggle of pursuers: Ronnie Peterson, Denny Hulme and a young driver in only his third Grand Prix, James Hunt. By now alternating the Grand Prix with Brands Hatch, Silverstone had a chicane at Woodcote for the next visit in 1975. There were also new pit garages.

Apart from Grand Prix it stages a multitude of events ranging from Owners' Clubs meetings to World Sportscars (the famous 1000km) and, of course, the Tourist Trophy — the world's oldest motor race. Outstanding among the memories are the F1 home victories of James Hunt (1977), John Watson (1981) and Nigel Mansell (1987) — with huge crowds roaring them home. When crammed with people as it is for the Grand Prix, it

does have atmosphere, excitement and expectation. The sky is filled with helicopters ferrying in the rich and famous, none too keen to spend their days sitting in the seemingly endless traffic jams which build up in the lanes around the area as 150,000 people try to find their way in and then out. For one day a year Silverstone is the busiest airport in Britain.

Each year there are changes to the circuit: new bridges and tunnels; new pits; new press centre; the chicane, which replaced the old Woodcote sweeper, in turn replaced by a dog-leg which has yet to be fully accepted by the drivers; and in 1989 major revisions that allow two independent circuits to be used simultaneously. Much work has gone into making Silverstone a premier circuit, but it remains above all a working track. When there is no race meeting the track is constantly busy with testing, and the industrial areas hum with the daily life of the racing teams based there. But while Silverstone buzzes around the Woodcote area, the essence of the track is away out at the back, at Stowe, Club and Abbey, where the cars are just a blur of speed.

Goodwood

A month after Silverstone opened, another wartime airfield was unveiled for racing. This was at Westhampnett in Sussex, which had been an important satellite field for the Tangmere fighter base during the Second World War. At the foot of the South Downs, it took the name of Goodwood after the nearby stately home and the racecourse perched high in the chalky downland hills above. The track had been a perimeter road of 2.38 miles. It opened in 1948 with the Goodwood Trophy, won by Reg Parnell in a Maserati. Indeed, Parnell managed to win the first three trophies before the international aces started to arrive; and he was twice runner up — to Nino Farina (soon to be F1 world champion) in 1951 and to Gonzalez in 1952, earning himself the nickname 'The

Emperor of Goodwood'.

More than any other track, Goodwood doled out trophies and cups with abandon: the Glover Trophy; Chichester Cup; Lavant Cup; Madgwick Cup; Woodcote Cup; Richmond Trophy; St Mary's Trophy; Sussex Trophy and, for a time, the Tourist Trophy as well. It was the home of the British Automobile Racing Club (BARC) for many years and the venue of a 9-hour sportscar race in the mid-1950s.

The fast sweeps of the perimeter road were the scene of many fine triumphs but also a share of tragedy. It was here that Stirling Moss's career ended after a huge accident at Fordwater in 1962. Eight years later Bruce McLaren died while testing one of his own CanAm cars. More recently, Canada lost its designated successor to Villeneuve when Bertrand Fabi was killed in an F3 testing accident. Today racing has left Goodwood behind, though it remains a test track.

'The best corner in the world?' muses Denny Hulme. 'St Mary's at Goodwood in a CanAm. Now that was something . . . .'

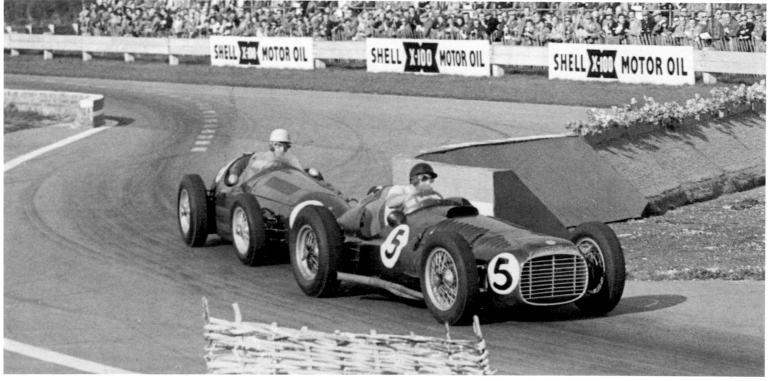

Aintree

If Goodwood has ceased to be a racing circuit, another of the major post-war tracks barely survives, for Aintree now holds only the occasional club event. Lying alongside the famous Aintree racecourse, home of the Grand National, in the northern suburbs of Liverpool, the track was a fast and flat three miles. At a time when there were few well-organised and developed racing facilities, Aintree had a major advantage: it shared the grandstands with the racecourse. As a result it shot quickly to prominence after opening in 1954, staging the British Grand Prix of 1955. It turned out to be one of the most memorable of the national Grands Prix for in that first race Stirling Moss had the audacity to take on the Old Master Juan-Manuel Fangio, his idol and team-mate at Mercedes. In front of his own crowd Moss was shadowed by Fangio most of the way but in the closing laps the Argentinian closed right up to the Englishman's tail. The last laps were greeted with huge excitement which spilled over into rejoicing as Moss crossed the line just ahead — the second closest finish in F1 history at the time.

While Mercedes finished 1-2-3-4 on that occasion, the British racing industry was beginning to grow; and two years later, when the Grand Prix returned to Aintree, Moss and Tony Brooks scored the first win for a British-built car in the World Championship, their shared Vanwall outpacing the chasing Ferraris. The Grand Prix returned on three further occasions, the final one being in 1962 when a young Scot by the name of Jim Clark won his second Grand Prix victory. That day British cars filled the top six places.

Aintree had served its purpose well, but with the coming of the permanent circuits it faded gracefully away, leaving its 1.64-mile (2.64 km) club circuit as a memory of those exciting days.

Left Goodwood chicane in the early 1950s: a packed grandstand watches Fangio in a V-16 BRM hounded by a McLaren 250F. The chicane was less substantial than it appeared, and little harm came to some drivers who inadvertently tried to 'straight-line' it.

Above Sportscars four abreast on a grid almost fill the track in the early 1950s. Jaguars to the fore, with three C-types on the front row.

Right An auspicious occasion at Aintree as the Mercedes of Fangio and Moss lead the 1955 Grand Prix field away at the start. Moss was to be the first British driver to win this race.

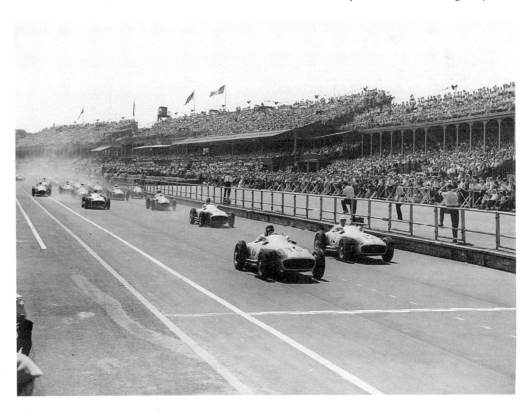

Brands Hatch

'For me,' says Ferrari ace Gerhard Berger, 'the best circuit in the world is Brands Hatch. But it's a bit dangerous now for Formula 1.' The Brands organisation would like to believe otherwise and continues to lobby for a return of the British Grand Prix, to which it played host in alternation with Silverstone from 1964. The history of the track, on the Kentish downs to the south-east of London, dates back to 1926, when a group of passing cyclists noticed a natural bowl, a mushroom field, beside the road. It belonged to Brands Hatch Farm, and after discussion with the farmer agreement was reached for a track to be used by the cyclists. Motorcyclists arrived two years later and throughout the 1930s there were regular events on the chalky tracks in the bowl.

In 1947 Brands Hatch Statium Limited was created and two years later the track was surfaced, so that in April 1950 the first race took place on a kidney-shaped circuit resembling the modern Indianapolis circuit (the Druids loop was not yet in existence). At first the new circuit was used only for 500cc Formula 3 racing, and it ran anticlockwise. Among the early winners was the intrepid Stirling Moss, who in June that year entered five races on the same day, won them all and took a lap record.

Although fine as a club-racing track, it was too short for international events. So in the winter of 1953 a major programme of changes began. The racing was switched to a clockwise direction and the track was widened with the addition of the uphill-downhill Druids section. Pits and spectator banks were also built. In the summer of 1955 a permanent grandstand was bought from the Northolt

Brands Hatch Formula 1	
1964	J. Clark (Lotus)
1966	J. Brabham (Brabham)
1968	J. Siffert (Lotus)
1970	J. Rindt (Lotus)
1972	E. Fittipaldi (Lotus)
1974	J. Scheckter (Tyrrell)
1976	N. Lauda (Ferrari)
1978	C. Reutemann (Ferrari)
1980	A. Jones (Williams)
1982	N. Lauda (McLaren)
1983	(Europe GP) N. Piquet (Brabham)
1984	N. Lauda (McLaren)
1985	(Europe GP) N. Mansell (Williams)
1986	N. Mansell (Williams)

trotting course which was closing down. A racing drivers' school was founded. And so it went on.

Central to the history of Brands Hatch has been John Webb, the first press officer. In 1961 he negotiated a takeover of Brands by Grovewood Securities and he took a seat on the board of Brands Hatch, heading the Motor Circuit Developments company that took over management of the track. A regular Formula 2 venue by now, the decision was taken to upgrade the track to Grand Prix status and the new loop was built out in the woods, bringing the track length to

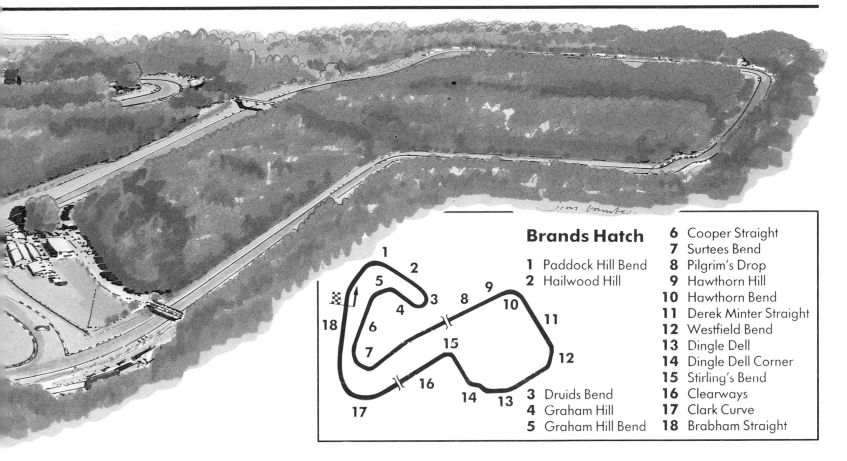

Brands Hatch

1. Paddock Hill Bend
2. Hailwood Hill
3. Druids Bend
4. Graham Hill
5. Graham Hill Bend
6. Cooper Straight
7. Surtees Bend
8. Pilgrim's Drop
9. Hawthorn Hill
10. Hawthorn Bend
11. Derek Minter Straight
12. Westfield Bend
13. Dingle Dell
14. Dingle Dell Corner
15. Stirling's Bend
16. Clearways
17. Clark Curve
18. Brabham Straight

Left Formula Ford drivers trying to use the same piece of track at Druids, the hairpin. The track runs down the hill, then left into the short straight shown in the picture at right.

Above Lotus and McLaren behind the pits about to turn onto the back straight on the long circuit.

2.65 miles in total. In the meantime the empire-building Grovewood acquired Mallory Park in 1962, Snetterton a year later and subsequently Oulton Park as well.

The burning ambition of Webb was at last realised in 1964 in the first British Grand Prix at Brands Hatch. Thereafter until the present decade the race alternated between the Kent circuit and Silverstone. And some great races there have been. That first event resulted in victory for Jim Clark. Four years later Brands witnessed a nail-biting battle between Jo Siffert and Chris Amon. Jack Brabham, who had won the 1966 race, ran short of fuel at the end of the 1970 race, handing victory to Jochen Rindt. In 1972 Fittipaldi and Stewart chased each other for the entire race.

From the earliest days Brands had seen a number of fatal accidents but in the winter of 1965-6 Paddock Hill Bend acquired a dreadful reputation. Within a matter of months George Crossman, Tony Flory and Stuart Duncan were killed there and two others were seriously hurt. The death of Jo Siffert in October 1971 led to major safety work in 1972, and new pits and grandstands appeared.

Brands had by now grown into one of the major international circuits in the world and was the venue for numerous important races, such as the Race of Champions and the BOAC 500. The track was also a vital part of British club racing. It provided the best spectator viewing in the country and facilities were improved with each year. The character of the track, however, remained: a superb mix of fast and slow corners, drops and rises. To get a perfect lap at Brands was a much sought-after experience by the finest drivers.

Paddock Hill Bend remains one of the great racing corners in the world, plunging downhill and with its difficult double apex and lack of run-off. The

Below left Coming out of Paddock Hill Bend, a double-apex corner that is one of the most demanding on any British circuit.

Below right A saloon field lines up for the start on Brands' top straight – which is by no means straight.

Left Druids offers overtaking opportunities, if a driver's approach is right. This is a pair of the short-lived Ford C-100s.

Below Porsche pit stop at Brands Hatch.

downhill sweep leads into Hailwood Hill rising to Druids, curling and dropping down to the fast left sweeper at Graham Hill Bend and on to the short Cooper Straight. At Surtees the 'Indy' circuit peels off, curling towards Clearways; the Grand Prix track sweeps left uphill and out to the fast back section, through the plunging Pilgrim's Drop to the high-speed Hawthorn Bend and the equally tricky Westfield, before dropping into Dingle Dell and up again for Dingle Dell Corner and Stirling's Bend, leading on to the straight back to Clearways, which curls on to the pit straight. There is little run-off anywhere on the circuit and while drivers love it, the thought of an accident is pushed, necessarily, to the back of their minds.

When packed with people at Grand Prix time, Brands bubbled, with the roar of the engines bouncing between the hospitality suites and the South Bank. The circuit always put on a fine show, its air displays in the 1980s matching even major air shows. When Nigel Mansell won his first Grand Prix in the autumn of 1985 at the European Grand Prix the place lit up – though the aficionados were rightly more impressed by the fact that a Frenchman called Alain Prost had won his first World Championship title.

Since then Brands has lost the British Grand Prix to Silverstone; and with the carnage of the Formula 3000 race of 1988 its reputation for safety took a bad knock. But Webb is still there – and if we doubted it – the ambition still burns within him . . . .

Oulton Park

Right Using all the road, a saloon nears the end of a lap at Oulton in a 1980s touring car race.

Oulton Park

1 Old Hall
2 The Avenue
3 Cascades
4 Shell Oils Corner
5 Foulstons
6 Clay Hill
7 Water Tower
8 Lodge
9 Deer Leap

Below F2 Coopers set off through rural Cheshire in the glorious environs of Oulton Park in the 1950s.

A s with many of the stately homes of England, Oulton Hall, some 35 miles to the south-east of Liverpool in Cheshire, suffered a sad decline in the 20th century. It was burned down in 1926, and its land was taken over by the military during the Second World War and used as a camp for the troops gathered for the invasion of mainland Europe. As such it had roads laid out on private ground, the perfect ingredients for a potential racing circuit. The Cheshire Car Club was quick to notice this in the immediate post-war days; but the army huts were still inhabited by Polish refugees, and it was not until they had been moved out and Sir Philip Grey Egerton had been persuaded to lease his land that work could begin on a circuit. Consent came in 1951 and the first motor races followed in August 1953. A year later the track had twice been extended and the Gold Cup had been established. Though the regulations

have chopped and changed over the years, the Gold Cup still continues, though its heyday was in the early years when Stirling Moss won five victories, the fourth in the four-wheel drive Ferguson in 1961.

Although a venue for international races — and for a time the Tourist Trophy — Oulton Park has always been essentially a national circuit; it has also acquired an important place in the motorcycling world with the annual Transatlantic Trophy meeting. In 1964 Oulton was sold to Grovewood Securities and became part of the Brands Hatch empire; it remains such to this day.

It's a scenic spot, with the challenging righthander Old Hall Corner, the Avenue and the swooping Cascades and the high-speed Knickerbrook. Over the years there has been considerable change but its essential character remains — a great challenge and one not to be underestimated. Roy Salvadori succeeded in putting his big Jaguar 3.8 into the lake in 1962; and, sadly, Paul Hawkins died here in a sportscar accident during the Tourist Trophy of 1969.

Snetterton

The third of the Brands Hatch-owned tracks is another old airfield, 18 miles south-west of Norwich at Snetterton. Opened in the autumn of 1951, the track was the brainchild of Oliver Sear and its 2.71 miles have remained substantially unchanged since the first races. With such competition in Britain to stage international races, Snetterton has taken on the role of a national track: in the 1980s international racing has not made the trek north through the forests of Thetford to the flat and windswept circuit.

Snetterton is the home of the famous Jim Russell School and the base for world-renowned Formula Ford constructor Van Diemen. As with

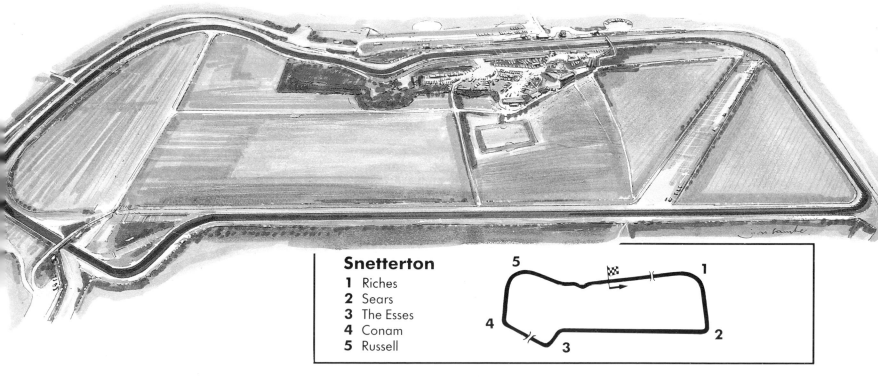

Snetterton
1 Riches
2 Sears
3 The Esses
4 Conam
5 Russell

many British tracks, Snetterton is permanently busy with teams testing between race meetings. The track supplies a good combination of turns to try out every tweak. There is the fast, bumpy double-apex at Riches, which you always think could be quicker, and then on to the tighter Sear, which leads you on to the main straight. The back section is unspectacular in comparison with the section from the Esses to the Bombhole, Coram and Russell — one of the most demanding series of corners in British racing. Many have got it wrong in the past — and you don't have a minor shunt when you do.

Today the track's biggest event of the year is the Willhire 24 Hours, the day-long thrash for British production racing cars. Hurtling around the mere 1.92 miles of the circuit, dodging the slower cars in the dark can be quite interesting. The track held an annual

Formula 1 race, the Lombank Trophy, in the early 1960s, but memories of those days seem very distant now as if they have been blown away by the cold east winds off the North Sea.

Below Sierras line up on the grid in front of Snetterton's pits, rebuilt after the October storms of 1987.

Thruxton

Thruxton in Hampshire is similar in many ways to Snetterton and the other airfields: fast, relatively flat, and always windy. While other tracks have had unbroken histories, life at Thruxton has been in fits and starts. It was opened in 1950 and the first car races began three years later. Financial difficulties, however, caused closure in 1965 and Thruxton did not reopen until 1968.

Taking over from Goodwood as the home of the British Automobile Racing Club (BARC), the 2.356-mile circuit allows only limited access to spectators, who crowd into the area around the start line and 'the Complex' — the corners of Campbell, Cobb and Segrave. Beyond this tricky section is the really fast motoring through Kimpton

and Goodwood to Church and up Woodham Hill (really only a rise) to the chicane, where much of the overtaking is done. From here it is past the pits and off through the teetering Allard and back to the Complex. It is a

Above The Thruxton chicane before the pits area. A mix of cars files through during a historic cars race.

track that requires compromise, for the fast sweeps are offset by the two twisty sections and, with most of the track being flat, for modern single-seaters all the time is made or lost at the Complex and the chicane. An untidy exit from Segrave will be costly.

From 1968 a European Formula 2 Championship event was staged at Thruxton, a track where Jochen Rindt was unbeatable (he won three in a row). With the advent of Formula 3000 in 1985 the traditional Easter Monday race disappeared from the calendar despite various attempts to finance international events. Since then Thruxton has been a purely national racing circuit. Still an operating airfield, Thruxton's future remains uncertain. The track needs change but there is never the money available to bring it about.

Thruxton

1 Allard
2 Campbell
3 Cobb
4 Segrave
5 Goodwood
6 Village
7 Church
8 Brooklands
9 Woodham Hill

Above The start of an F3 race at Thruxton. The fast right-hander leads up to the tricky 'Complex' section.

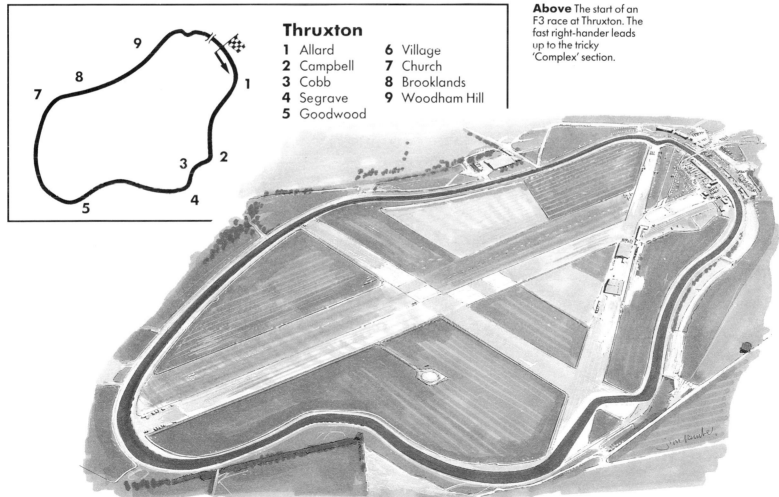

Birmingham

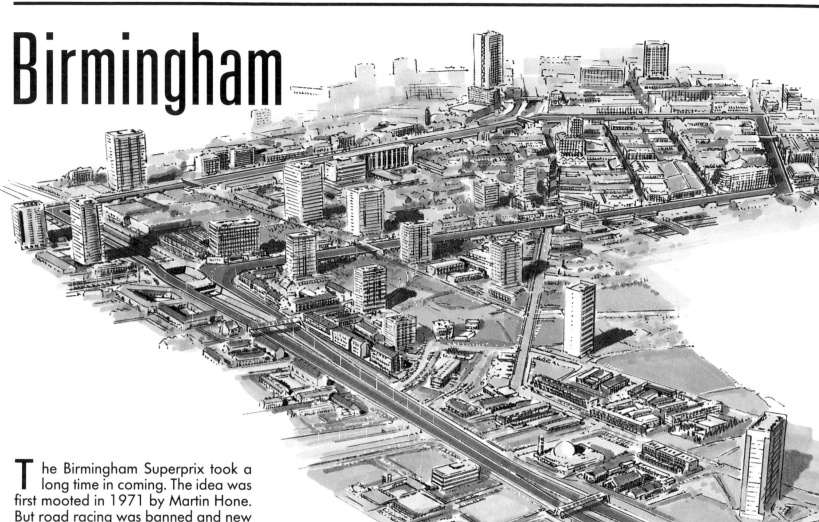

The Birmingham Superprix took a long time in coming. The idea was first mooted in 1971 by Martin Hone. But road racing was banned and new legislation was necessary before a race would be allowed. The supporters of the race raised their hopes in 1975 but the legislation was torpedoed. There followed a series of 'On the Streets' parades with racing cars, driven (presumably sedately) by celebrities of assorted vintage such as Fangio, Moss, Brabham and Hunt, around the streets. In April 1985, however, the Birmingham Road Race Bill passed through Parliament, despite considerable opposition from the permanent circuits, and street racing arrived on mainland Britain a year later in the form of Formula 3000.

Glamorous is not a word you readily associate with Britain's second city, a huge mainly industrial sprawl. As at Long Beach and Adelaide, the idea of racing on the streets was in part a conscious attempt to improve the image of the place. Motor racing is

perceived – at least by its fans – to be glamorous and Birmingham City Council hoped that perception would rub off on the city itself. Once the race was established it even went as far as to declare Birmingham a 'holiday resort'.

As luck would have it, the first Superprix of 1986 coincided with the arrival in Britain of Hurricane Charley! Splashing through the deluge Luis Sala, minus the nose of his Ralt, was adjudged the winner when spinning cars blocked the track. Despite the weather and the initial organisational hiccoughs, the race was deemed to be

a success. A year later things were considerably better. As at Adelaide, the race was integrated into a festival and the crowds flocked to every available viewing point to see Stefano Modena win, notwithstanding a hair-raisingly brilliant drive by Roberto Moreno. It was fast, too, with an average speed of 105mph. There

Birmingham

1 Bristol Street
2 Belgrave Middleway
3 Sherlock Street
4 Pershore Street
5 Bromsgrove Street

Left F3000 field at the start of the Birmingham Superprix, the first major street race on the British mainland.

Above The first corner on the Birmingham circuit, turning towards the roundabout and the outward and return straights on a dual-carriageway road.

take the track through Pershore Street, Bromsgrove Street and back to the top of Bristol Street — 2.47 miles at over 100mph!

While the roads are mainly wide, the hotshots in Formula 3000 in 1988 proved that, no matter what you do, if they can have an accident, they will. They had several. On the first lap David Hunt launched his Lola into the air and over the barriers into a brick wall. The Englishman wasn't quite sure where he was but at least he was unscathed, unlike his car which was in several pieces. The race was stopped and they tried again. The result was another accident and another red flag. Finally at the third attempt the field got away and Roberto Moreno, the unrewarded hero of the previous year, scored a fine victory. Birmingham came in for much criticism, however, and there were threats to take away its F3000 licence from the sport's governing body FISA. The future remains clouded, which is a pity for the Superprix has brought racing to the people on their own doorstep.

were some fearsome bumps but unlike many street tracks the fast straights (170mph for Formula 3000 cars) followed by slow corners meant overtaking was possible.

The pits are situated on the forecourt of Bristol Street Motors and from there the track is fast and wide to the first corner, where much of the over-taking can be done. A narrow chicane lies ahead and then, passing the mosque, is the long blast up the Belgrave Middleway to the hairpin (actually a roundabout) at Halfords Corner and back down the other carriageway of the Middleway to Sherlock Street — a fast righthander, leading to the three lefthanders that

Other British Circuits

Below A holiday crowd enjoys an F2 race in the glades at the Crystal Palace circuit in the late 1960s.

The remaining modern British tracks are used only for national race meetings, although **Lydden Hill** (off the Canterbury-Dover road) has staged international rallycross events. More recently, **Pembrey** (to the west of Llanelli in Wales) has become an increasingly important test track in spite of its small size and relative remoteness. In May 1989 it received official BARC approval to hold race meetings.

One much-lamented facility was **Crystal Palace** in the southern suburbs of London. Opened in 1937, the track ran through parkland which had surrounded the Crystal Palace, the huge glass building (hence the name) which had stood in Hyde Park for the Great Exhibition in 1851 and was subsequently moved lock, stock and barrel to Sydenham and was destroyed by fire in 1936. Being close to the nightclubs of London, this was a popular track with racers and staged the London Grand Prix and the Coronation and Imperial Trophies before the war. The two-mile track ran around a lake and was the scene of several victories for the Siamese Prince Birabongse Bhanubah, who drove under the pseudonym of B. Bira, in his famous ERA 'Romulus'.

During the war the track was closed and it was to remain so until 1953 when it reopened in modified form with a new link cutting the original length to just 1.39 miles. Essentially an oval with twists and kinks, Crystal Palace became a hugely popular track in the 1950s and 1960s, staging some breathtaking races. The track was a regular Formula 1 and Formula 2 track beginning in 1953, when Stirling Moss won the first London Trophy event. F1 continued until 1962, but Crystal Palace slipped

quietly away as that decade wore on.

Mallory Park in Leicestershire was opened in April 1956, threading its 1.35 miles around a lake. It hosted many major single-seater races including several Formula 1 events but today it remains a club circuit, unsuitable for the big cars of the modern era. **Castle Combe**, between Bristol and Chippenham, was another war-time airfield but in July 1950 it opened as a 1.84 mile racing track, only to be closed down five years later in the wake of the Le Mans disaster. In 1962 it was reopened by the British Racing and Sports Car Club (BRSCC) and it has fought for its survival ever since against local

opposition. Finally, the battle won, work was done to improve the facility, although the political fighting has militated against it being any more than a club circuit.

Some think **Cadwell Park** the best circuit in the country, though it is tucked away in the Lincolnshire Wolds south-west of Louth. It was opened in 1934 as a motorcycle track of 0.7

Left The bottom of the hill on the one-mile circuit at Lydden, with a rather primitive paddock in the background.

Right Formula Ford action at Knockhill, the Scottish circuit opened in the mid-1970s.

miles, was widened and lengthened in 1952 to 1.3 miles and Formula 3 racing began to take an interest; further extension in 1962 brought it to 2.25 miles in length. Although still strongly associated with motorcycles, it is used regularly by club racers. However, even Formula 3 has shunned the track they call 'England's Nürburgring'. Foremost among its

Right A Formula 3 grid at Mallory Park in the circuit's heyday as the 1960s drew to a close. At the end of the lap they swooped down the curving slope in the background.

challenging corners is 'The Mountain' where vitrually any racing car in existence will take off.

Lydden Hill is a tiny 1-mile track, though it rises and falls dramatically and is well known owing to its televised rallycross meetings.

In addition to Pembrey, Wales also has a track at **Llandow** though this bumpy near-oval with a chicane built in to make it interesting has failed to attract any major events.

North of the border in Scotland are two tracks, neither of which has figured on the international scene. Built on the Royal Showground just outside Edinburgh, **Ingliston** is another club circuit, serving the Scottish racers. At 1.03 miles in length it is suitable for little more than club rac-

ing. Further to the north is **Knockhill**, near Dunfermline, opened in the mid-1970s amid plans to turn it into a major international racing facility. To date that hasn't happened and it remains a domestic-standard track of 1.3 miles in length.

Other tracks still exist, although they are not now used for competition. One such is **Boreham**, the home of Ford Motorsport. It held major races for just two seasons in the early 1950s but has since been used by Ford to test its competition cars in privacy.

There is intermittent talk of building new tracks here and there in Britain, but few become reality. Though overloaded with testing work, the circuits of Britain have difficulty surviving financially despite the modern trend of using the tracks for company days, driver-training schemes and training schools. Any new facility would need to be of the very highest standard to make any impact on the establishment, even if the established tracks continue to squabble among themselves.

UNITED STATES

If ever there was a country where the expression 'Have car, will race' is true, it is in America. Racing has taken place anywhere and everywhere from the whiskey-runners in the Deep South, who built fast cars to outrun the police and ended up racing each other, to the teenagers who would (and still do) indulge in 'burn-ups' at midnight on deserted stretches of road. There have been sand races, trans-continental Cannonball Runs — you name it, the Americans are you sure have done it.

Of all the traditions, however, oval racing is the best established. Across the continent there are thousands of clay, dirt and paved ovals. Some have grown into the superspeedways of today, others have remained much as they always were, with their own heroes and their individual quirks. Occasionally a national series pays a visit, adding to what is already a larger than life atmosphere.

In the earliest days, motor racing in the United States began in much the same way as in Europe, with events from one town to another. It is generally accepted that the first road race took place in Wisconsin between Green Bay and Madison in July 1878 — an event of 201 miles won by a steam-powered Oshkosh travelling hell-for-leather at an average speed of 6mph! The first challenge for petrol-engined cars did not occur until Thanksgiving 1885 when a race sponsored by the *Times-Herald* was planned between Chicago and Waukegan, Illinois, a distance of 94 miles. Snowstorms forced abandonment of the race at Evanston but victory was awarded to Frank Duryea in a home-built Duryea.

Thereafter American racing went its various ways and today those traditions remain diverse. There remains a strong seam of showmanship running through all American racing people. A circus really does come to town, in the spirit of the great racer-cum-showman Barney Oldfield.

The National Championship (today the CART series) has been running since 1909. Initially it was regulated by the American Automobile Association (AAA), though it would be superseded in the mid-1950s by the United States Auto Club (USAC), which itself gave way to the rebel Championship Auto Racing Teams (CART) organisation in 1978-9. The National Championship retains its own unique character. From the start the series featured both road and oval races and although road racing died out for many years, today it is again an important part of the series. In the interim the series incorporated the wooden board tracks, Pike's Peak hillclimb and even the first airport race in the world at Mines Field in 1934.

Under USAC, racing on the dirt ovals came to the fore — tracks like Duquoin and Springfield, Illinois, Indiana State Fairgrounds in Indiana, Langhorne, Pennsylvania, and Sacramento, California. But in the 1960s when rear-engined cars arrived and more superspeedways were built, the dirt ovals were gradually phased out and road courses reintroduced alongside the paved ovals.

Road racing in the States has had its peaks and troughs. It began with the Vanderbilt Cup in 1904 held on a 28-mile course on Long Island, just outside New York City. This attracted many of the European racers of the era. Four years later came the Grand Prize held at Savannah, Georgia,

Milwaukee, Wisconsin and Santa Monica, California. Ultimately the event was combined with the Vanderbilt Cup but both died out with the First World War.

In the 1920s the board tracks at such places as Sheepshead Bay, Uniontown, Beverley Hills and Altoona shot to prominence, but these were expensive to run and serious fire hazards and they too faded into oblivion. The ovals, road courses, airfields, streets, board tracks, beaches and even parking lots are now — and have always been — overshadowed by the greatest American track of them all, Indianapolis Motor Speedway.

Left International event at Roosevelt Raceway just prior to World War II. Auto Unions, Mercedes and (at left) Maseratis fill the first seven places.

Indianapolis

H ow can you even begin to describe Indianapolis in a few short pages? This is the oldest surviving race track in the world. Once a year it holds the world's largest one-day sporting event of any kind, a race that attracts around 400,000 people on Memorial Day — The Indianapolis 500. Here in the suburb of Speedway is The Brickyard, a huge, daunting, four-corner track. This is the backbone of American racing, a vital part of the National Championship.

'If it weren't for Indianapolis Motor Speedway,' says four-times 500 winner A.J. Foyt, 'you really wouldn't have a good championship circuit. You'd have a lot of road courses, but it would be more or less like Formula 1. Indianapolis makes it championship automobile racing.' This huge motor racing facility holds only one race a year, though this is all it needs to continue to be a profitable enterprise. Come the month of May, Indianapolis bubbles and after endless trials and saturation promotion a race finally

Right Bill Vukovich (Kurtis) heads the field in the 1952 Indianapolis 500. His car broke down nine laps from the finish.

takes place.

The story of Indianapolis goes back to 1908 when for the princely sum of $75,000, Carl Fisher, James Allison, Arthur Newby and Frank Wheeler financed the construction of a rectangular 2.5-mile crushed stone and tar track. The first race at Indy was held in June 1909 — but this was for balloons, another of Fisher's passions. Motor racing turned up in August but a series of fatal accidents convinced the owners that a paved surface was necessary. And thus they came up with

the idea of bricks — 3.2 million of them! Thus was born the Brickyard, with its fast straights, its nine degree banking and its legend. Although Fisher was later to develop the resort city of Miami Beach, his greatest monument is undoubtedly the Speedway.

The first Indy 500 took place in 1911 and it has been an annual feature in the racing calendar ever since except in times of war. The first 500 was won by Ray Harroun who emerged from retirement, built his

own car — a Marmon Wasp — took the chequered flag and promptly retired again! The following year was a classic race as the Mercedes of Ralph DePalma and his mechanic broke down with five and a half laps to go while in a five lap lead. The two pushed the huge car from the back straight as Joe Dawson swept by time after time. The Mercedes was on the final straight when Dawson flashed by to take victory.

The reputation of Indy had already spread far and wide and in 1913 the event was won by a Frenchman, Jules

Indianapolis

turn 4

turn 1

turn 3

turn 2

Above Jim Clark (Lotus) in the 1965 race. His victory, the first for a rear-engined car in the 500, signalled the end of the roadster at Indy.

Indianapolis 500

Year	Winner		Year	Winner	
1911	Ray Harroun	74.59 mph	1952	Troy Ruttman	128.922 mph
1912	Joe Dawson	78.72 mph	1953	Bill Vukovich	128.740 mph
1913	Jules Goux	75.93 mph	1954	Bill Vukovich	130.840 mph
1914	René Thomas	82.47 mph	1955	Bob Sweikert	128.209 mph
1915	Ralph DePalma	89.84 mph	1956	Pat Flaherty	128.490 mph
1916	Dario Resta	84.00 mph	1957	Sam Hanks	135.601 mph
1919	Howard Wilcox	88.05 mph	1958	Jim Bryan	133.791 mph
1920	Gaston Chevrolet	88.62 mph	1959	Rodger Ward	135.857 mph
1921	Tommy Milton	89.62 mph	1960	Jim Rathmann	138.767 mph
1922	Jimmy Murphy	94.48 mph	1961	A.J. Foyt	139.130 mph
1923	Tommy Milton	90.95 mph	1962	Rodger Ward	140.293 mph
1924	L.L. Corum & Joe Boyer	98.23 mph	1963	Parnelli Jones	143.137 mph
1925	Peter DePaolo	101.23 mph	1964	A.J. Foyt	151.207 mph
1926	Frank Lockhart	95.904 mph	1965	Jim Clark	150.686 mph
1927	George Souders	97.545 mph	1966	Graham Hill	144.317 mph
1928	Louis Meyer	99.482 mph	1967	A.J. Foyt	151.207 mph
1929	Ray Keech	97.585 mph	1968	Bobby Unser	152.882 mph
1930	Billy Arnold	100.448 mph	1969	Mario Andretti	156.867 mph
1931	Louis Schneider	96.629 mph	1970	Al Unser	155.749 mph
1932	Fred Frame	104.144 mph	1971	Al Unser	157.735 mph
1933	Louis Meyer	104.162 mph	1972	Mark Donohue	162.962 mph
1934	William Cummings	104.863 mph	1973	Gordon Johncock	159.036 mph
1935	Kelly Petillo	106.240 mph	1974	Johnny Rutherford	158.589 mph
1936	Louis Meyer	109.069 mph	1975	Bobby Unser	149.213 mph
1937	Wilbur Shaw	113.580 mph	1976	Johnny Rutherford	148.725 mph
1938	Floyd Roberts	117.200 mph	1977	A.J. Foyt	161.331 mph
1939	Wilbur Shaw	115.035 mph	1978	Al Unser	161.361 mph
1940	Wilbur Shaw	114.277 mph	1979	Rick Mears	158.899 mph
1941	Floyd Davis & Mauri Rose	116.338 mph	1980	Johnny Rutherford	142.862 mph
1946	George Robson	114.820 mph	1981	Bobby Unser	139.084 mph
1947	Mauri Rose	116.338 mph	1982	Gordon Johncock	162.026 mph
1948	Mauri Rose	119.814 mph	1983	Tom Sneva	162.117 mph
1949	Bill Holland	121.327 mph	1984	Rick Mears	163.612 mph
1950	Johnnie Parsons	124.002 mph	1985	Danny Sullivan	152.982 mph
1951	Lee Wallard	126.244 mph	1986	Bobby Rahal	170.722 mph
			1987	Al Unser	162.175 mph
			1988	Rick Mears	144.809 mph
			1989	Emerson Fittipaldi	167.581 mph

Goux in a Peugeot. The French scored again in 1914 with René Thomas in a Delage. DePalma won in 1915 to make up for his earlier heartbreak and England-based Italian Dario Resta won the final Indy 500 before the First World War dragged in the United States. Indianapolis served as a military landing strip and repair depot during the conflict, but in 1919 the race was on again.

A new generation of stars arrived in the form of Gaston Chevrolet, Tommy Milton, Jimmy Murphy, Peter DePaolo and Frank Lockhart. Speeds increased

and in 1925 DePaolo recorded the first finish at an average speed of over 100mph. There were accidents too but these were precursors of those of the 1930s, when the Brickyard became a graveyard. The track had been sold in 1927 to First World War flying ace Eddie Rickenbacker, but in the Depression years it remained much the same as had always been, with little money available for maintenance and improvements.

At the time Louis Meyer and Wilbur Shaw emerged as the stars, the Speedway began claiming souls at a

frightening rate: there were two in 1931; two more in 1932; five in 1933; two more in 1934; four in 1935. Finally as the Depression was beginning to pass major changes were made with sections of track resurfaced with tarmac. The same year (1936) Meyer gained his third victory, then an unrivalled achievement. Wilbur Shaw was the next hero, winning in 1939 and 1940, the first man to score consecutive victories. Going for a third in 1941, he crashed and broke several vertebrae. Thus began an enduring legend: no man

Right General view during the 1988 race. The tower at right indicates the positions of all the cars throughout the race; the leader at this point is number 5.

Below 'Fish-eye' view of the circuit from a grandstand as the cars approach Turn 1.

belonged to Mauri Rose, who won in 1947 and 1948. Going for the treble the following year, his car broke down just eight laps from home while shadowing the leader. After Rose retired in 1951 a new star emerged in the formidable shape of Billy Vukovich, the Mad Russian. With nine laps of the 1952 race remaining his car broke down and 22-year-old Troy Ruttman swept by to become the youngest winner of the Indy 500. Vukovich won in 1953 and 1954 and was leading in 1955 when he was killed, flipping on the back straight. The tradition held: no one ever won three in a row. . . .

With speeds for a single lap creeping ever closer to 150pmh, the Indy 500 continued to pack in the crowds. They were thrilled by the speeds and the crashes. A spectacular pile-up in 1958 made the largest crash in the Speedway's history with car after car shunting in, and Jerry Unser going over the wall in the chaos! Amazingly no one was seriously injured.

Since 1950 Indy had been a nominal round of the Formula 1 World Championship inaugurated in that year, and although this association with European F1 ceased in 1960, the following years saw the beginnings of a foreign invasion. In 1963 the great Jim Clark arrived with his nimble rear-engined Lotus and the big roadsters were given notice that their days were numbered. A. J. Foyt won the last front-engined victory in 1964 and a year later Clark outclassed the field to win. In 1966 Graham Hill provided another British winner in a Lola, avoiding a huge 11-car pile-up at the start.

In the late 1960s, the Americans fought back with the new generation who would dominate Indy through to the present: Foyt, Mario Andretti, Johnny Rutherford, Gordon Johncock and the Unser brothers, Bobby and Al. By 1988 Foyt competing that year in his 30th Indy 500, had won four; Al Unser had matched that, while brother Bobby had three to his name, as had

ever wins three in a row at Indy. The race that year was significant in many ways: it marked the first victory for Mauri Rose, while half of Gasoline Alley (the track's fuel depot) burned down on race morning! The depot was rebuilt but by then war had broken out and once more Indianapolis was forgotten.

By 1945 the Speedway was in a sorry state, partly overgrown and crumbling. Rickenbacker decided to sell and the Speedway was bought by

Tony Hulman. Major redevelopment began with new grandstands, followed over the years by a museum, tunnels, a control tower, hospitality suites, a huge four-lane tunnel between Turns 1 and 2, the Hall of Fame and offices. By the 1970s the Speedway property was like a miniature city: it included two golf courses (nine-holes inside the oval and full-size 18-hole outside), not to mention a 96-room motel!

On the racing front, the late 1940s

Rutherford; Johncock was on two wins and poor Andretti, the distinguished F1 driver who never had much luck at the Speedway was still trying to add to his triumph of 1969. In recent years, with speeds up to 200mph, a Californian called Rick Mears emerged to win three times, while the 1985 winner Danny Sullivan spun at high speed on his way to an incredible victory.

Today the bricks have gone, replaced by asphalt in 1961, leaving just a strip of bricks at the start — finish line; and Gasoline Alley has been rebuilt. But still they come to inhabit the famous Snakepit between Turns 1 and 2 and to see the Indycar aces do their own peculiar thing. It is something that every true race enthusiast should try to witness at least once. The legend and the festival that is Indianapolis continues to grow. Despite the atmosphere of razzmatazz an anxious anticipation remains. Empty, the Speedway must be frightening: full it is unbelievable.

Daytona

While Indianapolis stands head and shoulders above the other American tracks in history, the folks of Daytona Beach, Florida, would like to believe otherwise. Here is another classic oval track, the Daytona International Speedway. Though a comparative upstart in age, Daytona has become the Mecca for fans of the big NASCAR stockers.

The hard sands of Daytona Beach have been used since the turn of the century for speed-record attempts. It was and remains one of the world's most famous beaches at some 23 miles long, centred on the holiday resort on the Florida coast. It was here that many of the great speed records of the 1920s had been set, where Henry Segrave had clocked 203.79mph in his Sunbeam and where Frank Lockhart somersaulted into the sea, survived intact and died later trying to beat his compatriot Ray Keech's mark of 207.552mph.

While these men strove to beat the land speed records, the first beach races at Daytona did not take place until the mid-1930s. Legend has it that Bill France, heading south for a new life in Miami in 1934, had his car break down here on the way. He decided to settle in Daytona, raced there on the beach in 1935 and took over the promotion of the beach races

Edwardian prelude: Barney Oldfield in a Benz at Daytona Beach, venue for many international attempts on the world land-speed record.

in 1938. When the war ended, France and others set up NASCAR to organise stock-car racing. This was a success but France had another dream, to build a great speedway. It took some time to raise the necessary money but in October 1955 he leased 377 acres of swampland inland from the beach and set about building a superspeedway. Money remained a problem but by 1959, at a cost of $3 million the track was finally finished.

Away from the now trashy Atlantic Avenue — a four lane highway running beside the beach flanked with seemingly endless neon, fast-food joints, unsavoury clubs — the Speedway is the pride of the area, a big lazy bowl around a lake. A 2.5 mile anticlockwise tri-oval with the front straight banked to 18 degrees and the imposing East and West Turns at 31 degrees, it was far beyond anything the NASCAR men had ever seen.

The first Daytona 500 was one of the greatest races in the history of a sport peppered with close finishes. Among the 59 runners at the start were NASCAR heroes Lee Petty, Joe Weatherly, Cotton Owens and Fireball Roberts. As the race developed Petty, Weatherly and Johnny Beauchamp fought a tooth-and-nail battle at the front, constantly switching positions. Weatherly dropped back and as the finish drew close, the three found themselves together again, Weatherly a lap down. The three crossed the line side by side. Beauchamp was awarded the trophy. Three days later a photograph proved otherwise and Petty was given the cup!

How do you follow that? Well, Bill France, always a skilful exponent of promotion, managed and the France family continues to manage to this day. The Pettys did much to help, although Lee went over the Daytona banking in 1961, ending his own

Left Daytona at night: a view from the grandstands of pits activity during the 24-hour race, which uses the infield loop as well as the banked oval.

Cars in the 1989 24-hour race turn into the infield section on the opposite side of the circuit from the pits. Here the winning Porsche 962, driven by Derek Bell, Bob Wollek and John Andretti, is about to overtake the second-placed Cobb/Nielsen/Wallace/Lammers Jaguar.

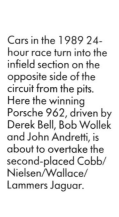

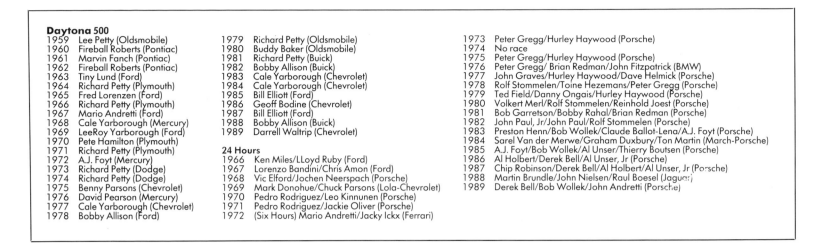

Daytona 500

1959	Lee Petty (Oldsmobile)	1979	Richard Petty (Oldsmobile)	1973	Peter Gregg/Hurley Haywood (Porsche)
1960	Fireball Roberts (Pontiac)	1980	Buddy Baker (Oldsmobile)	1974	No race
1961	Marvin Fanch (Pontiac)	1981	Richard Petty (Buick)	1975	Peter Gregg/Hurley Haywood (Porsche)
1962	Fireball Roberts (Pontiac)	1982	Bobby Allison (Buick)	1976	Peter Gregg/ Brian Redman/John Fitzpatrick (BMW)
1963	Tiny Lund (Ford)	1983	Cale Yarborough (Chevrolet)	1977	John Graves/Hurley Haywood/Dave Helmick (Porsche)
1964	Richard Petty (Plymouth)	1984	Cale Yarborough (Chevrolet)	1978	Rolf Stommelen/Toine Hezemans/Peter Gregg (Porsche)
1965	Fred Lorenzen (Ford)	1985	Bill Elliott (Ford)	1979	Ted Field/Danny Ongais/Hurley Haywood (Porsche)
1966	Richard Petty (Plymouth)	1986	Geoff Bodine (Chevrolet)	1980	Volkert Merl/Rolf Stommelen/Reinhold Joest (Porsche)
1967	Mario Andretti (Ford)	1987	Bill Elliott (Ford)	1981	Bob Garretson/Bobby Rahal/Brian Redman (Porsche)
1968	Cale Yarborough (Mercury)	1988	Bobby Allison (Buick)	1982	John Paul, Jr/John Paul/Rolf Stommelen (Porsche)
1969	LeeRoy Yarborough (Ford)	1989	Darrell Waltrip (Chevrolet)	1983	Preston Henn/Bob Wollek/Claude Ballot-Lena/A.J. Foyt (Porsche)
1970	Pete Hamilton (Plymouth)			1984	Sarel Van der Merwe/Graham Duxbury/Ton Martin (March-Porsche)
1971	Richard Petty (Plymouth)	**24 Hours**		1985	A.J. Foyt/Bob Wollek/Al Unser/Thierry Boutsen (Porsche)
1972	A.J. Foyt (Mercury)	1966	Ken Miles/LLoyd Ruby (Ford)	1986	Al Holbert/Derek Bell/Al Unser, Jr (Porsche)
1973	Richard Petty (Dodge)	1967	Lorenzo Bandini/Chris Amon (Ford)	1987	Chip Robinson/Derek Bell/Al Holbert/Al Unser, Jr (Porsche)
1974	Richard Petty (Dodge)	1968	Vic Elford/Jochen Neerspach (Porsche)	1988	Martin Brundle/John Nielsen/Raul Boesel (Jaguar)
1975	Benny Parsons (Chevrolet)	1969	Mark Donohue/Chuck Parsons (Lola-Chevrolet)	1989	Derek Bell/Bob Wollek/John Andretti (Porsche)
1976	David Pearson (Mercury)	1970	Pedro Rodriguez/Leo Kinnunen (Porsche)		
1977	Cale Yarborough (Chevrolet)	1971	Pedro Rodriguez/Jackie Oliver (Porsche)		
1978	Bobby Allison (Ford)	1972	(Six Hours) Mario Andretti/Jacky Ickx (Ferrari)		

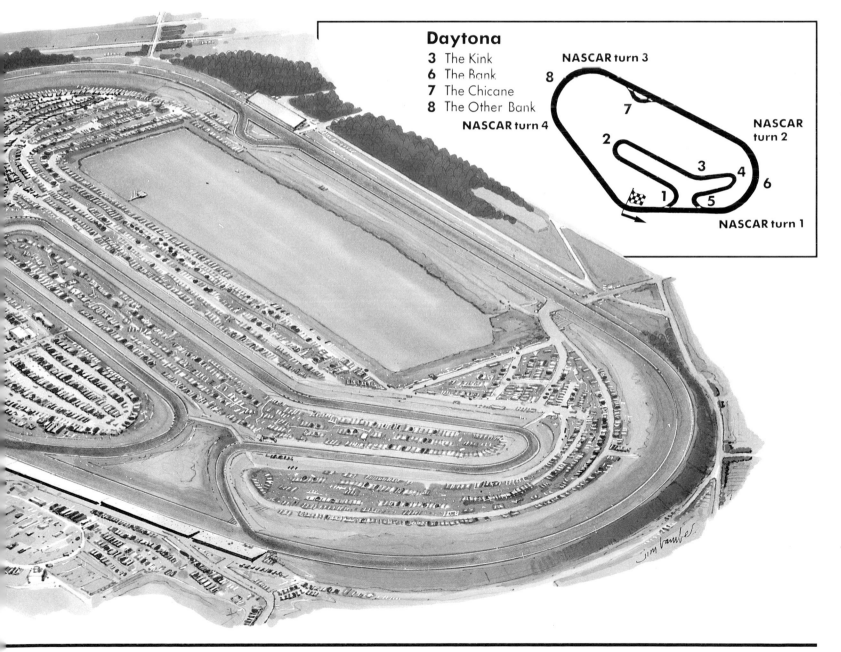

Daytona

3 The Kink
6 The Bank
7 The Chicane
8 The Other Bank

NASCAR turn 3
NASCAR turn 4
NASCAR turn 2
NASCAR turn 1

career. His son Richard, who had been a runner in the first Daytona 500, won seven 500s and three Firecracker 400s, the latter being the second annual NASCAR event at the track, held on Independence Day, 4 July. This began in 1959 as a 250-mile race, but in 1963 it was extended to 400 miles. No one has come close to Petty's record at Daytona, the nearest challenger being Cale Yarborough with four 500 victories and four Firecrackers. Today the 500 is not merely a race meeting, it has become a Speed Week with qualifying races and the Busch Clash money race.

Daytona also has a road course laid out in the infield and it is this which is used each year, in combination with the banking, for the Daytona 24 Hours, a sportscar classic which began in 1966. The road course peels off the oval after the pits, twisting back behind the paddock to a hairpin, a quick straight with a left kink before a second hairpin and a sweeping left back to the base of Turn 1.

The Daytona 24 Hours was the opening round of the World Sportscar Championship in 1966 and remained such until 1971, when Buenos Aires

hosted a race earlier in January. Today it is one of the major events in the IMSA championship calendar. As with nearby Sebring, the race attracted the top sportscar drivers and their fearsome machines — Porsche 917s, Ford GT40s and Ferrari 512s. Though the overseas drivers stole much of their thunder, locals Peter Gregg, Hurley Haywood and Al Holbert were all able to score multiple victories. The Porsche team dominated for many years before the TWR Jaguar team's remarkable debut American win at Daytona in 1988.

Daytona is an electrifying place, crammed with people who have spent the nights before the races in the infield, partying until in hurts. To see a full grid of thunderous NASCARs curling through Turn 4 as the green flag is waved is to experience a sensation which is hard to describe. The ground shakes as 40 cars thunder by at 200mph, just inches apart. It takes your breath away. To witness one of Daytona's occasional high-speed pile-ups is to be granted a preview of the Day of Judgement — you leave Florida chastened. Such is the violence of the accidents here that today the televi-

sion cameraman, perched in the notorious hole-in-the-wall on Turn 4, is clad in full baseball protection gear in case of flying debris.

In 1988 Daytona opened a new grandstand some 14 storeys high which dwarfs even the grandiose tri-oval, bringing the seating capacity to almost 90,000. With the ever-enthusiastic promotion there seems little doubt that crowds will continue to fill the track at every opportunity.

Curiously, considering the mild climate of sunny Florida, Daytona suffers from the weather. Not from rain, though that has been known — but from heat and humidity.

'You cannot run the same set-up in July [for the Firecracker] as you can in February [for the 500],' points out famed NASCAR engine builder Waddell Wilson. The engines lose power and the cars drift more in the heat, thus reducing speeds. Walking around Daytona in July in the shimmering heat is like swimming through the air, heavy with the scent of Florida flowers. And when the engines fire up, I cannot imagine that there is a more exhilarating place for a racing enthusiast to be.

The new 14-storey grandstand at Daytona. The circuit's expertly promoted meetings have ensured capacity crowds at the big events.

Watkins Glen

An early street race at Watkins Glen. The field is headed on the start line by a Stutz Bearcat (left) and a Lagonda.

Upstate New York has a very different atmosphere from the hothouses of Daytona and Indianapolis. Yet here in the Finger Lakes region in the hills above Lake Seneca is the undisputed home of American road racing. Daytona, Indianapolis and others might quibble about who's the best speedway, but there is no doubt that America's most influential road track is Watkins Glen.

The Watkins Glen of today is the third circuit to have that name. The original idea for a track in this popular tourist region came from Cameron Argetsinger who, in 1947, set about persuading the local authorities of the value of a race to the tourist industry. Evidently, they agreed with him and

the first races took place on 2 October 1948 on a 6.6-mile course of public roads running through the town and including such excitements as railway crossings! The first race, won by Frank Griswold in an Alfa, was such a success that it immediately became an annual event. In 1951, however, Sam Collier ran off the road in a Ferrari and rolled into the fields to his death. In the aftermath Argetsinger was censured by the SCCA and the AAA and he resigned. But the popular annual event continued and in the following year Fred Wacker's car left the road and killed a child and injured 12 other spectators. The original track at the Glen was condemned. As plans were drawn up for a permanent replace-

ment, a transitional 4.6-mile circuit was selected out in the hills and this was used from 1953 to 1955. While this was in operation Bill Milliken designed the new permanent circuit in conjunction with the computer department of Cornell University. The result was a 2.3-mile track winding around a wooded hilltop. Work on the new Glen was finished just in time for its first race in 1956. Although the surface broke up that day, it was the new Watkins Glen that was chosen to stage its first United States Grand Prix in October 1961.

This was the year of American triumph in Formula 1 with Phil Hill (Ferrari) the World Champion but at the Glen the victor was Innes Ireland

Watkins Glen Formula 1

1961	I. Ireland (Lotus)
1962	J. Clark (Lotus)
1963	G. Hill (BRM)
1964	G. Hill (BRM)
1965	G. Hill (BRM)
1966	J. Clark (Lotus)
1967	J. Clark (Lotus)
1968	J. Stewart (Matra)
1969	J. Rindt (Lotus)
1970	E. Fittipaldi (Lotus)
1972	J. Stewart (Tyrrell)
1973	R. Peterson (Lotus)
1974	C. Reutemann (Brabham)
1975	N. Lauda (Ferrari)
1976	J. Hunt (McLaren)
1977	J. Hunt (McLaren)
1978	C. Reutemann (Ferrari)
1979	G. Villeneuve (Ferrari)
1980	A. Jones (Williams)

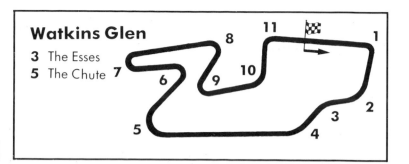

Watkins Glen

3 The Esses
5 The Chute

U.S. Grand Prix (East) 1978: Alan Jones in the unreliable Williams FW06, in which he took second place at the Glen's final appearance as an F1 venue.

(Lotus) in his first and only Championship F1 victory. The following year the Glen provided Jim Clark with his third F1 win and another for Lotus and following the Norfolk marque's successes there was a hat-trick of wins for Graham Hill and BRM. In 1966 and 1967 it was Clark again followed by Jackie Stewart in 1968. The British seemed to have a lock on the race. It

took until 1969 before Jochen Rindt shut out the British drivers, following up in 1970 – but the latter race is now unhappily remembered for Graham Hill's, accident. Hill then 40, was seriously injured.

A year later Rindt was dead by the time the Grand Prix circus arrived at the Glen; his team-mate Emerson Fittipaldi won, defending the Austrian's title from the Ferrari of Jacky Ickx.

That was the last Grand Prix at what was by then the old Glen, for during the following summer major redevelopment took place. 'Actually,' recalls Denny Hulme, ' the old Glen was a nothing circuit. We all went to play golf. It was all right, the trees looked lovely in the autumn. When they modified the track it became a good circuit.'

At a cost of $2.3 million, the track was widened and resurfaced and the pits re-sited. More important, however, was the addition of a new 1.1-mile section, making a total 3.377 miles. Again designed with the help of computers at Cornell University, this featured four new corners, making 11 in all. The new extension departed from the old circuit at the exit of Loop-Chute section, diving down through the trees into a descending, curling left-hander leading on to a downhill stretch along the edge of the hillside to the lowest point of the track. From there it climbed to a 180-degree right-hander and on to a straight where the track levelled off, before dropping to a righthander leading back on an undulating stretch. Here the old circuit was rejoined with a long lefthanded curve with a blind brow.

The first U.S. Grand Prix on the new layout was won by the brilliant young French driver, François Cévert. A year later his team-mate Jackie Stewart scored but then, in 1973, tragedy struck when Cevert was killed in a practice accident in the fast sweeper behind the pits. Stewart withdrew from what would have been his 100th race and retired for good – a sad end to a great career. A chicane was

installed the following year but there was more tragedy when young Austrian Helmut Koinigg died.

For 1975 newly crowned World Champion Niki Lauda scored another triumph but a year later as he and James Hunt struggled for the World Championship, he would come only third to the Englishman, setting up the final showdown for a new race at Fuji in Japan. The era of Grand Prix racing at the Glen ended in 1978 with Jean-Pierre Jarier dominating for Lotus, just weeks after Ronnie Peterson's death. But the Lotus car broke down and Carlos Reutemann won for Ferrari. A year later Gilles Villeneuve, having failed to win at home in Canada, took consolation at Watkins Glen. But by then Long Beach was established as a Grand Prix venue and Las Vegas was waving dollars at the F1 circus. Watkins Glen was left behind.

This traditional end-of-season event had been popular but the harsh winters had taken their toll on the track. The spectators had not helped either, the infamous Bog being a squalid place. Not at all the image Formula 1 sought to promote. So the circuit moved on to Vegas. CART was quick to pick up the Glen and it remained an Indycar venue until 1981.

Of course, the track had been the setting for many important races beyond the Grands Prix: it was a regular CanAm and Formula 5000 venue and also staged a major sportscar fixture.

In the 1980s, however, only IMSA remained. NASCAR returned in 1986 for the first time since 1965 and the Budweiser at the Glen has since become an exciting addition to the calendar. The spectators who once crammed in with their tents and campers at Grand Prix time have returned to see the southern Good Ol' Boys heaving their mighty cars around the sweepers of the Glen. An exciting spectacle this may be, but a far cry from the days of Clark and Hill and the aristocrats of Formula 1.

Early Oval Racing

The oval racing tradition is strong right across America but nowhere more so than in the Deep South.

Darlington, in the heart of the cotton country of South Carolina, is the granddaddy of the great NASCAR superspeedways, dating back to 1949 when a group of locals formed a stock corporation to build a 1.25-mile paved oval. The first race, the Southern 500, took place on Labor Day 1950. In the years that followed, the Southern 500 emerged as the top meeting of the NASCAR season.

Darlington itself was rebuilt between 1952 and 1953 with the first turn being altered and the track length increased to 1.37 miles. This allowed higher speeds and drew larger crowds, forcing the organisers to increase the grandstand capacity. To-day the race remains one of the four big races in the calendar, with a great carnival atmosphere.

As with many of the NASCAR venues, Darlington stages a second event each year. Beginning in 1957 as the Rebel 300, this increased first to 400 miles and ultimately to a full 500 miles. Today the pressures of sponsorship have meant that the name Rebel 500 has been dropped. Darlington also features a Joe Weatherly Museum in honour of the great NASCAR racer.

Two other NASCAR speedways date back to the late 1940s: North Wilkesboro and Martinsville. A tiny, flat 0.62-mile oval in the foothills of the Blue Ridge Mountains in North Carolina, **North Wilkesboro** lies deep in the NASCAR heartland — moonshine country. The home of Junior Johnson and his team, North Wilkesboro hosted its first races in May 1947 and the track was paved in 1959. Today it runs two 400-lap races a year over this short track where Richard Petty truly is 'The King' with 15 victories.

Martinsville (north-east of North Wilkesboro across the state line in Virginia) is even shorter at 0.52 miles, a flat oval similarly dating from 1947. Lee Petty was the star in the early years, winning 6 of the 12 events before the track was paved in 1955. Thereafter his son Richard took over and matched his tally from North Wilkesboro in the two annual Martinsville 500-lappers in the stadium that in another age would have been excellently suited to chariot racing.

Bridgehampton

While the NASCAR speedways were beginning to develop in the Deep South in the immediate post-war era, some 100 miles from New York City, on the eastern tip of Long Island (once famous for Vanderbilt Cup racing), a four-mile road course for sports cars was introduced in the Hamptons. The course, which included the long Ocean Road concrete straight, remained unchanged until 1953 when the increasing popularity meant that crowd control was becoming a major problem. A series of accidents forced a switch in 1955 to the Westhampton Airforce base until a new purpose-built track was ready in 1957. This was Bridgehampton, one of the classic early CanAm venues.

A picturesque 2.85-mile course undulating and twisting through giant sand dunes with a panoramic view of Peconic Bay, Bridgehampton was a great driver's circuit and in the mid-1960s, as CanAm was born, so Bridgehampton had its moment of international glory. The finest CanAm drivers of the day — Dan Gurney, Denny Hulme, Bruce Mclaren and Mark Donohue — all raced here. Hulme tells a story of Bridgehampton and the year the Hell's Angels came to visit, threatening to wreck the meeting. A bright spark in the organisation came up with a novel way of keeping the bikers from causing aggro: he appointed them all marshals, and they patrolled the verges of the track, seemingly unaware that Maclaren M8Bs were whistling past their ears!

Bridgehampton hosted NASCAR and TransAm races, until the circuit ran into financial trouble in the 1970s and faded from the international scene, although Formula Atlantic paid it a couple of visits as recently as 1979-80.

Left Darlington, 1988: Geoff Bodine in the yellow Chevy crashes into the circuit's outer wall in this NASCAR race incident.

Below
Bridgehampton, mid-1960s: a King Cobra (left) and a Chaparral head a pair of Cobras in an SCCA event.

Sebring

H ighway 27 runs down the spine of Florida passing through the endless lakeland. If you turn off eastwards on U.S. 98 towards Okeechobee, you will stumble upon Sebring Air Terminal.

This Second World War airfield became the home of the first American Grand Prix and the world-renowned Sebring 12 Hours, America's oldest sportscar race. The old bomber training base, dotted with old aircraft and hangars, has seen several different tracks laid out on the runways and local roads since it was opened for racing in December 1950. The second race meeting at Sebring, in March 1952, featured the first 12 Hours and the race has enjoyed an unbroken run since.

In 1953, with the introduction of the World Sportscar Championship, Sebring was the venue for the opening round of a series which included the

The Sebring 12 Hours has been the United States' greatest sportscar race since the inaugural event of 1952. Here a very mixed bag accelerate away from the start line in the early 1960s.

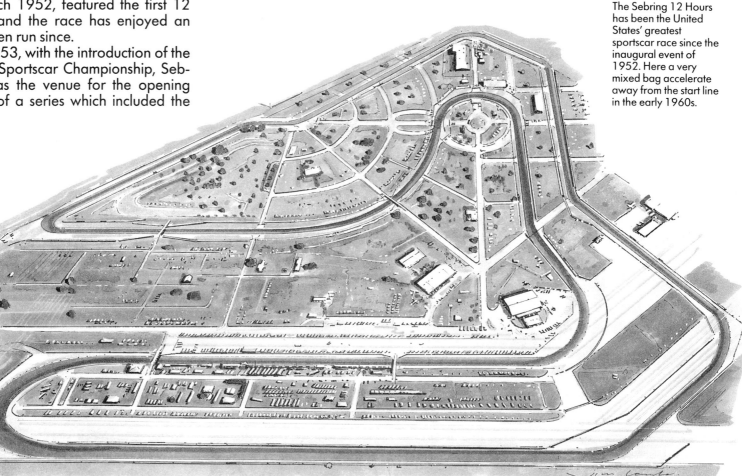

backdrop as the Ford, Porsche and Ferrari teams slugged it out with their GT40s, the 917s and the 512s. Mario Andretti and Bruce Mclaren gave Ford victory in 1967 but a year later Porsche triumphed with Hans Herrman — repeating a victory at Sebring from eight years before — and co-driver Jo Siffert leading the way.

A close race was fought in 1969 with the Jacky Ickx/Jackie Oliver Ford GT40 taking the lead from the prototype 312P Ferrari of Chris Amon and Andretti with just an hour to run. A year later Andretti was back in a 512S, sharing victory with Nino Vaccarella and Ignazio Giunti. Vic Elford and Gerard Larrousse won in their Porsche 917 in 1971, before Andretti (this time sharing with Jacky Ickx) returned to the victory podium. In the mid-1970s the Sebring 12 Hours dropped from the World Chanpionship calendar, though it remains an important round of the IMSA sportscar series.

It is a hard race, starting in the late morning and continuing until the late evening. Until recently it was run on a 5.2-mile track laid out on bumpy concrete runways with lap speeds averaging 120mph. Of the runways, the back straight was the most formidable with the cars sweeping on to it through Warehouse Turn, a 90 degree righthander taken very quickly. The straight was almost a mile long

Above Mario Andretti (Ferrari 512S) passes a backmarker BMW in the 1970 12 Hours. This car later broke down, but Andretti took over another 512S and went on to win.

Millie Miglia, Le Mans, Spa, Nürburgring, Dundrod and the Carrera Panamericana. The best sportscar drivers in the world began to arrive, helping to establish the race as one of the classic events in the sportscar

calendar, with a traditional March date. Victory in 1954 went to Stirling Moss in an OSCA, and in the following years the names Hawthorn, Fangio, Collins, Phil Hill, Gendebian, Bonnier, Bianchi, Surtees and Parkes were added to the victory roll.

The track was changed in 1966 after an accident caused the deaths of four spectators. Despite the changes, the international racers continued to visit in what was a great era of sportscar racing. Sebring was a fitting

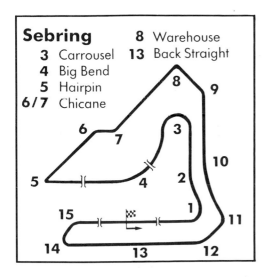

Sebring
3 Carrousel **8** Warehouse
4 Big Bend **13** Back Straight
5 Hairpin
6/7 Chicane

24 Hours

1966	Ken Miles/LLoyd Ruby (Ford)	1980	Volkert Merl/Rolf Stommelen/Reinhold Joest (Porsche)
1967	Lorenzo Bandini/Chris Amon (Ford)	1981	Bob Garretson/Bobby Rahal/Brian Redman (Porsche)
1968	Vic Elford/Jochen Neerspach (Porsche)		
1969	Mark Donohue/Chuck Parsons (Lola-Chevrolet)	1982	John Paul, Jr/John Paul/Rolf Stommelen (Porsche)
1970	Pedro Rodriguez/Leo Kinnunen (Porsche)	1983	Preston Henn/Bob Wollek/Claude Ballot-Lena/ A.J. Foyt (Porsche)
1971	Pedro Rodriguez/Jackie Oliver (Porsche)		
1972	(Six Hours) Mario Andretti/Jacky Ickx (Ferrari)	1984	Sarel Van der Merwe/Graham Duxbury/Ton Martin (March-Porsche)
1973	Peter Gregg/Hurley Haywood (Porsche)		
1974	No race	1985	A.J. Foyt/Bob Wollek/Al Unser/Thierry Boutsen (Porsche)
1975	Peter Gregg/Hurley Haywood (Porsche)		
1976	Peter Gregg/ Brian Redman/John Fitzpatrick (BMW)	1986	Al Holbert/Derek Bell/Al Unser, Jr (Porsche)
		1987	Chip Robinson/Derek Bell/Al Holbert/Al Unser, Jr (Porsche)
1977	John Graves/Hurley Haywood/Dave Helmick (Porsche)		
1978	Rolf Stommelen/Toine Hezemans/Peter Gregg (Porsche)	1988	Martin Brundle/John Nielsen/Raul Boesel (Jaguar)
1979	Ted Field/Danny Ongais/Hurley Haywood (Porsche)	1989	Derek Bell/Bob Wollek/John Andretti (Porsche)

and so wide that the drivers had little point of reference for braking for the double-apex turn at the end, a corner taken with a wide — and often wild — variety of cornering lines. Things have changed now. The new layout of 1987 features less of the abrasive old concrete runways and more new asphalt sections linking portions of the old track. The 1988 race was the 13th consecutive Porsche victory at Sebring, including the remarkable triumph in 1986 when the Coke Porsche of Bob Akin/Hans Stuck/Jo Gartner arrived in victory lane on three wheels!

The first U.S. GP took place at Sebring in 1959, marking the debut Fl victory of Bruce Mclaren (Cooper Climax). In the same race Jack Brabham secured the World Championship by pushing his car to the finish after running out of fuel. A year later the event moved to Riverside in California before settling in 1961 at Watkins Glen. Sebring, however, is best remembered as a sportscar venue, although today the Indycar teams use the track to make the best of Florida's mild winter. Not a bad place for a test drive!

Right Though no longer a World Sportscar championship, the Sebring 12 Hours remains a key event in the IMSA calendar. Here the Nissan GTP of Geoff Brabham, Chip Robinson and Arie Luyendyk is on its way to victory in the 1989 race.

Laguna Seca

Laguna Seca is a track for the brave. It rises and falls around a natural hollow of ground in the hills of California's Monterey Peninsular and has long been one of the foremost road courses in the United States. Nearby was the former public-road course of Pebble Beach, which wound a sinuous path through the pine forest of Del Monte. When this closed in 1956, Laguna was planned and built in collaboration with the U.S. Army.

Laguna is a wonderful and spectacular track for the fans. But its remoteness from major urban centres — it is some 100 miles south of San Francisco — means that attracting crowds has sometimes been difficult and the access roads leave much to be desired. The struggle to get there is worth it, for this is how racing should be. Instead of wasting years on miser-

Right Start of a 1960s CanAm event at Laguna Seca. Two McLarens (Bruce McLaren, 5, and Denny Hulme, 7) lead; Jackie Stewart (38) is in a Lola.

able street circuits or car parks, Formula 1 might have been better established in America had it visited venues such as Laguna, where the cars are able to been seen at their best. The track has an elevation change of 300ft, leaving the pits and blasting through a series of fast tricky lefthanders. Turn 2 is downhill before the climb up, bordered by rock-strewn banks and barriers alongside the road — run-off was minimal until recently. At the top is the infamous Corkscrew (Turns 5 and 6), a twisting left dropping into a curling right, where the camber change can catch the driver off guard. From there it is downhill left and right under the famous bridge to the abrupt Turn 9 at the bottom of the course, a tight lefthander back on to the pits straight.

Hopeful of attracting a Formula 1

Above Brian Redman (Lola), followed by two Porsche 935s, negotiates Laguna's perilous Corkscrew in an IMSA race.

Left Pits scene at Laguna during practice for a CART race. The car is Bobby Rahal's Lola.

Grand Prix after the demise of Detroit, the track underwent major revisions in 1988 to include a new infield section around a lake, extending the original 1.9 miles to 2.2. Inside the old Turn 1 is a new hairpin, followed by a fast right across an artificial lake by causeway before another fast right, feeding back into another fast left at the old Turn 2.

The first races at Laguna took place in 1958 but true international racing arrived with the Monterey sportscar Grands Prix of the early 1960s, the first two being won by Stirling Moss. When CanAm was launched Laguna was an obvious venue and it hosted the championship through its greatest

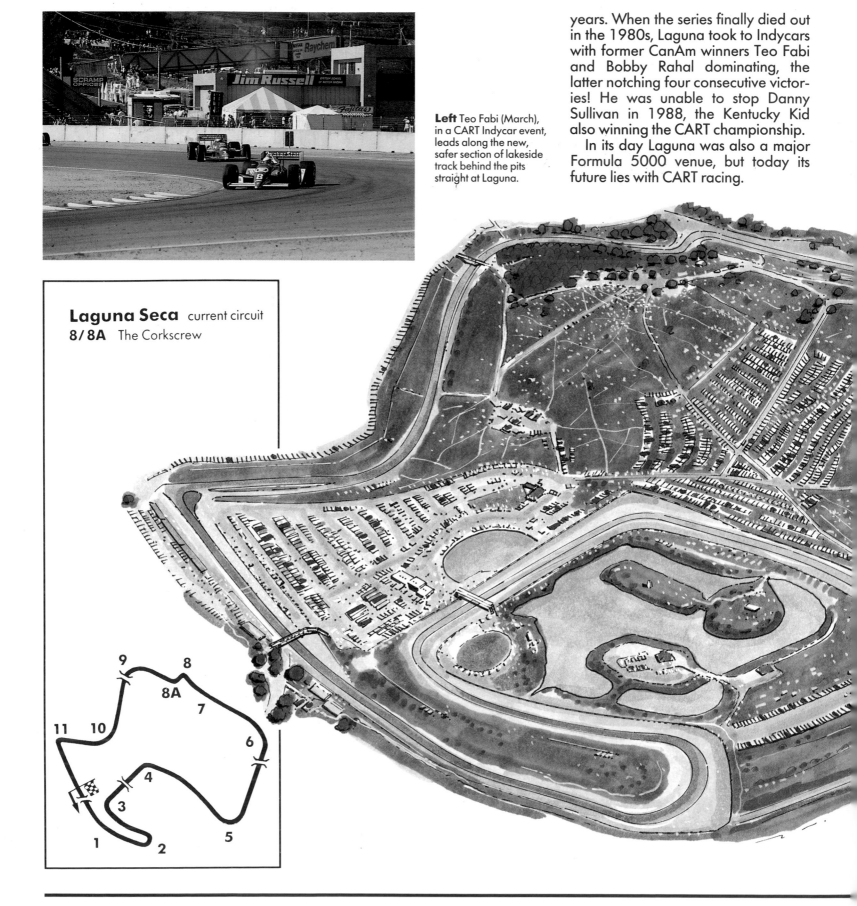

Left Teo Fabi (March), in a CART Indycar event, leads along the new, safer section of lakeside track behind the pits straight at Laguna.

years. When the series finally died out in the 1980s, Laguna took to Indycars with former CanAm winners Teo Fabi and Bobby Rahal dominating, the latter notching four consecutive victories! He was unable to stop Danny Sullivan in 1988, the Kentucky Kid also winning the CART championship.

In its day Laguna was also a major Formula 5000 venue, but today its future lies with CART racing.

Laguna Seca current circuit
8/8A The Corkscrew

Riverside

Another track of the same era as Laguna, Riverside is about 50 miles east of Los Angeles. In the hot, dusty desert below California's San Bernardino mountains, Riverside staged the second U.S. Grand Prix in 1960, a race won by Moss in a Lotus 18. Built in 1957, Riverside had several different layouts and a drag strip doubling as the main straight. It was primarily a sportscar venue and featured regularly in the CanAm years with the *LA Times* GP race. Riverside was always Dan Gurney's track: he won in 1967 and 1968 when the Indycars visited first and dominated the early NASCAR Motor Trend 500 event, winning four consecutive races.

Riverside was bumpy with blind brows, difficult cambers and unmarked track edges. It was fast and spectacular, with a dominant main straight and the famous uphill Esses. But it was also a place for large accidents: the great NASCAR driver Joe Weatherly died here in 1964 and in the 1980s it took the life of German sportscar ace Rolf Stommelen, and there were others... When the nearby

Ontario Motor Speedway closed down, Indycars returned after a 12 year break in 1981 and it was local hero Rick Mears who won two in a row; but after 1983 CART departed. NASCAR was a regular visitor to the track from its earliest days and continued until the track closed in 1988. In its later years affected by the Los Angeles smog, Riverside fell victim to urban expansion, although a smaller track was retained for local competition.

Away to the north in Washington state is **Seattle**, another combined road track and drag strip of the same vintage. Situated 25 miles south of the city of Seattle, it was called Pacific Raceway on its opening in 1960 but has also been known as both Kent (the nearest town) and Seattle. It is 2.25 miles in length and anticlockwise, a bumpy track with a taxing carousel corner. Always overshadowed by the more famous tracks to the south, it staged TransAm, SuperVee and Formula Atlantic races but it never really broke into the big time occupied by Riverside and Laguna Seca.

Right Riverside 1960: F1 cars power through the tricky Esses on the only occasion the U.S. Grand Prix was held at this desert circuit. Moss and Ireland made it a 1-2 for Lotus; Brabham (Cooper), who took the drivers' title that year, came fourth after teammate McLaren.

Road America

At the same time as Laguna Seca, Riverside and Pacific Raceway were making their reputations in the west, Wisconsin's Road America was emerging as another major American road circuit. Built in the mid-1950s near the village of Elkhart Lake to the north of Chicago and close to the Canadian border, Road America is set in rolling wooded countryside and at 4 miles is one of the longest tracks in America.

Road America's biggest race meeting of the year used to be held annually in late July or early August. Initially this was a CanAm track ruled over by the mighty McLarens until the fifth visit of the big sportscars in 1971

when George Follmer ended a run of five McLaren wins in his Porsche. At the same time Formula 5000 was regularly seen on the sweeps and swerves of Elkhart, a track where David Hobbs, Brian Redman, Graeme

Right Road America, host to a variety of events, is one of the most important road circuits in the United States' domestic racing programme.

Road America (Elkhart Lake)

4	Moraine Sweep
7/8	Hurry Downs
9/10	The Carrousel
12	Kettle Bottoms
13	Canada Corner

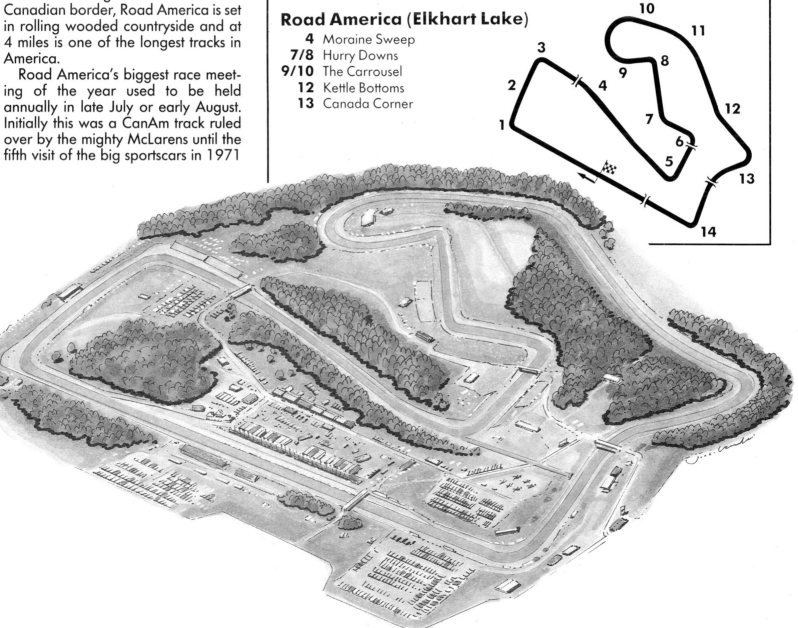

McRae and even Mario Andretti and Al Unser all shone in F5000. TransAm too was a regular visitor and Mark Donohue was the ace in the early period before the days of the late great Peter Gregg. Also in action were the SuperVees and Formula Atlantics, underlining Elkhart's claim to being one of the most important national venues in American road racing.

Internationally, Road America made little impact despite CanAm and Formula 5000. It was not until the final demise of CanAm in the mid-1980s that Indycar racing began to show interest in the fast Wisconsin track with its sweeping back straight, its endless trees and the evocatively named corners: Moraine Sweep, Hurry Downs,

the Carrousel, Kettle Bottoms and Canada Corner. In September 1982 Indycars headed for the swooping hills of Wisconsin for the first time. And it was an extraordinary affair with leaders dropping out all the way through until, a couple of miles from the flag, the Longhorn of Al Unser ran out of fuel, leaving Mexican journeyman Hector Rebaque to win. A year later they were all chasing another Mexican, Josele Garza. He spun out a few laps from the flag and Mario Andretti grabbed his chance to win. A year later Andretti repeated the victory, this time in rather more emphatic style.

The weather in Wisconsin had always been somewhat unpredictable and in 1985 a wet/dry race resulted

in victory for Gilles Villeneuve's brother Jacques, though Al Unser Jr damaged his legs in a hefty accident. Unser crashed out again the following year, in the rain again, when his accident — this time without undue hurt — ended the race after a handful of laps. It was postponed to be run in October, when it duly poured with rain again and amid much drama and dodging of puddles Emerson Fittipaldi won, chased across the line by Michael Andretti just 0.3 second behind. His father Mario won in 1987, once more in the rain. Road America is like that, never short of surprises and upsets. Although until recently there was talk of a Formula 1 race, Elkhart Lake continues to be the backbone of American national racing.

New Ovals of the 1960s

NASCAR stock car racing was taking off dramatically in the late 1950s. Daytona International Speedway was built and with it came a new generation of paved speedways. One of the first of the second generation tracks was **Atlanta International Raceway** in Georgia which was built in 1959, 20 miles south of the now burgeoning state capital. A high-banked 1.522-mile superspeedway, with 24-degree banking in the corners and a slight bank on the straights, was built in a dip in the ground providing spectators with a fine natural arena in which to view the action. This was to be the home of the Atlanta 500 (latterly the Coca-Cola 500) and the Dixie 500 (now the *Atlanta Journal 500*) NASCAR races. Indycars were a regular fixture in the mid-1960s but not returning until 1978.

At the same time **Charlotte Motor Speedway**, North Carolina, arrived. Today, it is one of the most complete motor sport facilities in the world. In America ostentation ain't no crime and Charlotte has plenty of that with its chandeliers, rosewood spiral staircases and condominiums overlooking the track! It will seat 171,000 people and there are no traffic hold-ups as the track has umpteen exits on to a passing freeway. Back in 1960 both Curtis Turner and Bruton Smith wanted to build speedways in the area and finally the two were persuaded to get together. The result was a 1.5-mile oval with 24-degree banking and a trioval section similar to that at Daytona. There was also a 2.25-mile road course.

The track broke up at the first meeting, which featured a race under the title of World 600. This would become one of the big four NASCAR events and was held deliberately on the same day as the Indianapolis 500. It was on this track in 1964 that Fireball Roberts was killed and here also that superspeedway king David Pearson took 10 consecutive pole positions between 1974 and 1978. The World 600 is augmented each year by the National 500 (though the sponsors' naming rights have long since gone to the brewing corporation, Miller) Charlotte remains, as it was intended, a thorn in Daytona's side; it is a track with promotional skills to rival even those of the France.

While the short oval track at **Bristol**, on the Virginia-Tennessee state line, dates from 1961, the home of the Volunteer 500 and Southeastern 500 did not emerge as a front line track until 1969 when the half-mile track had its banking raised to 24 degrees. The same is true of the superspeedway (tracks must be at least a mile long to qualify for that grandiose tag) at Rockingham, the **North Carolina Motor Speedway**. In sandhills close to U.S. Highway 1, it was completed in 1965 and used as the venue

Left Atlanta International Raceway: pits action in a CART race in 1981. Atlanta is one of the second-generation superspeedways.

Right The field at Turn 3 at the start of a NASCAR race at the Charlotte Motor Speedway.

Charlotte

NASCAR turn 2

NASCAR turn 3

NASCAR turn 4

4 5 6
3 2 7 8
1

for the Peach Blossom 500. In 1969 the banking was increased and the speeds increased. On this track Richard Petty has scored 11 victories in the two annual events, the American 500 and the Carolina 500.

The grandest and most majestic of the superspeedways of the 1960s was Talladega, the **Alabama International Motor Speedway**, 2.66 miles in length and the fastest of them all. Another track conceived by the France family, Talladega had a staggering 199.466mph qualifying speed at its first race in 1969 and although the drivers were unhappy that the high speeds were causing tyres to shred, the race took place nonetheless, being won at a more conservative average of 153.778mph! In March 1970 Buddy Baker broke the 200mph closed circuit record and Talladega has been used since then for a number of record attempts. In August 1975, just a few days before his death at the Austrian GP, Mark Donohue clocked 221.12mph in a Porsche 917. The huge lazy speedway also stages twin NASCAR races each year, the 'big Four' Winston 500 and the Talladega 500. Speeds of 200mph in the mighty stock cars are not unusual here.

Other Ovals

Ovals in America have come and gone, with some impressive facilities. These range from one of the most historic, the flat one mile oval in **Wisconsin State Fair Park**, Milwaukee, dating back to its first National Championship races in 1933 and still in use today; to long-gone locations such as **Asheville-Weaverville** in the Blue Ridge Mountains, the fastest half-mile stock car track of its era but unused since 1969. Of today's survivors, the most notable are Michigan and Pocono, which hold the two 500-mile Indycar races besides that at Indianapolis.

Michigan International Speedway at Brooklyn, to the west of Detroit, is owned by Roger Penske and is as fast as Indianapolis. Only the back stretch is flat here and the steeply banked two-mile oval was famed for its rough surface until resurfaced in 1986. Featuring not one but two road courses, neither is used today, MIS sees average speeds in excess of 220mph when the CART men visit. It first staged a 500 in 1981, though it had been used for 200-mile races since 1970 and NASCAR one year before that. It was here that Derek Daly survived a horrendous accident in 1984.

Pocono has been running 500 races since it opened in July 1971. Up to the Pocono Mountains near Long Pond, Pennsylvania, it is another track to have a road course built inside, though as with many other ovals this has seldom hosted any major events. Pocono is unusual in that it is an irregular 2.5-mile tri-oval, each of its three turns different in angle and steepness of banking. To the driver it is interesting but unfortunately it is also dangerous because of a bumpy surface unmatched anywhere in the modern CART calendar.

Once a popular venue attracting large crowds from Philadelphia and New York, Pocono is now rundown for both spectators and drivers. Sporadic resurfacing has made little difference for the drivers and virtually nothing has been done for the spectators. Built in the late 1960s, Pocono looks likely to fade away unless refurbishment is carried out. Pocono has a wide front straight lined by flat metal barriers (they call it 'boiler plate') and it has seen some immense accidents in recent years, including Johnny Rutherford's miraculous escape in 1981. There was carnage in 1982 from which all emerged unscathed. Others have not been as lucky and there are numerous contemporary Indycar and NASCAR drivers who have been hurt here.

While the future of Pocono is threatened, other superspeedways have disappeared, notably the extraordinary **Ontario Motor Speedway**, not far from Riverside in California. Built in the late 1960s as the West Coast's answer to Indianapolis, Ontario cost a fortune to construct yet it was lack of finance that finally killed it in 1981. In its day Ontario hosted

Above A pit stop in a NASCAR event at the Pocono tri-oval. The circuit's future is put in doubt by the notoriously bumpy surface of the track.

Above right Phoenix International Raceway, hemmed in by arid Arizona scrubland, hosted regular Indycar events like this one in the 1980s.

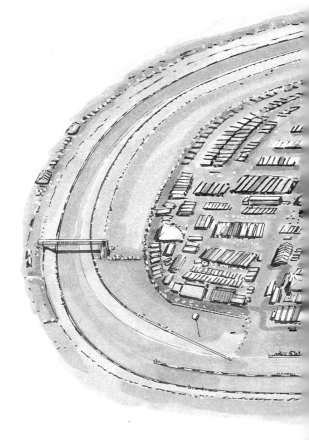

Phoenix International Raceway

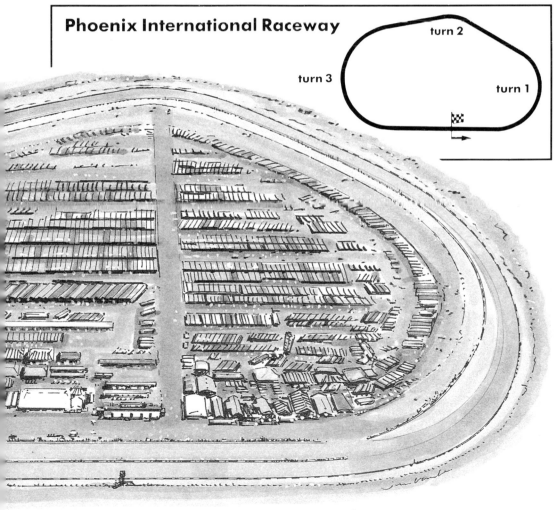

major Indycar races, although its first event in 1971 was a bizarre F5000 versus F1 race.

Texas World Speedway at College Station, close to Dallas-Fort Worth, was an Indycar and NASCAR track in the 1970s and is another oval that has faded away, as has **Trenton**, New Jersey, a National Championship oval from 1958 until 1979. **Nashville**, Tennessee, had a famous speedway, dating back to 1958. This was just over half a mile in length and the original 35-degree banking had to be eased to 18 degrees. At one time this was the home of NASCAR Nashville and Music City 420s but now it is forgotten. Until recently there was the half mile at **Richmond**. Paved over in 1968, this was the home of the NASCAR Richmond 500 and the Capitol City 400. Richard Petty's winning score here is double that of his nearest rival. That track was demolished in 1988 to make way for a bigger and better facility, so at least the name will survive.

Aside from its new F1 street circuit **Phoenix** has its International Raceway — a regular Indycar track in the 1980s and today the venue of the annual CART season-opener.

Other ovals struggle on, notably the 'Monster Mile' at **Dover Downs**, a bumpy and vertiginous high-banked track on the Delaware pensinsula near Washington DC, home for the Mason-Dixon and Delaware 500s, where NASCAR machines lap at 140mph.

While some fade, others emerge, most notably in recent years at Nazareth, home town of the Andretti family. Refurbished in 1987 by Roger Penske, it has been renamed the **Pennsylvania International Raceway** and holds a CART event each year.

Though they are highly dangerous if they are not suited to the cars racing on them, it is probable that ovals will continue to come and go as the demands on them alter.

Road Circuits

The major American road circuits of the modern era date for the most part from the 1960s. The trend today is to create total racing facilities that combine as many disciplines as possible. This has been done at Moroso, Indianapolis Raceway Park and Memphis, where drag strips and ovals are combined with road courses. This isn't a new trend as speedways such as Michigan International, Pocono, Daytona, Charlotte and College Station all featured both combined road and oval courses, though many of the road sections fell quickly from regular use and have never been resurrected.

In addition to Laguna and Road America, the list of true road courses must include such facilities as the **Mid-Ohio Sports Car Course**, opened in 1962 in the rolling hills of central Ohio, between Columbus and Cleveland. It was bought in 1981 by the late Jim Trueman, who set about transforming the track from a relatively unimportant track into a major facility. Today there are wide spectator banks all around the tight 2.4-mile track. If the tarmac is narrow, the circuit still provides a challenge with its abrupt changes of elevation and direction. Some drivers find it hard to adjust to the idiosyncrasies of Mid-Ohio but few doubt it is a course to reckon with.

Although not a track with a great international history, Mid-Ohio played an important role in the latter days of CanAm and during the F5000 years. Since its refurbishment it has become a CART track and a national racing venue with as much importance as Road America. It too has hopes for a more international future.

Portland International Raceway in Oregon, where on a clear day you can see the snow-capped Mt Hood to the east and the remains of Mount St Helens to the north, is built on a flood plain. This combined drag strip and race track today also stages an annual CART race, although previously it was a regular IMSA and TransAm venue.

Sears Point, near Sonoma in California's Napa Valley, is another such circuit. Opened in 1969, it is hilly and tortuous for its entire 2.52-mile length, with scarcely a straight to speak of. Again, this track has come into its own with the 1980s, though it served its time as a latter-day CanAm venue. It has also long been the home of the famous Bob Bondurant school.

Road Atlanta in Gainesville, Georgia, is now the only major road racing track in the Deep South, that

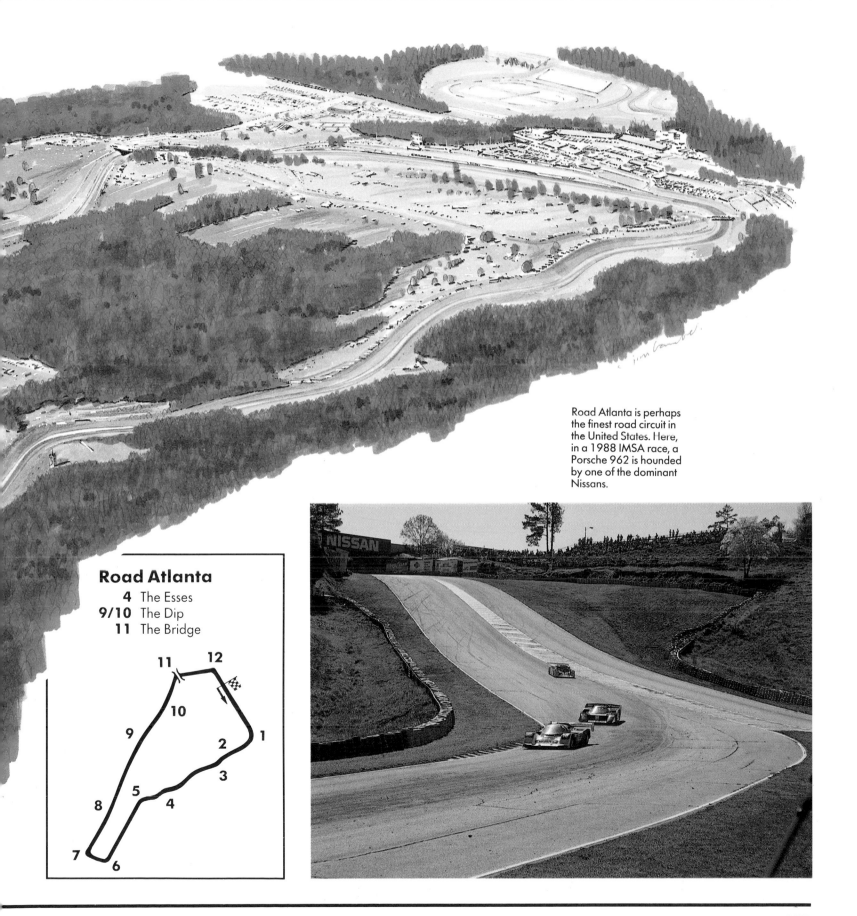

Road Atlanta is perhaps the finest road circuit in the United States. Here, in a 1988 IMSA race, a Porsche 962 is hounded by one of the dominant Nissans.

Road Atlanta

4 The Esses
9/10 The Dip
11 The Bridge

Below Start of an IMSA GTO race at Road Atlanta in 1988. Front row, from the left: Mustang, Camaro, Toyota Celica.

NASCAR stronghold. Built in 1970, it is a roller coaster track with blind brows and steep climbs and runs to 2.52 miles in length. 'Road Atlanta is probably the best road course in the United States of America,' says David Hobbs. 'It's undulating, there's not enough run-off, but it's good for the spectators.' And he points out that though it is stuck out in the middle of nowhere Atlanta is moving ever closer as it expands.

Road Atlanta has an immensely long straight leading back towards the pits, dipping away and swinging slightly left before flying uphill, going right under a bridge in a cutting where it dips downhill again, with a very quick righthander at the bottom. It's a stern challenge in any kind of car, particularly the big 1970s CanAm sportscars, the Formula 5000s which visited only occasionally and the modern IMSA prototypes. Every autumn Road Atlanta plays host to the Run-Offs, an annual gathering of the club-racing clans during which as many as 20 or more national titles can be settled over one bewildering weekend.

There are many less important road courses spread across the country, some with their best days behind them, others looking ahead. The evocatively named **Donnybrooke** at Brainerd, Minnesota, opened in August 1968 was a popular track in the 1970s, despite being 140 miles from Minneapolis and a million miles from anywhere else. Donnybrooke has a long, wide straight with long, slightly banked bends. The three-mile track staged early F5000 races, CanAm from 1970 and more recently IMSA, although the sportscar series moved elsewhere after 1983 when Kathy Rude was grievously hurt in an accident. Today Brainerd (as it is now called) is no more than a club track.

Lime Rock Park in the foothills of the Berkshire Mountains in the north-west corner of Connecticut has fared better, despite being short (at 1.53 miles), narrow and very fast. An irregular oval in shape, it features a series of fast corners, diving descents and dramatic crests, one of which sent the IMSA Nissan of John Morton flying skyward in 1988. Its quaintly named West Bend, No name Straight and Uphill betray little of its character. Unusually, racing at Lime Rock is restricted to Saturdays, in deference to the nearby church.

There is the **Continental Divide** track at Castle Rock, Colorado, another tight and rolling circuit that had its moment of glory in 1970 when it staged the National Championship; the once snake-infested **Dallas International Motor Speedway**, designed for Indycar racing but never host to more than a single Formula 5000 event; **Bryar** at Loudon, New Hampshire, essentially a bike track around a hillside but also a TransAm venue.

Of course, you could go on forever finding race tracks in the United States: the long forgotten Thompson Speedway near Hartford, Connecticut, one of the earliest of closed permanent tracks in the USA; Stardust Raceway outside Las Vegas, Nevada; Hallett, Oklahoma; Green Valley, Texas; Meadowdale, Illinois; Mid-America Raceways at Wentzville; War Bonnett Park, Oklahoma; Modesto Air Station, California; Danville, Virginia; Waterford Hills, Michigan; Pueblo, Colarado; Willow Springs, California; Summit Point, West Virginia.... Tracks as varied as the landscape of this vast country.

Below The Geoff Brabham/John Morton Nissan leads assorted machinery through an S-curve in a 1988 IMSA Sportscar championship race at Road Atlanta.

Long Beach

Aside from the speedways and permanent road circuits, American racing history has often been made on temporary track, though not in the same way as Europe's Targas Florio or Pescara Grand Prix. On the contrary, these are the street tracks — the up-a-block, left, down-a-block races. In recent years there have been many such tracks but none has had the success of Long Beach, California, home of the United States Grand Prix (West). If the title was ungainly, the track itself was something of a success.

Originally a rather drab seaport with an elderly population, Long Beach yearned to be as glamorous as its near neighbours San Diego and Los Angeles. It had the *Queen Mary* berthed in the harbour and Howard Hughes' vast flying-boat *Spruce Goose*, but it needed a little razzmatazz. When Englishman Chris Pook approached the City Fathers with the suggestion that the streets be turned into a race track, they coughed and spluttered, but eventually sat up and listened. Could they make this the Monaco of the West Coast? It didn't

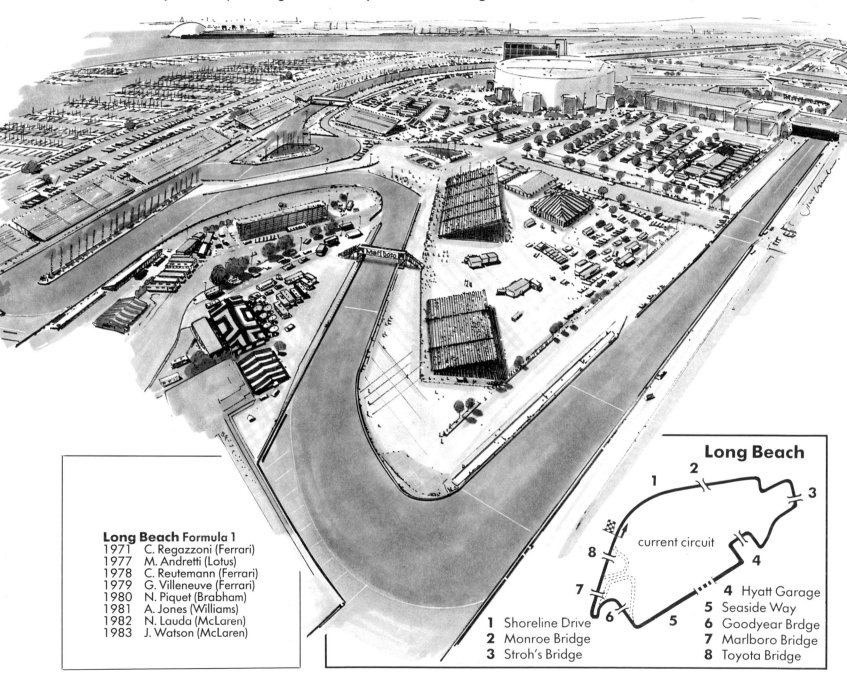

Long Beach Formula 1

1971	C. Regazzoni (Ferrari)
1977	M. Andretti (Lotus)
1978	C. Reutemann (Ferrari)
1979	G. Villeneuve (Ferrari)
1980	N. Piquet (Brabham)
1981	A. Jones (Williams)
1982	N. Lauda (McLaren)
1983	J. Watson (McLaren)

Long Beach

current circuit

1 Shoreline Drive
2 Monroe Bridge
3 Stroh's Bridge
4 Hyatt Garage
5 Seaside Way
6 Goodyear Brdge
7 Marlboro Bridge
8 Toyota Bridge

work out quite like that, but in September 1975 Long Beach staged an excellent all-star Formula 5000 race won by Brian Redman, in a dress-rehearsal for the arrival the following year of the Formula 1 Grand Prix circus. It was a tough track, where automobile gymnastics seemed more in order than aerodynamic tuning; a place where cars were abused, where concrete barriers were perpetually being thumped by errant machines.

If the Formula 5000 event had been a fine race and a great success, the first F1 Grand Prix was not. To put it briefly, Clay Regazzoni disappeared into the distance while everyone else foundered, crashed or waved fists at one another. Financially, it was a disaster. But Long Beach hung on, hoping for better things. Fortunately the next year saw a great race, with victory going to Mario Andretti's Lotus after a close-fought battle with Jody Scheckter's Wolf and Niki Lauda's Ferrari. An American victory was warmly applauded by audience, sponsor and TV alike. It was here in 1980 that a promising young Brazilian called Nelson Piquet won his first Grand Prix and, at the same meeting, where Clay Regazzoni survived an awful accident which ended his career.

In 1983, after the track had undergone a number of modifications to slow down the fast sweeping Shoreline Drive, John Watson scored a remarkable victory after starting 22nd on the grid. Not to be outdone, his McLaren team mate Niki Lauda started 23rd and finished second! A year later, however, Formula 1 had moved on, leaving Long Beach to CART and the Andretti family: Mario winning in 1984, 1985 and 1987 with his son Michael winning in 1986! It took another son of a famous father, Al Unser Jr, to break the Andretti domination. Today Long Beach is booming, with massive redevelopment taking place around the track as pavilions and convention centres are built. It may not be Monaco but it goes down well in California. . . .

Left De Angelis (Lotus, 11), Tambay (Ferrari, 27), Rosberg (Williams, 1) and Laffite (Williams, 2) line up for a right-hander in the 1983 U.S. Grand Prix (West) — the last, and best, to be held at Long Beach.

Below Plenty of vantage points for spectators at Long Beach: a scene during the 1988 Toyota Grand Prix, a CART event.

Other Street Circuits

Since Long Beach there have been three other attempts to take Formula 1 racing on to the streets and into the car parks of North American cities at Detroit, Las Vegas and Dallas. None has been wildly successful, all held on frustrating stop-go tracks with the ubiquitous concrete barriers. Some drivers, like Mario Andretti, excel in such circumstances, others hate them. Once the novelty value has worn off, moreover, the street tracks find it hard to survive.

Las Vegas was perhaps the epitome of the genre, a concrete 'tunnel' in a huge car park. This was the

Right Carpark contender: Carlos Reutemann (Williams) in the 1981 U.S. Grand Prix at Las Vegas, where his listless performance cost him what had seemed an inevitable F1 drivers' title.

Detroit street circuit, viewed from the grandiose Renaissance Center. Most F1 drivers (Senna the obvious exception) detested the bumpy track and hoped for something better at Phoenix.

Las Vegas Formula 1	
1981	A. Jones (Williams)
1982	M. Alboreto (Tyrrell)

Detroit Formula 1	
1982	J. Watson (McLaren)
1983	M. Alboreto (Tyrrell)
1984	N. Piquet (Brabham)
1985	K. Rosberg (Williams)
1986	A. Senna (Lotus)
1987	A. Senna (Lotus)
1988	A. Senna (McLaren)

Dallas Formula 1	
1984	K. Rosberg (Williams)

Phoenix Formula 1	
1989	A. Prost (McLaren)

inauspicious setting for the World Championship showdown of 1981 with Carlos Reutemann and Nelson Piquet tussling for the title and Alan Jones marking his retirement (the first one) with a superb win. A second event, won by Michele Alboreto's Tyrrell, ended F1 racing in Vegas, and no one mourned for long. **Detroit** survived longer, the streets of Motown being used from 1982-1988. Senna thrived there and won; Prost and Piquet detested it. **Dallas** was another flash in the pan, arriving and disappearing in 1984.

While F1 is in this strange phase, looking to **Phoenix** for salvation, Indycar racing has moved into car parks, airports and on to the streets, beginning with Cleveland's soulless **Burke Lakefront** airport in 1982. The organisation took over Las Vegas from F1 in 1983 — a brief love affair — and Long Beach in 1984. The same year Indycars went to a car park glorified by the name Meadowlands GP in New York and a year later took up in Miami, followed in 1986 by Toronto. It seems that a city decides it is a good idea to boost tourism and a car park or street track is found. There is rarely a good track and almost never a long-term commitment from the organisers. It is a quite different situation from the immensely successful Adelaide race, an event which shows how street racing should be done.

Good street racing is wonderful, but few tracks measure up to the job. Better the magnificent sweeps of Laguna or Road Atlanta than pottering around in a car park, bouncing off concrete blocks.

Above Mario Andretti (1, Lola) heads Danny Sullivan (4) in New York's Meadowlands GP, an Indycar event, in 1985.

Phoenix City

1	Jefferson St	**8**	3rd Ave
2	1st St	**9**	Adams St
3	Madison St	**10**	5th Ave
4	5th St		
5	Monroe St		
6	3rd St		
7	Washington St		

Below Miami has become established as a round of the IMSA series despite its unforgiving concrete walls.

CANADA

International motor racing is comparatively new to Canada. The country is huge and the population concentrated mainly into the eastern cities of Quebec, Montreal and Toronto. Even today, the national racing championships are fragmented by the distance across the continent and further confused by the rivalry between the French-speaking Quebecois and the English speakers from the rest of the country. Motor racing is at its strongest in Quebec, where they have an almost Italian devotion to the sport. The weather in the region does not help matters, although, like the country's greatest driver Gilles Villeneuve, many of the youngsters cut their teeth in snowmobile racing.

The first attempts at professional racing took place on the aerodrome at Harewood Acres in 1959, although there had previously been races at Abbotford, near Vancouver. The first international competition, however, came with the 1960s and the circuits at Mosport Park in Ontario and Mont Tremblant, Quebec. With little racing tradition of its own, Canada has tended to look to both Europe and the United States and the result is a curious synthesis of events from the two retions: Formula Ford, Formula Atlantic and, in its day, CanAm. There are rounds of the American championships at Canadian circuits and the European-based FISA championships come and go.

With the outstanding exception of Villeneuve, few Canadian drivers have made it into Formula 1 on anything close to a regular basis. Some have gone south to the United States, and others have looked to Europe. Some have even done both! Canada did not stage a Formula 1 Grand Prix until as recently as 1967 but in later years, notably when Villeneuve was still alive, this was a popular end-of-season fixture, if at times a little on the cold side with winter coming on.

Mosport Park

The first major racing facility in Canada was Mosport Park, opened in 1961. Near Bowmanville, 60 miles east of Toronto, Mosport is set in hills close to the north shore of Lake Ontario and is a scenic and spectacular track, plunging between the trees. The inaugural race, and the first international race to be held in Canada, the Player's 200, took place in 1961 and was won by Stirling Moss in a Lotus.

The same meeting saw the first Canadian Grand Prix, for sportscars. The visitors, among them Pedro Rodriguez, Jo Bonnier and Olivier Gendebien, found Mosport to be a tricky, undulating 2.4-mile track, up hill and down dale. 'Turn 2 was a ballbreaker,' remembers regular visitor David Hobbs, 'a downhill righthanded sweeper with guard-rails close in, as the track crossed a pedestrian tunnel at that point. It was a great circuit, and a good place to go racing.'

The Player's 200 and the Canadian Grand Prix continued through the 1960s as sportscar races until the first Formula 1 event and the introduction of the Canadian American Challenge (CanAm).

The Formula 1 Grand Prix arrived in 1967 and with it came a regular feature at Mosport — rain! The race was won by Jack Brabham from his Repco-Brabham team mate Denny Hulme. CanAm began in 1966 and until the series finally fell apart in the mid-1980s, Mosport was a regular venue — and a popular one, for this was a driver's track.

As at all driver's tracks, there were some monumental accidents at Mosport, smashes that would ultimately drive international racing away. John Surtees had the worst accident in his racing career at the track in 1965 after a suspension breakage caused

Mosport Park

1 Corner One
2 Tunnel
3 Corner Two
4 Corner Three
5 Corner Four
6 Player's Bridge
7 Corner Five A
8 Moss Corner (Five B)
9 Corner Five C
10 Corner Six
11 Corner Seven
12 Mario Andretti
   Straightaway

13 Corner Eight
14 The Esses
15 Tunnel
16 Corner Nine
17 White's Corner

Left Mosport Park: a fast but tricky circuit amid spectacular scenery. Here Laffite (Ligier), Pace (Brabham), Peterson (March) and Regazzoni (Ferrari) go into a fast right-hander during the 1976 Grand Prix.

Mosport Formula 1

1967	J. Brabham (Brabham)
1969	J. Ickx (Brabham)
1971	J. Stewart (Tyrrell)
1972	J. Stewart (Tyrrell)
1973	P. Revson (McLaren)
1974	E. Fittipaldi (McLaren)
1976	J. Hunt (McLaren)
1977	J. Scheckter (Wolf)

his CanAm Lola to crash violently, leaving the World Champion with extensive injuries. Two years later Ian Ashley was hurt in a violent shunt during qualifying for the Grand Prix.

Over the years Mosport has changed little, while the cars have been lapping ever faster. When the World Sportscar Championship visited the track in 1985 — the race in which Jaguar returned to sportscar events — Manfred Winkelhock was killed after an accident at the downhill sweeping Turn 2. World Sportscar racing did not return. The winner on that tragic day was Jacky Ickx, one of the stars of Mosport. He had won the Canadian GP in 1969 and would win again in CanAm in 1979, proving himself the master of Mosport under three codes.

The Canadian Grand Prix alternated between Mosport and Mont Tremblant until 1972 when the sponsors Player's gave way to Labatt Breweries and Mont Tremblant faded away. Thereafter Mosport would be the home of the Canadian race until it moved to Montreal in 1978. In that period Jackie Stewart won twice (once in the rain and once in fog), while Peter Revson in a McLaren scored his second and last Formula 1 victory on the circuit's twists and turns, again in the rain. McLaren also won in 1974 and 1976 courtesy of Emerson Fittipaldi and James Hunt and Jody Scheckter in a Wolf closed the era. Patrick Depailler twice finished runner up by just a few seconds on each occasion.

In recent times Mosport has staged many American events, including rounds of the IMSA, TransAm, Super-Vee and Formula Atlantic championships. It has become bumpy and increasingly shabby although new owners who bought the track in December 1987 have announced their intention to develop the site from a pure race track into a recreational park — always assuming the money can be found.

Pit work on Al Unser's Lola-Cosworth DFX during a 1978 CART race at Mosport. Hawaiian driver Danny Ongais sits on the wall at right.

Mont-Tremblant

The Mont-Tremblant circuit at St Jovite, Quebec, is a scenic spot set in the beautiful rolling woodland of the Laurentian Mountains. As at Mosport, the track swerves and dives through the hills. 'That was a hell of a frightening place,' recalls David Hobbs, 'with its undulating main straight and sweeping corners. There was a famous jump, too, where Paul Hawkins looped the loop in the old days and where Brian Redman hurt himself so badly in 1977.'

Opened in September 1964 and extended soon afterwards to its full 2.65-mile length, Mont-Tremblant played host to the first ever CanAm race in 1966, an event won by the Lola of John Surtees at an average speed of 96mph. Even then the track was narrow and bumpy and its arrival in Grand Prix racing in 1968 coincided with the tail-end of the 'anything goes' era. That year Denny Hulme won by a lap from Bruce McLaren but the tragedies in the following years would mean that almost from its start Mont-Tremblant was living on borrowed time as the campaign to improve safety in Formula 1 grew. After the 1970 race (won by Ickx in the wake of Jochen Rindt's death at Monza) the circuit was strongly criticised on safety grounds and the Canadian Grand Prix never returned. Indycar racing also had a brief flirtation with the track, holding two races in both 1967 and 1968 with Mario Andretti winning all four!

Start of the CanAm Labatt 50 Race at Mont-Tremblant in the 1960s

Montreal

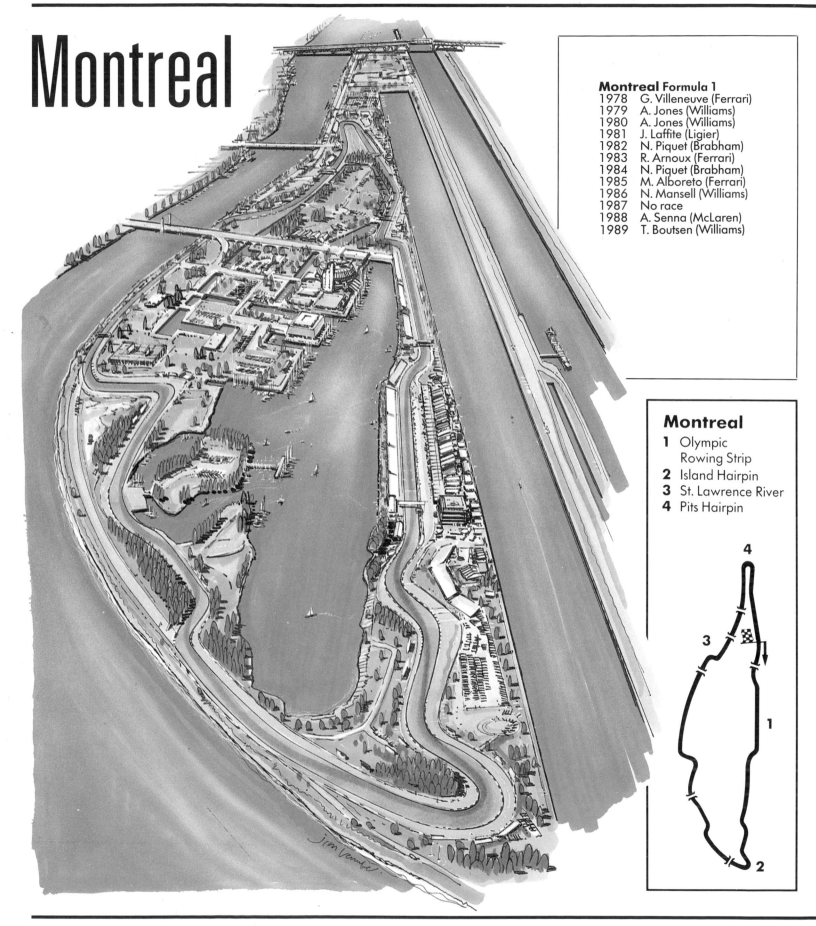

Montreal Formula 1

1978	G. Villeneuve (Ferrari)
1979	A. Jones (Williams)
1980	A. Jones (Williams)
1981	J. Laffite (Ligier)
1982	N. Piquet (Brabham)
1983	R. Arnoux (Ferrari)
1984	N. Piquet (Brabham)
1985	M. Alboreto (Ferrari)
1986	N. Mansell (Williams)
1987	No race
1988	A. Senna (McLaren)
1989	T. Boutsen (Williams)

Montreal

1 Olympic Rowing Strip
2 Island Hairpin
3 St. Lawrence River
4 Pits Hairpin

Island circuit: the outward leg from the start/finish line at Montreal culminates in a sharp right-hander, seen here during the 1981 Grand Prix.

You could hardly have asked for a better script for the first Canadian Grand Prix to be held on the Île de Nôtre-Dame circuit in Montreal. A talented young driver in his first full season in Grand Prix racing — with the Ferrari team no less — gains his first Formula 1 victory in front of his home crowd. Enter Gilles Villeneuve . . . . The French-Canadians, in search of a Formula 1 track after the demise of St Jovite and aware of the fact that Mosport could no longer cope with the F1 cars of the day, had never had a Formula 1 Grand Prix driver to cheer before then. With undue haste they prepared a track in 1978 for him to show his fellow countryman his talents.

The circuit on the Île de Nôtre Dame is one of the more bizarre racing circuits in the world. It is laid out in the parkland among the futuristic pavilions of Expo 67, around a lake on a man-made island in the middle of the St Lawrence Seaway! The track was completed, to the design of Roger Peart, in double-quick time. It sufficed, but drivers complaints led to changes before the 1979 event. This was the race which saw Niki Lauda walk off

the block, retiring from the sport after the first practice. Villeneuve drove mightily, but this time he had to give best to the Williams of Alan Jones.

A year later Jones won again, clinching the World Championship, despite finishing second on the road to the Ligier of Didier Pironi. On the same day Mike Thackwell became the youngest-ever Grand Prix driver, though he reached only the first corner before being involved in an accident. In this race Jean-Pierre Jabouille's F1 career effectively ended in a leg-breaking accident.

Being an end-of-season event meant that the weather in Canada in late September was not always pleasant, as the 1981 race proved; Jacques Laffite used effective Michelin tyres, a progressive Matra engine and no little skill to score what turned out to be his last Grand Prix victory. But Villeneuve was in the limelight once again, battling hard all day in a pig of a car to finish third, his front wings mangled after a series of incidents. Twelve months on Villeneuve was dead and, although the circuit was named after him, Montreal seemed doomed to be an unhappy race.

Moved forward in the year to June, the race came not long after Villeneuve's fatal accident at Zolder. The crowd was down, no longer having their hero to cheer. Didier Pironi sat in pole position but at the start the red car stalled and was ploughed into from behind by the Osella of Riccardo Paletti. Pironi leapt out to help the grievously injured youngster only for the car to burst into flames around him. The fire was put out and Paletti extracted from the wreck, though he would die later in hospital. This inauspicious day ended with a 1-2 finish for the BMW-powered Brabhams of Nelson Piquet and Riccardo Patrese.

The race continued until 1987 when a dispute between sponsors Labatts and the rival Molson Brewery caused the cancellation of the race. Once the dispute was sorted out and major modifications made, the track returned to the World Championship in 1988. But it must be admitted that as a race meeting Montreal has never recovered the joy of the early meetings. It has become just another race in the Formula 1 calendar. More than anything, the Circuit Gilles Villeneuve needs another Gilles Villeneuve.

Toronto

Although there had been several previous attempts, going back to the 1960s, to stage a race on the streets of Canada's financial capital, it was not until 1986 that a race in Toronto materialised. With Formula 1 on the streets of Montreal, sponsored by Labatts, there was a joint effort by rival brewery Molson, rival city Toronto and rival championship CART to organise a competing attraction. A race was to be staged on a 1.78-mile track laid out in the parkland of the Canadian National Exhibition Grounds between the Lake Ontario shoreline and the Gardiner Expressway. CART had held an annual race at Sanair but the tight tri-oval at St Pié, Quebec, was unpopular; so when the opportunity arose to race in Toronto the organisation was quick to accept.

The CART men had grown used to visiting temporary street circuits at the time but few had impressed the driv-

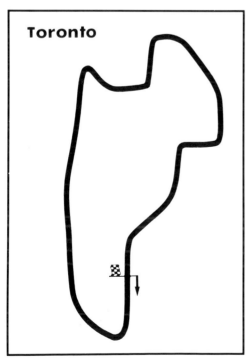

Toronto

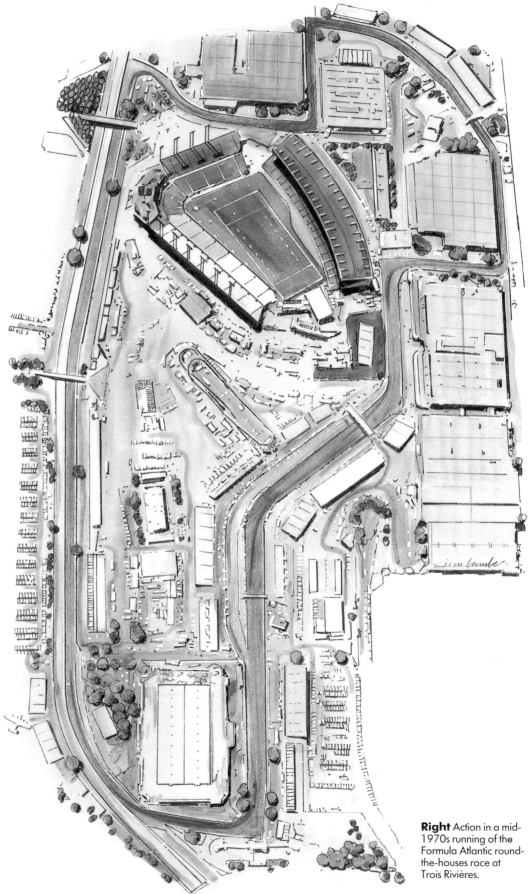

Right Action in a mid-1970s running of the Formula Atlantic round-the-houses race at Trois Rivières.

ers, who complained of driving through concrete tunnels created by the huge blocks positioned around the tracks. Toronto was different. There were no bumps and, unusually for a street track, it was fast, the 11-turn course being lapped at an average speed of around 100mph. It was immediately well received by the top Indy runners, who ranked Toronto alongside Long Beach as one of the best street races on the North American calendar.

The first event saw Emerson Fittipal-di on pole but victory to Bobby Rahal (not surprisingly, Villeneuve's rival in their Formula Atlantic days). The second year roles were reversed: Rahal was on pole and victory went to the Brazilian. Toronto is now an established round of the CART series, as Montreal is of the F1 circus. Montreal has its weird Expo pavilions, Toronto its stadiums, museums and the huge gateway, which when surrounded by concrete barriers could be mistaken for the old Brandenberg Gate in East Berlin.

Other Canadian Circuits

Of Canada's other racing circuits the most outstanding is the North American continent's oldest street race at **Trois Rivières**, midway between Quebec and Montreal on the St Lawrence River. The round-the-houses race was a regular on the Formula Atlantic and CanAm circuit and will probably be best remembered as the track where Gilles Villeneuve launched his meteoric career when he trounced James Hunt and Alan Jones in Formula Atlantic in 1976.

On the west coast near Vancouver is **Westwood**, perched on the side of a wooded mountain, a challenging, narrow, fast and bumpy track which has staged Formula Atlantic races since 1974. Then there is **Shannonville** in Ontario, owned by Ray David who in recent years has pumped large sums of money into upgrading the facility. The track has been extended with a new section named after David's young protégé Bertrand Fabi, who was killed in an F3 accident at Goodwood in 1986; this section can be linked to the old circuit or run independently.

In the eastern Montreal suburb of St Pié is the tiny tri-oval of **Sanair Superspeedway**, the shortest and tightest oval ever used by modern CART Indycars. Rick Mears was seriously hurt here when CART first visited in 1984 and it fell into disuse when CART moved to Toronto after just three annual events.

Beyond these there are **Edmonton International Speedway**, Alberta, a venue for CanAm and Formula Atlantic until the late 1970s; **Atlantic Motorsports Park** at Schubenacadie, Nova Scotia; **Gimli** in Manitoba; and **Quebec City**. The last three faded with Formula Atlantic. There is also a number of small ovals such as **Race City Speedway** and **Cayuga** — but these hold only local events.

CARIBBEAN

In recent years racing has all but died out in the Caribbean, although from the mid-1950s the Nassau Speed Week in the **Bahamas** was an event of major international importance, featuring the best sportscars and drivers from around the world. Held on New Providence island, the first Speed Week took place in 1954, the brainchild of Captain Sherman F. 'Red' Crise, who saw the idea as a means of bringing tourists to the islands. Its annual November-December date was popular, the climate and the cocktail-party atmosphere attracting many of the leading European racers to compete against the American racers of the era.

Originally held at Windsor Field, a very primitive 3.5-mile track on a disused airfield, the events moved in 1957 to Oakes Field, another aerodrome albeit a mile longer than the original venue. There were two major races disputed during the Speed Week: the Governor's Trophy and the Nassau Trophy and their rolls of honour are testament to this interesting blend of the European and American scenes: Alfonso de Portago, Masten Gregory, Carol Shelby, Phil Hill, Stirling Moss, Dan Gurney, the Rodriguez brothers, Innes Ireland, A.J. Foyt, Roger Penske and Bruce McLaren are among the winners.

In the early 1960s Formula Junior was also imported, but by 1966 the Speed Week had run into trouble of a most unusual nature. Each year, the cars were transported to the islands by an ancient landing craft, which that year the customs saw fit to impound. As a result, the Nassau Speed Week came to an untimely end. There was a lacklustre attempt in 1967 to transfer the races to Freeport on Grand Bahama island and, despite a Formula Vee race which was won by Jean-Pierre Beltoise, the event fizzled out, to be revived as an historic meeting in 1984 in Freeport.

The Cuban Grand Prix at **Havana** had a brief and somewhat bizarre history between 1957 and 1960; on one occasion Juan-Manuel Fangio was kidnapped by Fidel Castro's guerrillas. In the 1980s there were races in **Barbados**, at the Bushy Park track, and in **Guyana** on the South Dakota circuit at Atkinson Field, Timehri. After almost a decade without any racing in the Caribbean, the Sports Car Club of America organised a Formula 3000 race in 1985 on a bumpy street circuit around Willemstad in the tiny oil-rich former Dutch colony of **Curaçao**. The race was won by the Dane John Nielsen in a Ralt, but it was not repeated.

In 1988 the British car manufacturer Reynard announced that it was planning to supply cars for a Caribbean Formula 3 Championship, to be based at San Juan in **Puerto Rico**, where in 1962 there was a one-off sportscar and Formula Junior meeting. It remains to be seen whether the initiative will bring mainstream racing back.

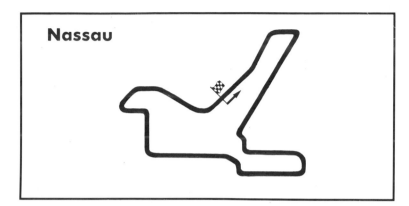

Nassau

Right Heavy traffic in the 1965 Tourist Trophy race at Nassau, Bahamas. Winner Roger Penske (Corvette Sting Ray) is at right front; Ken Miles (427 Cobra), at left front, led by 8 seconds at the end of the first lap, but later retired.

MEXICO

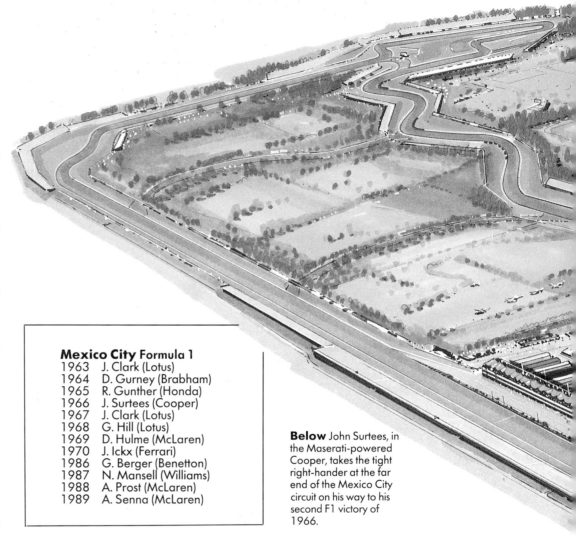

The history of Mexican racing is dotted with fervent spectators, appalling accidents and safety deficiencies. The great Carrera Panamericana road race, which began in 1950, was briefly a round of the World Sportscar Championship; its victors included such as Fangio, Piero Taruffi, Maglioli and Kling. Later, in 1962, came the Baja — 920 miles of roads from Tijuana to La Paz. With the usual spectator interventions this became an off-road race five years later.

At the same time as the Baja began, Mexico held its first Grand Prix, initially a non-championship race. In those days the two Rodriguez brothers, the wild 20-year-old Ricardo and his older brother Pedro, were making their names on the international racing scene. What should have been a joyful event for Mexican racing turned into a nightmare when Ricardo was killed during qualifying. Built in a public park near the airport, the 3.1-mile Mexico City track staged its first championship event the following year, won by Jim Clark. Mexico became the traditional end-of-season GP until 1970. In 1964 Dan Gurney won one of his few F1 victories on a gripping day when the World Championship was settled on the last lap of the final race of the year! There was a triple confrontation between Jim Clark, Graham Hill and John Surtees. Hill was involved with a collision while Clark took off into the lead. In the closing laps the Scot's Lotus developed an oil leak and on the last lap Gurney swept by. Surtees, who finished second, took the title! A year later Mexico was the venue for Honda's first Formula 1 victory as Richie Ginther scored his only Grand Prix

Mexico City Formula 1
1963	J. Clark (Lotus)
1964	D. Gurney (Brabham)
1965	R. Gunther (Honda)
1966	J. Surtees (Cooper)
1967	J. Clark (Lotus)
1968	G. Hill (Lotus)
1969	D. Hulme (McLaren)
1970	J. Ickx (Ferrari)
1986	G. Berger (Benetton)
1987	N. Mansell (Williams)
1988	A. Prost (McLaren)
1989	A. Senna (McLaren)

Below John Surtees, in the Maserati-powered Cooper, takes the tight right-hander at the far end of the Mexico City circuit on his way to his second F1 victory of 1966.

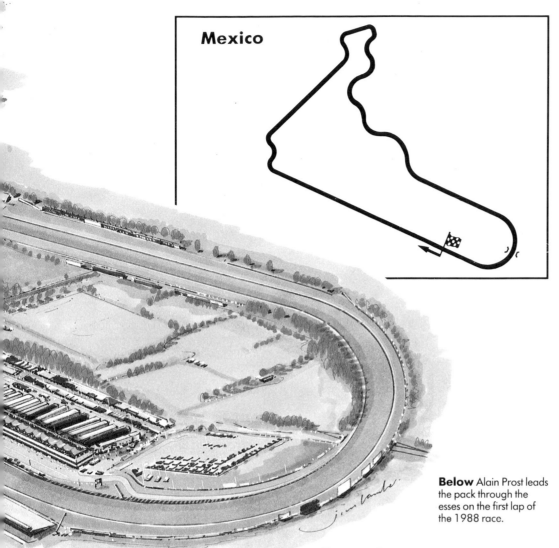

Mexico

major work was done to revise the track. A great deal of money was spent and the result was a fundamentally altered circuit. There were modern pits, high fences and ferocious guard dogs to keep the excitable crowds at bay. It was still bumpy but the slightly banked final corner taken in fifth was a real challenge.

At 6000ft above sea-level, the thin air of Mexico City suited the turbocharged machinery of 1986, but that first race was decided by tyres with the Pirelli rubber of Gerhard Berger's Benetton-BMW the right stuff to have. It was the first victory for both the team and the skilful young Austrian. The bumpy surface led to the stopping of the 1987 race after Derek Warwick had a huge accident in his Arrows car. A year later it was Philippe Alliott's turn to emerge unscathed from a monumental accident. But the enthusiasm for the sport is unstinting and at present it seems that Mexico will remain a round of the modern World Championship.

Elsewhere in the country, the local Formula K championship visits a number of speedways, almost all under a mile long: the tri-oval at Jalisco; Vera Cruz; Puebla; Coahuila; and León.

Below Alain Prost leads the pack through the esses on the first lap of the 1988 race.

triumph. 'The crowds were always beside the track,' recalls Denny Hulme. 'We used to have to use them as marker posts. It wasn't much fun.' The race survived, despite the nightmarish possibility of crowds on the track, until 1970, when the international authorities decided that enough was enough. A year later Pedro Rodriguez was dead, victim of a sportscar accident. The Mexicans renamed their track after the two brothers.

Formula 1 did not return to Mexico City for 16 years, though the American Formula Atlantic and Indycar men were brief visitors during the CART/USAC war, Rick Mears winning both Indycar events. Finally, in 1986,

SOUTH AMERICA

South Americans have an enthusiasm for motor racing similar to that of the Italian *tifosi*. It is a macho sport and, in a culture where machismo is all-important, the men who race are treated as gods. None more so than local drivers who manage to win on the international stage – and there have been plenty of them. At the start of each British Formula Ford season you will hear the same complaint: 'Another bloody South American!' They often win, you see.

British drivers have won 10 World Championships between them since 1950 while South Americans have won 11. No other country or region comes close to these totals. The greatest of all the South American champions was, without doubt, Juan-Manuel Fangio, the only five-times World Champion in the history of Formula 1 and (with 24 F1 victories in 51 starts) a man who dominated his era as few have done since. While Fangio remains the only Argentinian to have won the F1 title, Carlos Reutemann came close (within one point in 1981) only to be beaten by the Brazilian Nelson Piquet, who would later add two more titles to his tally. Emerson Fittipaldi took two championships while Ayrton Senna seems extremely unlikely to settle for one.

This, however, is only the tip of an iceberg. Young South Americans have been arriving in Europe with each passing year intent on breaking into the big time. They have to do it. The whole world remembers Fangio, but how many know of Oscar Galvez, his great rival in Argentina? Some of these international gypsies like Fittipaldi, Piquet and Senna have triumphed but many others have not had it as easy: Roberto Moreno, Chico Serra, Roberto Guerrero, Alex Ribiero, Ingo Hoffman, Maurizio Sandro Sala and a multitude of others. It is a formidable history.

The safety record of South American racing has been scarred by crowd indiscipline. The sport in Latin America has suffered badly from the macho posturing of its fans. The first Argentinian Grand Prix meeting pushed the point home to the visiting Europeans. Nino Farina had to swerve to avoid a spectator trying to get closer to the cars than anyone else, and the Italian crashed into the crowd; 9 people died and 40 were injured. There have been numerous horrendous accidents which have overshadowed the history of the sport in South America, where life is considered cheaper than it is elsewhere in the racing world.

Road racing in various forms has been taking place for many years in South America, much of it not sanctioned by any official bodies. These *turismo de carretera* road races, in which both Fangio and Reutemann competed in their early careers, are extremely dangerous as local heroes in tuned-up road-cars fly along public roads. There have been some awful accidents involving spectators in this form of racing but it remains untroubled by the authorities and popular with the locals. The modern Grand Prix tracks have to be heavily fenced off to keep the enthusiastic crowds at bay.

While the great racing heroes have travelled abroad to make their mark on the international scene, racing in South America has always been a victim of the political instabilities that characterise this region. Military men with guns are not an unusual sight at races. One famous example of this turbulence occurred when a fire extinguisher exploded inside Mario Andretti's Lotus as he powered past the pits in Buenos Aires. It was time to take cover, in case the guns being waved around returned fire! In this volatile political environment and with intermittent financial crises, racing has

been disjointed. But the tradition is strong. As each generation of drivers comes and goes, interest is sparked anew.

When the great Argentian drivers of the 1950s faded away — Fangio, José-Froilan Gonzalez and Carlos Menditeguy retiring and Onofre Marimon to his grave — it took years for the Argentian Grand Prix to be re-established with the arrival in international racing of Carlos Reutemann.

The Brazilian Grand Prix, for its part, was not staged as an F1 Grand Prix until after Fittipaldi had won the country's first World Championship title.

Road racing had been taking place for many years before these permanent tracks were built. The largest of the great road races was the International GP of the North in the late 1930s, won in 1950 by a young Fangio. This was a 5920-mile dash across the pampas from Buenos Aires to the Andes, on to Lima in Peru and then back again. It took 13 days. That tradition continued into the 1960s with the Bolivian Grand Prix, a 1200-mile road race in the Andes.

Genuine international racing in South America had begun in 1934 with the Formula Libre Río de Janeiro Grand Prix at Gávea (just outside Río), a race which in later years saw men such as Hans Stuck and Carlos Pintacuda make the trip from Europe. In 1936 a similar event was tried at São Paulo. Racing flourished after the war with Buenos Aires organising international road races in the forests of Palermo from 1947. The framework for a series was created with another event at Rosario, won by Achille Varzi. In 1948 the series was repeated with four races: two in Buenos Aires, one at Mar del Plata and another at Rosario. This was christened the Temporada series and became a regular fixture in the international racing calendar in January and February.

The Temporada series has had a chequered history after those glorious early years. Competition for races at the same time of year came from the Tasman Championship in Australia and New Zealand, and although a variety of Formula 2 and Formula 3 series did take place there was never any certainty that there would be continuity from year to year. In its various forms the racing continued until the late 1970s before finally dying out. Since then local competition has increased with the Codasur F2 series and more recently the SudAm Formula 3, which operates in line with the international F3 regulations.

Optimism is high that this will expand in the years to come to provide South America with its own international championship; allowing foreign visitors to compete means that the locals can judge their performances against international yardsticks and perhaps earn a plane-ticket to Europe. The early races at Buenos Aires, Mar del Plata, Rafaela, Costanero and Rosario all proved that point for they introduced to the European visitors a man called Fangio and they went back to Europe full of tales about this 36-year-old who would set the circuit on its head when he arrived.

Rosario, 1964: Silvio Moser (Brabham) in one of the Temporada series of international races.

Buenos Aires

Below Winner Fangio leads Mercedes team-mate Moss in the 1955 Grand Prix. Most teams allocated two or three drivers per car owing to the searing heat of Buenos Aires that day.

Dictators are obviously good for motor racing, if for nothing else. As Hitler galvanised the German motor industry before the war, so President Juan Perón pushed Argentina's sportsmen on to the international stage in the late 1940s and early 1950s by supplying international races with trophies in his name and that of his wife Eva. The Perón Cup races of 1947, which were dominated by Gigi Villoresi, laid the groundwork for what would later become the Temporada series. Villoresi was the force behind the construction of the first proper international-standard racing circuit in South America, the Autodromo 17 Octobre at Buenos Aires.

Built on swamp-land on the outskirts of Buenos Aires, today it has been engulfed by the city and racing takes place against the backdrop of modern skyscrapers. The Autodromo featured 12 possible different circuits and in its day saw racing in both directions. In true dictatorial style Perón left his modest mark with the huge white Almirante Brown arch at the entrance.

Opened in March 1952, the Autodromo staged the final Perón races the same year (won by Fangio); but after the death of Eva Perón the President's popularity began to slump, and he was forced into exile in 1955. Before then, however, the Perón Cup had been replaced by the Argentian Grand Prix, the first, in 1953, being the opening round of the World Championship that year. Fangio retired and the race was won by Alberto Ascari. His triumph, however, was overshadowed by Farina's ghastly accident.

A year later Fangio won and he repeated the victory in front of his adoring fans for the next three years.

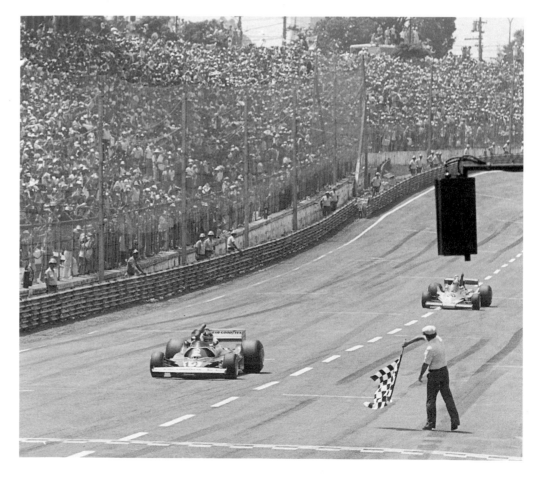

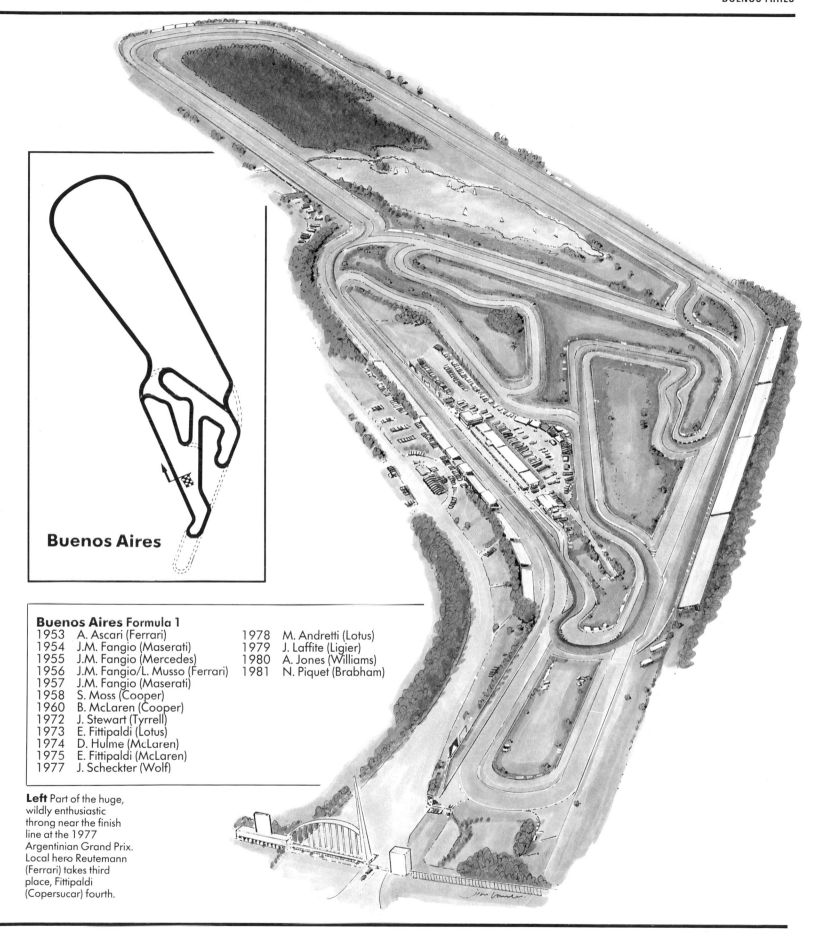

Buenos Aires

Buenos Aires Formula 1

1953	A. Ascari (Ferrari)		1978	M. Andretti (Lotus)
1954	J.M. Fangio (Maserati)		1979	J. Laffite (Ligier)
1955	J.M. Fangio (Mercedes)		1980	A. Jones (Williams)
1956	J.M. Fangio/L. Musso (Ferrari)		1981	N. Piquet (Brabham)
1957	J.M. Fangio (Maserati)			
1958	S. Moss (Cooper)			
1960	B. McLaren (Cooper)			
1972	J. Stewart (Tyrrell)			
1973	E. Fittipaldi (Lotus)			
1974	D. Hulme (McLaren)			
1975	E. Fittipaldi (McLaren)			
1977	J. Scheckter (Wolf)			

Left Part of the huge, wildly enthusiastic throng near the finish line at the 1977 Argentinian Grand Prix. Local hero Reutemann (Ferrari) takes third place, Fittipaldi (Copersucar) fourth.

It was not until 1958 that anyone else had a look in. Having recorded the fastest lap, Fangio retired from what would be his last home Grand Prix and Stirling Moss squeezed home to record the first victory for a rear-engined car, the tiny Cooper Climax, just clear of the Ferrari of Luigi Musso. There was no Argentian race in 1959 but the 1960 event marked Bruce McLaren's second *grande épreuve* win. Thereafter the Argentian Grand Prix disappeared.

A similar fate befell the Auto-dromo's major sportscar event, the Buenos Aires 1000, which had begun in 1954 and remained a round of the World Sportscar Championship for its duration; it was won by such luminaries as Farina, Moss, Menditeguy, Peter Collins and Phil Hill.

After a 10-year break international racing made a tentative return to Argentina in 1971, the Autodromo having been modernised. The Buenos Aires 1000 of 1971 was, however, an unhappy race for it witnessed the death in a controversial accident of the Italian Ferrari driver Ignazio Giunti, killed when he ran into the Matra which Jean-Pierre Beltoise, in contravention of the rules, was pushing down the track. Two weeks later a non-championship Formula 1 race took place with Chris Amon winning for Matra. In this event the state oil company YPF hired an old McLaren M7C for Carlos Reutemann and he came home third in his first F1 outing. A year later 'el Lole' had been signed by Brabham, and at the Autodromo he took pole on his Grand Prix debut.

Patrick Depailler (Ligier) passes a familiar landmark on the Buenos Aires circuit during the 1979 Grand Prix.

The Argentian GP would never be won by Reutemann, who ironically won three times in Brazil. But among landmarks in this race were Denny Hulme's last F1 victory in 1974, the sensational debut triumph for the Wolf team in 1977, and the surprisingly dominant Ligier victory of 1979. In 1980 the track broke up badly and in 1981 Brazilian Nelson Piquet won what was the last Argentian GP.

Interlagos

The Brazilian city of São Paulo held a race as early as 1936 when Carlo Pintacuda and Attilio Marinoni shipped their Alfas out from Europe. After the war the exercise was repeated and in 1952 racing found a new home at Interlagos, a hilly natural amphitheatre, close to São Paulo's ever-expanding urban sprawl. Like everything in South America's largest city, Interlagos had to fit a good deal into the smallest possible space, which was done proficiently when the track was built in 1940. Winding around itself and twice crossing a lake, this anticlockwise track was just under five miles long with all manner of flat and banked corners, fast straights and fast corners and hairpins.

By the time Formula 1 finally arrived for the first of two annual non-championship races in 1971, São Paulo was bursting with people, the fastest expanding city in the world with vast, glittering skyscrapers at the centre and dismal (favelas) shanty towns around the edges. It is a city where a gas mask and ear plugs might come in handy, unless of course you have a nice air-conditioned limousine or a helicopter.

Into this bizarre sprawl of humanity came the world's greatest capitalist circus, averting its eyes from the poverty and feeling distinctly uncomfortable in designer clothes. The 1972 race, another non-championship event, was won by Reutemann but a year later Emerson Fittipaldi, coming home from Europe a World Champion and having won in Argentina, proceeded to show the same dominance for his own people. There were tears in the eyes as the fans streamed home — and for once it wasn't the pollution that caused them.

Fittipaldi pulled off the same feat a year later, setting himself up for a second World Championship title by the end of the year. But when he returned to Interlagos in 1975 he had

181

to make way for another local, Carlos Pace, who wrote his name indelibly into the Brazilian history books with his debut F1 victory. To round off a perfect day Fittipaldi was second and Brazil's first home-made Grand Prix car – the Fittipaldi – driven by Emerson's brother Wilson, made its first home appearance. Sadly Pace never won another Grand Prix, for he died in a plane crash in March 1977. By then Reutemann had scored another Brazilian victory, repeating the Ferrari triumph of the previous year when Lauda had been at the wheel.

In 1978 Formula 1 tried Jacarepaguá (down the road from Río) for the first time and Reutemann, unable to win at home in Argentina, did it again; the race then reverted once more to Interlagos. But times had changed: the ground-effect revolution had arrived and the bumps of the São Paulo track were magnified by the cars. That day France scored a memorable victory, with the Ligiers of Jacques Laffite and Patrick Depailler riding the bumps better than the rest. There would be another French success in 1980 as the Renault team tweaked the turbos and outblasted everybody, Jean-Pierre Jabouille taking pole and René Arnoux winning the race, his first Grand Prix victory.

By now, however, the slums of São Paulo were becoming too much for the refined sensibilities of Formula 1's beautiful people. So in 1981 they took themselves off to Jacarepaguá again. After all, that was enticingly close to Copacabana and Ipanema and a long way from the smog and bumps of Interlagos.

Interlagos Formula 1
1973	E. Fittipaldi (Lotus)
1974	E. Fittipaldi (McLaren)
1975	C. Pace (Brabham)
1986	N. Lauda (Ferrari)
1977	C. Reutemann (Ferrari)
1979	J. Laffite (Ligier)
1980	R. Arnoux (Renault)

Interlagos

Regazzoni (Ensign) leads a quintet through fast curves at Interlagos in 1980's Grand Prix. Of this group only Patrese (Arrows), immediately behind Regazzoni here, scored a championship point that day.

Jacarepaguá

Away from Guanabara Bay and the lush green mountains rising abruptly around it; away from Sugar Loaf mountain and the huge white statue of Christ at Corcovado; in short, away from everything beautiful in Río de Janeiro, is Jacarepaguá. Now called the Autodromo Nelson Piquet, the track was built on reclaimed marsh land beyond the city's south-west outskirts. It isn't a particularly inspiring place, flat as a pancake and just a mile from the Atlantic shore, though overlooked by the hills. The city has a throbbing energy, released annually at Carnival time and, by the racing fans, when the Formula 1 Grand Prix comes visiting. Aside from that it is as overcrowded, noisy, polluted and crime-ridden as São Paulo. The track is of the modern uniform style, cursed with constant radius corners and dominated by the long back straight. On race day the huge grandstands are packed with screaming Brazilians. When it gets hot, they cool the crowd down with fire hoses and no one seems to mind much as it does not douse the delirium of the fans.

It was to Jacarepaguá that the Grand Prix circus made its first visit in 1978 when Reutemann disappointed the Brazilians by winning their Grand

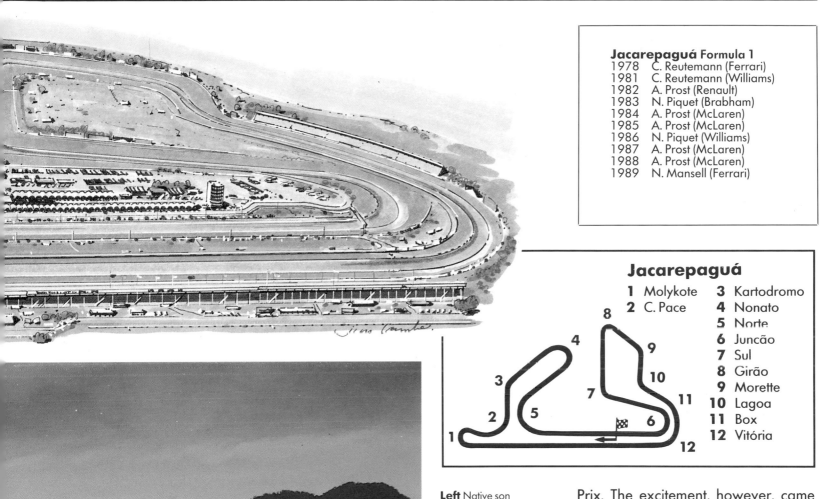

Jacarepaguá

1	Molykote	**3**	Kartodromo
2	C. Pace	**4**	Nonato
		5	Norte
		6	Juncão
		7	Sul
		8	Girão
		9	Morette
		10	Lagoa
		11	Box
		12	Vitória

Left Native son Piquet (Williams) on Jacarepaguá's Norte curve, the bend that leads onto the long back straight, in the 1987 Grand Prix, when he took second place.

Prix. The excitement, however, came from Emerson Fittipaldi who steered home his own car, the Fittipaldi F5A, to be second to the Argentian. The race did not return for three years but since then it has stayed. Fittipaldi had retired from F1, leaving his cars to be driven by Keke Rosberg and Chico Serra. Nelson Piquet, however, was there and he did not disappoint, putting his Brabham on pole ahead of the dreaded Reutemann. Serra could only make 22nd on the grid. And then it rained. Piquet selected dry tyres and ended the first lap in 15th place. Serra did not get that far for he was eliminated at the start. And who was leading? Why, Reutemann of course, and he did so for the entire afternoon, ignoring pit signals to yield to his team-mate, World Champion Alan Jones, who followed him home. The Brazilians went home grumpy — and wet.

Things could hardly have been

more different a year later for it was a scorching day, hot and humid. Riccardo Patrese, Piquet's Brabham teammate, blacked out from exhaustion and spun wildly out of the race. Gilles Villeneuve in the ungainly turbocharged Ferrari blasted away at the start but as the race drew on it was clear that Piquet and Rosberg (now with Williams) were a match for Gilles in their normally-aspirated cars. For much of the afternoon the two duelled, at last overhauling the Ferrari and fighting it out for the victory. By the end Piquet had won, to the delight of the crowd and such was the World Champion's exhaustion that he could not stand up, 'I was the World Champion in front of my home crowd,' he

remembers, 'and I was destroyed, but it was really fantastic.'

Months later he would be deprived of the win by FISA, but it didn't matter to the crowd; he had won at home. And to make sure, he did it again in 1983. For the next five seasons he and Alain Prost would share the Brazilian Grand Prix, the Frenchman winning in 1984, 1985, 1987 and 1988, and Piquet once more in 1986, a day when another new star in the Brazilian firmament, Ayrton Senna, followed his compatriot home. When Piquet won his third title in 1987 the locals celebrated by naming the track after him. Senna won the World Championship in 1988 — what will they rename after him?

Hot-air balloons and screaming Brazilian fans at least help enliven the flat and featureless environs of Jacarepaguá.

Other South American Circuits

There is another Autodromo Nelson Piquet in **Brasilia**, one of the many smaller tracks dotted across South America. As with the international tracks, most of these are concentrated in Brazil and Argentina, although there have been races of some form or other in most Latin American countries. Peru has a daunting road circuit at **Santa Rosa** to the north of Lima. This is the home of the annual Seis Horas Peruanas. On the Pacific coast, the track came about literally by accident. Plans for a major holiday resort were cancelled when it was discovered that the local ocean currents were too dangerous. The builders conveniently left a road behind them.

Bogotá in Colombia has a track some 8000ft above sea level, that is used today by the SudAm Formula 3 racers, although way back in 1971 the city staged a pair of international F2 races won by Jo Siffert and Alan Rollinson. **Guyana** used to boast the 1.98-mile South Dakota circuit at Timehri airport, not far from Georgetown. Meanwhile a street track in **Caracas** hosted the Venezuelan Grand Prix for sportscars in 1955-7: Fangio, Moss, Collins and Phill Hill were all winners.

Sandwiched as it is between Brazil and Argentina, Uruguay has long been included in racing activities in the region, the powerbase of the modern SudAm Formula 3 series. Fangio dominated the first two races in Uruguay, held on a street track in **Montevideo** in 1952. Since then a street track in the seaside resort of **Punta del Este** has been a regular fixture in SudAm racing, while nearby **El Pinar** has also figured in this form of motorsport in recent years. Chile lags behind the other South American

Jaime Uribe's MG TD belches smoke after throwing a con rod in a street race in Bogotá, Colombia, in 1954.

states but the **Las Viscachias** track has been used recently for SudAm events and indications are that the Chileans would like greater involvement. Ecuador and Bolivia too have both been looking at becoming part of this growing championship. If progress continues as it has in the 1980s the SudAm series may yet attract some of the prestige attached to South American racing in the Temporada days. Some of the tracks from that era are still in existence such as **Taruma**, near Pôrto Allegre in Brazil, a sweeping anticlockwise 1.87-mile circuit built in 1971. It has been joined over the years by **Goiania, Cascavel** and **Guapore**.

While many of the early Argentian circuits were road circuits at places such as **Costanera, Mar del Plata, Mendoza** and **Rosario**, semi-permanent tracks began to arrive in the 1960s and 1970s: the

Oscar Calaban Aerodrome at **Córdoba** staged a Grand Prix of 1960 won by Maurice Trintignant in a Cooper. Today that is gone and Córdoba has a street circuit. Mendoza has a permanent track, built in the late 1970s. Argentina boasts events at **Salta** and at **El Zonda** in San Juan, the latter used for Temporada racing. There is also a race in the northern Argentian resort of **Puerto Iguazu**.

Soaring inflation and political instability permitting, South American racing in the years to come could change from the rather chaotic state in which it finds itself today. There are surely enough drivers with the raw talent to go round.

AFRICA

Since the decolonisation of the European empires in Africa, racing on that continent has been very restricted, although major international rallies, adventurous challenges through bush and desert (such as Paris–Dakar and the Safari Rally), are regular features of the African motorsport year in the modern era. Only in South Africa has racing truly survived.

Back in the 1920s and 1930s, Italian and French influences in North Africa resulted in a string of races which in their day attracted the best in the world. For the most part these were not repeated after the war, although the French colonies continued to hold races until the end of direct French control. The earliest North African races date back to 1925 and the Tripoli GP at the **Mellaha** course in Libya. Until 1933 the event took place on a rather slow track but changes in 1933 to make it considerably faster led to increased international interest. In the immediate

pre-war era Mellaha had become one of the fastest tracks in the world, its two straights joined by oval turns at each end. In the early days the Mellaha races had been won by Alfieri Maserati, Baconin Borzacchini and Claudio Biondetti, but the likes of Achille Varzi, Rudolf Caracciola and Herman Lang were to win on the new track in the 1930s. The race survived until 1940 when Nino Farina won the last race at Tripoli. It was not revived after the war.

The Moroccan GP for touring cars had begun in 1925 at **Casablanca** and continued until 1930, when racing switched to a new course at **Anfa**. Post-war **Ain-Diab** saw the Formula 1 machines of the era in action, with Jean Behra, Stirling Moss and Jack Brabham all winners. Until the end of the 1950s there were also regular sportscar events at **Agadir** and **Tangier**.

Algeria and Tunisia also had regular international events, beginning in the late 1920s. The Algerian GP was a regular feature at **Algiers**, while other races took place at **Bona** and

Right Luanda, capital of Angola, held regular round-the-houses races until the anticolonial civil war broke out in 1974. Here three Porsche 904s – one of which is careering backwards in a cloud of smoke – are involved in an event for GT cars.

Left Rudolf Caracciola (Mercedes W165) speeds past the grandstand in the Tripoli Grand Prix of 1939.

at the Arcole circuit near **Oran**. The first Tunisian GP took place at **Bardo** in 1928, although the action was to move to **Carthage** – used throughout the 1930s – and then briefly, in the post-war era at Belvedere. The tiny French colony of Sénégal also had a regular track in the 1950s, a section of extremely fast dual carriageway at **Dakar**, with triangular loops at the end of each straight.

During the 1960s the Portuguese colonies of Mozambique and Angola were linked in with South Africa to form the Springbok Series. These were sportscar tracks where wintering continentals found the sun and went racing. **Lourenço Marques**, the

Kyalami

If the rest of Africa had few permanent facilities, South Africa made up for it. The first racing in the country took place in 1934 on the Prince George road circuit at East London. The 15-mile track ran around the outskirts of the holiday port and the first South African GP was won here by Whitney Straight in a Maserati. The track was used between 1936–9, albeit in an 11-mile shortened form.

At the same time, the first meeting to hold the title Rand GP took the form of a handicap in Johannesburg in 1937 and that same year a 4.5-mile road circuit at Pollsmoor near Cape Town, was used to stage the Grosvenor House Grand Prix, named after the Grosvenor House company that financed the idea. This was won initially by Ernst von Delius in an AutoUnion and in 1938 by Earl Howe in an ERA; after one more event it faded away with the onset of war.

After the war it took a long time for racing to recover in South Africa. Three racing ciruits were active in the late 1950s at Gunner's Circle in Cape Town, Grand Central in Johannesburg and the Roy Hesketh circuit at Pietermaritzburg. At the end of that decade, however, came a new generation of tracks, while the Hesketh track soldiered on, despite being too narrow and too bumpy. A new facility at East London was opened in 1959, set in a natural amphitheatre in a parkland recreation area beside the ocean. The 2.43-mile track was based on sections of the pre-war circuit and had the full support of the local authorities.

The first post-war South African GP was held in 1960 and was for Formula Libre, but two years later the race became a round of the Formula 1 World Championship and until 1965 East London was the home of

capital of Mozambique, had a twisting 2.1-mile street circuit wandering through parkland close to the centre of the city. Its long straight ran along the tropical coastline, passing through the dunes where drivers had to watch out for crosswinds.

Luanda in Angola was another street track around the houses and along the waterfront. Hotel entrances were sandbagged and manhole covers were welded down. Practice started at 3am to miss some of the daytime heat and to avoid disrupting the town until race day. Come the race, of course, everything overheated but somehow a winner was always found. Later, as Angola fell

into civil war, motor racing became more difficult and the race faded away, the sandbags used for other purposes.

Political trouble has disrupted much racing in Africa, not least in Rhodesia (as it then was) which had staged regular Rhodesian GP meetings at **Kumalo** airfield track in the early 1960s. In 1969 a purpose-built track was opened at **Bulawayo**. This was 2.52 miles in length set in a natural depression on the edge of the city amid sandy hills and low scrub trees. There was plenty of run-off here. For a few years the Bulawayo Three Hours became a round of the Springbok series.

the race (a further event in 1966 not being a championship round). In 1967 East London lost the race to Kyalami, near Johannesburg, the replacement for the obsolete Grand Central. A consortium of local enthusiasts had got together in the late 1950s and had considered a number of potential sites. Finally, they chose a hillside 15 miles to the north of Johannesburg on an open plateau 5000ft above sea level at Kyalami.

The new circuit was opened in December 1961, its predominant features being the long main straight downhill into the first corner. Its initial major event was the re-established Rand GP, won by Jim Clark. The following year the Rand Nine Hours sportscar race — the major event of the Springbok series — also switched to the new track. But the South African GP itself stayed at East London. Kyalami was upgraded year by year, continuing to stage the Rand GP. Towards the end of 1966, when it was suggested that the track should host the South African Grand Prix itself, major

improvements were made including widening and resurfacing and on 2 January 1967 the South African GP came to Kyalami. Pedro Rodriguez triumphed in a Cooper-Maserati. Thereafter until 1972 the South African GP became the opening round of the Formula 1 World Championship.

Kyalami's permanent facilities were excellent and increasingly it was used as a winter testing track by the F1 teams. Although it was famous for having fast and slow days, Kyalami was a favourite with the teams. The track has seen some great races. Carlos Reutemann scored his first F1 victory in 1974; two years later Niki Lauda and James Hunt crossed the line just 1.3 seconds apart, so setting

Left The Renaults of Jabouille and winner Arnoux lead the field to the first corner at the start of the 1980 Grand Prix at Kyalami.

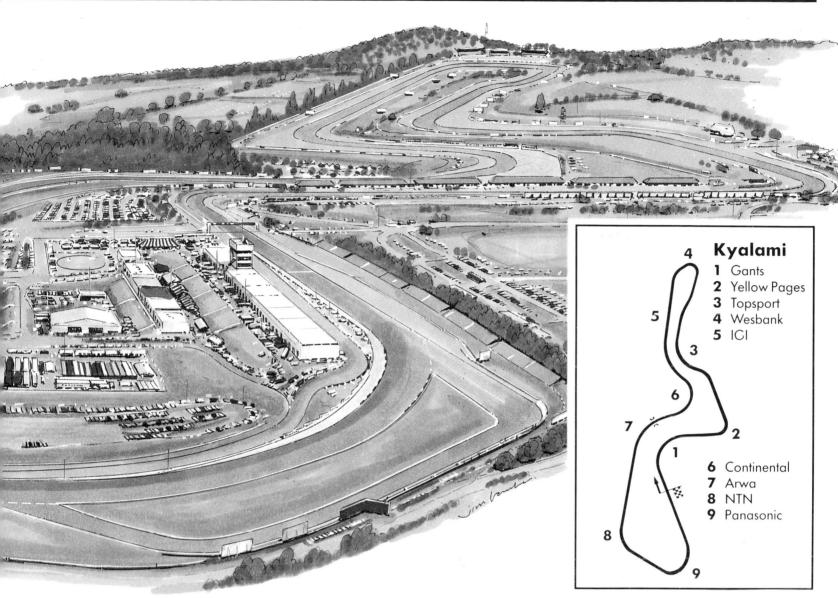

Kyalami
1 Gants
2 Yellow Pages
3 Topsport
4 Wesbank
5 ICI
6 Continental
7 Arwa
8 NTN
9 Panasonic

the trend for the season. It was at Kyalami that Riccardo Patrese put the new Arrows into a clear lead in the 1978 race, only to see his hopes dashed when the car blew up only a short distance from home.

There were also the inevitable tragedies: Peter Revson was killed in pre-race testing in 1974 and three years later Tom Pryce, very much a rising star at the time, died when he hit a marshal who was running across the track. With the arrival of the turbocharger, Kyalami's altitude made it a turbo circuit, with René Arnoux scoring his first win (and only the third for Renault) in 1980. The political situation in South Africa, however, was

deteriorating, making it more difficult to find money to stage the race and, ultimately, resulting in 1985 in several teams pulling out of what was the final South African GP because of political pressures at home.

Despite this, the South Africans, aware that changes were by then needed and that the urban expansion of Johannesburg threatened the area, decided to redevelop the track. In 1987 a new circuit was laid out lower down the hillside incorporating sections of the return leg of the old track but removing the famous straight once and for all.

Also active in South Africa today is the **Killarney** track, built to replace

Gunner's Circle in Cape Town in 1960. Situated in the sandy region, inland and cooled by breezes from the sea, the track has never really cracked the big time and is today used only for national level events. Up in the Johannesburg area is **Goldfields Raceway** at Welkom, a flat and featureless track prone to high winds and dust storms, while other smaller facilities can be found at **Aldo Scribante** near Port Elizabeth and **Zwartkops**. Other races have come and gone at Durban and Westmead but in the political climate of today, there seems no secure future for racing in South Africa.

Australasia
AUSTRALIA

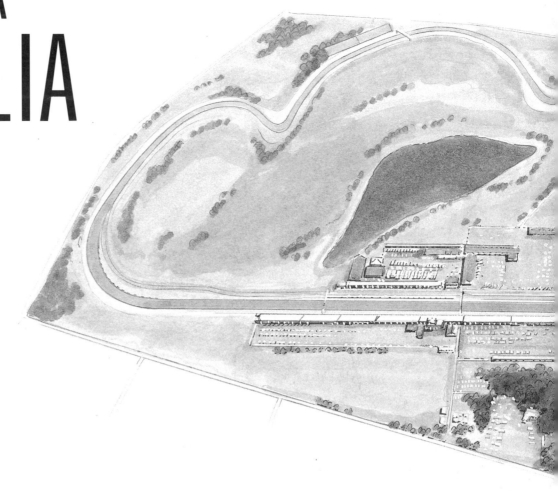

There has been considerable debate among Australians as to where the first race in their vast country took place. There were trials between Melbourne and Aspendale racecourse, a motorised tricycle race at Sydney cricket ground, and sundry other racecourses, including Melbourne's Sandown.

With no permanent facilities the Australians raced wherever they could on beaches and dry lakes and, of course, on the roads. The sheer size of Australia has made it hard for national championships to survive and the competition between the population centres of Sydney, Melbourne, Adelaide, Perth and Brisbane has meant that established races seldom had an established home. The Australian Grand Prix has taken place at the astonishing total of 23 venues in its 60-year history.

In the 1920s, with the international trend towards huge banked speedways, Australia was not left behind with the fearsome Melbourne Motordrome and Sydney's Olympia Speedway at Maroubra, out close to the sea to the south of Bondi. In remote Western Australia there was even an attempt to stage races at a track called Brooklands but this shut down after just a couple of events. The speedways were as dangerous as they were exciting and both the Motordrome and Maroubra claimed many lives. Financially, however, the great speedways proved difficult to sustain and both Maroubra and the Melbourne Motordrome fell from regular use. Both have long since vanished. By then, however, Australian racing had some tremendous venues, the first of which was opened in 1928 at Phillip Island.

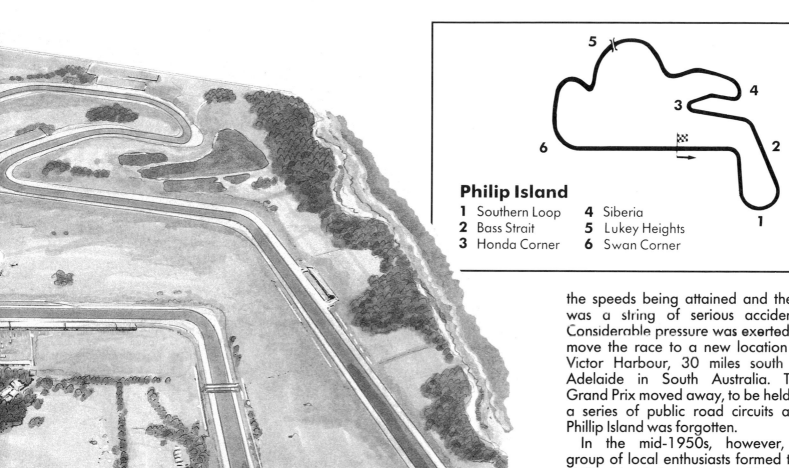

Philip Island

1 Southern Loop
2 Bass Strait
3 Honda Corner
4 Siberia
5 Lukey Heights
6 Swan Corner

The spiritual home of Australian motor racing is Phillip Island, off the Mornington Peninsula to the south of Melbourne in Victoria. The island, famous for its penguins, staged the first Australian Grand Prix in March

Left Phillip Island circuit, recently re-opened after closing down in 1980, has ambitions to regain its prominent role in Australian racing. Here Formula 5000 cars compete in a late-1970s event.

1928. Originally the idea of the Light Car Club, the race took place on a 6.5-mile dirt and gravel track on public roads at Cowes. There were 10,000 spectators for that first event and in the following years the popularity of The Island grew despite the fact that it could be reached only by ferry and, until the construction of a bridge, cars had to be transported to the track by boat!

The original track was altered over the years but by 1935 the rough and ready road circuit could not cope with

the speeds being attained and there was a string of serious accidents. Considerable pressure was exerted to move the race to a new location at Victor Harbour, 30 miles south of Adelaide in South Australia. The Grand Prix moved away, to be held at a series of public road circuits and Phillip Island was forgotten.

In the mid-1950s, however, a group of local enthusiasts formed the Phillip Island Auto Racing Club and found a site in a natural bowl over-looking Port Phillip Bay, where a new permanent circuit could be built. This was to be the home of the first Armstrong 500, an endurance event for touring cars that was to be the forerunner of Australia's biggest modern racing event, the Bathurst 1000 — 'The Great Race'. The 1962 Armstrong proved to be too much for Phillip Island to cope with and the track was destroyed as the cars tore up the tarmac. The following year the Armstrong 500 moved to Bathurst.

Phillip Island battled on under the ownership of former racer Len Lukey, but under considerable financial pressure it closed down in the early 1980s. It has since been bought, properly drained and resurfaced and now waits to regain its place as one of Australia's greatest tracks in the future. 'If they've resurfaced it properly,' says racer Allan Grice, 'it will be the greatest track in the world.'

Bathurst

There had been motorcycle races in the early 1930s at Bathurst, a small hill town in the Blue Mountains of New South Wales. These events had been held on closed public roads on a track known as the Vale circuit. The decision to build a scenic road for tourists across Mount Panorama in 1936 changed all that. In the course of the construction local engineer Hugh Reid quietly ensured that the corners were wider than had been planned and a couple of escape roads were added. A man of vision indeed. After leaving Phillip Island the Australian Grand Prix moved to Victor Harbour and then, in 1938, came to Bathurst for the first time. Held on the new dirt road, the race was won by a young English wool-buyer in an ERA, Peter Whitehead. The track was surfaced later that year and as no

Dust flies as the rear of the grid gets away in a 1951 race at Bathurst — all except the legendary, but unwell, Alfa Romeo Tipo B in the foreground.

comparable facilities existed elsewhere, the Grand Prix returned after the war in 1947 and then again in 1952 and 1958.

In addition to the Grands Prix, Bathurst hosted two traditional meetings. 'We lived for those two meetings each year — Easter and October,' remembers David McKay, the first Australian Touring Car Champion. 'Safety was confined to a few rotten old wooden fences at odd spots around the top of the mountain; but it was traditional, it was history.' With no facilities to speak of, at each meeting

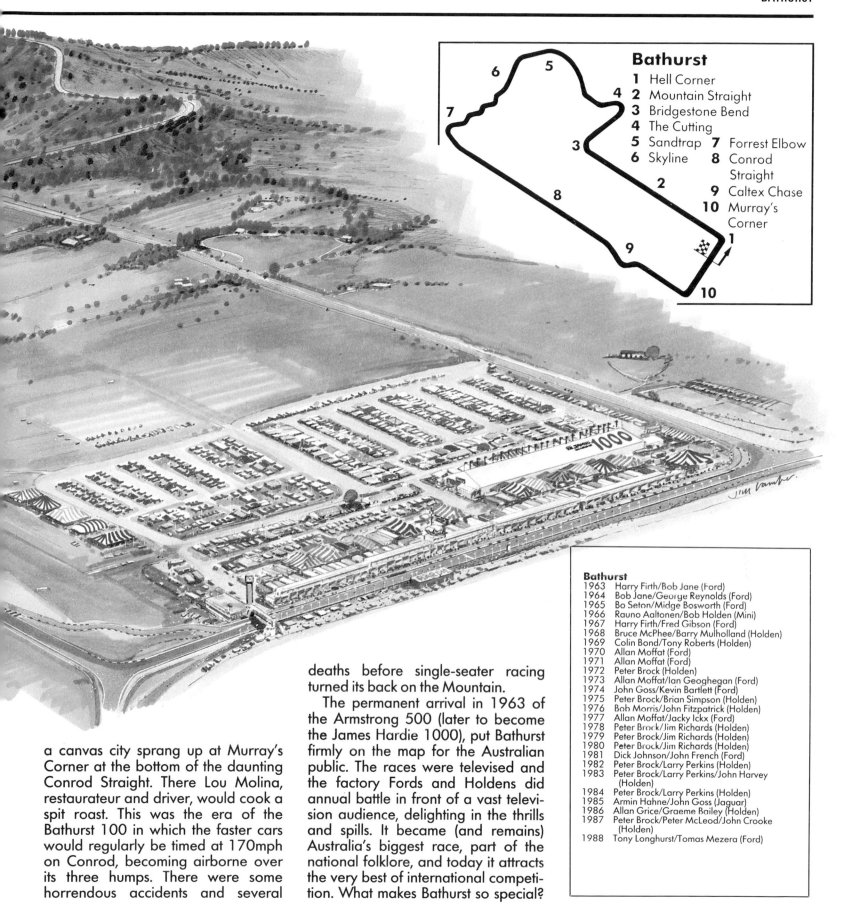

Bathurst

1 Hell Corner
2 Mountain Straight
3 Bridgestone Bend
4 The Cutting
5 Sandtrap
6 Skyline

7 Forrest Elbow
8 Conrod Straight
9 Caltex Chase
10 Murray's Corner

Bathurst

1963	Harry Firth/Bob Jane (Ford)
1964	Bob Jane/George Reynolds (Ford)
1965	Bo Seton/Midge Bosworth (Ford)
1966	Rauno Aaltonen/Bob Holden (Mini)
1967	Harry Firth/Fred Gibson (Ford)
1968	Bruce McPhee/Barry Mulholland (Holden)
1969	Colin Bond/Tony Roberts (Holden)
1970	Allan Moffat (Ford)
1971	Allan Moffat (Ford)
1972	Peter Brock (Holden)
1973	Allan Moffat/Ian Geoghegan (Ford)
1974	John Goss/Kevin Bartlett (Ford)
1975	Peter Brock/Brian Simpson (Holden)
1976	Bob Morris/John Fitzpatrick (Holden)
1977	Allan Moffat/Jacky Ickx (Ford)
1978	Peter Brock/Jim Richards (Holden)
1979	Peter Brock/Jim Richards (Holden)
1980	Peter Brock/Jim Richards (Holden)
1981	Dick Johnson/John French (Ford)
1982	Peter Brock/Larry Perkins (Holden)
1983	Peter Brock/Larry Perkins/John Harvey (Holden)
1984	Peter Brock/Larry Perkins (Holden)
1985	Armin Hahne/John Goss (Jaguar)
1986	Allan Grice/Graeme Bailey (Holden)
1987	Peter Brock/Peter McLeod/John Crooke (Holden)
1988	Tony Longhurst/Tomas Mezera (Ford)

a canvas city sprang up at Murray's Corner at the bottom of the daunting Conrod Straight. There Lou Molina, restaurateur and driver, would cook a spit roast. This was the era of the Bathurst 100 in which the faster cars would regularly be timed at 170mph on Conrod, becoming airborne over its three humps. There were some horrendous accidents and several deaths before single-seater racing turned its back on the Mountain.

The permanent arrival in 1963 of the Armstrong 500 (later to become the James Hardie 1000), put Bathurst firmly on the map for the Australian public. The races were televised and the factory Fords and Holdens did annual battle in front of a vast television audience, delighting in the thrills and spills. It became (and remains) Australia's biggest race, part of the national folklore, and today it attracts the very best of international competition. What makes Bathurst so special?

Perhaps it is the unforgottable sight of big touring cars skittering through the madness of Mcphillamy and across Skyline to the esses and the Dipper. Down at Forrest's Elbow you can still see the ruined trees through which Dick Johnson flew his Ford Falcon in 1983 – never was a man so lucky to step from the wreckage of his car.

This is a place where you don't have a small accident. Back in 1969 60 cars went up the Mountain on the first lap – just 15 came back. A year later Tony Roberts went over the edge at Mcphillamy, barrelrolling down the

Right Bathurst: the top of the circuit at Skyline, with the dangerous Esses ahead.

Left Four of the big touring cars that make up the field of the hair-raising James Hardie 1000 plunge down through the Esses.

'The reason why Bathurst is so difficult and fraught perhaps with a little danger,' Brock explains, 'is that it was built in the Depression by men with picks and shovels. They just drove the road across the top of the Mountain, they didn't worry about cambers and apexes. 'It's a real buzz if you can get the run across the top absolutely right. There are very few pieces of road on this planet where you can gain or lose so much time in such a short piece of road.'

The Great Race lost its rough and tumble innocence in 1986 when Mike Burgmann was killed on Conrod Straight. A year later the old Conrod was gone, replaced by a series of corners called Caltex Chase. The track was brought up to international standard – indeed it was the venue for a major round of the FIA World Touring Car Championship – but it would never be quite the same again.

mountainside until his car hit a tree. Twelve months later Bill Brown rolled his Falcon down the barriers at Mcphillamy, ripping it in two. The amazing thing was that neither Roberts nor Brown was hurt. The race was halted early in 1981 after a pile-up beyond a blind brow. Again, Mcphillamy was the culprit.

There have been some incredible races, as in 1975 when John Fitzpatrick freewheeled from the top of the hill to the finish line. Each year several books are written on that season's 'Great Race' and usually there is plenty to write about. Looming large in these stories is a man called Peter Brock, without a doubt the King of the Mountain, with nine James Hardie 1000 victories to his name.

Sandown

Australia's second classic touring-car event, the Castrol 500, takes place as a warm-up for Bathurst at Sandown, an equine racecourse out in the sprawling suburbs of Melbourne. One of the earliest motor races in Australia took place here but thereafter it reverted to horses until March 1962, when a perimeter tarmac track was opened for racing cars. It was fast and sweeping and popular with the drivers. Jack Brabham won the first Australian Grand Prix to be held at Sandown in 1964. This was the first Tasman Cup race in Australia and the track played an important part in that era with victories falling to such celebrated names as Jackie Stewart, Jim Clark and Chris Amon. After the Tasman series finished finally in the late 1970s, Sandown continued to stage major touring car meetings. But, in an effort to stage a World Sportscar event in 1984, major alterations were made that changed the character of the track with a new infield section to bring it up to the necessary international length. This was tight and twisty and drew little favourable comment. Worse still, the sportscar race was a disaster.

Beneath its towering 8000-seat grandstand, Sandown is still dominated by the pleasant setting of the racecourse, with its white rails, its lake inside the horse track and its green enclosures. The pits and paddock are scarcely noticeable from the grandstand. The 1984 changes did away

Left Sandown mounted a less than successful World Sportscar Championship event in 1984; in this picture Rothmans Porsches lead the field.

Above Sandown: a Tasman Cup race in the late 1960s, with Jim Clark (Lotus) leading Chris Amon (Ferrari); Graham Hill (Lotus) is in third place.

with two challenging corners, the fast lefthander out towards the Princes Highway and the crazy lefthander at the Dam where, in the old days, an accident might have landed you in the reservoir that is situated alongside the track behind a wooden fence. Some even tried to drive though it.

A second international event took place in the autumn of 1988, in which a dominant victory was scored by the two Sauber-Mercedes factory cars. However, with Phillip Island looming large in the years to come, Sandown's future is somewhat clouded.

Calder

Across Melbourne from Sandown is Calder (also known as Keilor), a track that fails to fit into the Australian mould. Originally it was short, little more than an oval of tarmac. It was opened in January 1962 but only after it was bought and developed by former racer Bob Jane in December 1974 did things begin to happen. The result was the first modern Australian Grand Prix to allow Formula 1 cars to be raced! In 1980, with Australia having a new World Champion in the burly shape of Alan Jones, Jane announced the AGP for Formula 1 cars. Only two arrived: a Williams FW07 for Jones and an out-of-date Alfa Romeo for the Italian driver Bruno Giacomelli. The field was bolstered by local F2 cars.

The result of the curious affair was unsurprising with Jones winning, following in his father Stan's footsteps as an Australian GP winner. Jane thought better of F1 in 1981 and opted for Formula Pacific cars and in the next four years attracted regular F1 runners to compete in his event, among them Nelson Piquet, Jones, Jacques Lafitte, Alain Prost, Keke Rosberg, Andrea de Cesaris and Francois Hesnault. In 1981 Piquet's protégé, a youngster called Roberto Moreno, won and he was to do the same twice more in the next three years, beating all the stars, although he failed to contain Prost in 1982.

With Adelaide taking the Australian Grand Prix in 1985, the ever ambitious Jane did something even more radical. He built an American-style banked speedway, the Thunderdome; his plan was to bring oval racing back to Australia. It cost multi-million dollar sums but at the start of 1988 Jane hosted a NASCAR race, complete with visiting American stars. It remains to be seen if the resourceful Mr Jane can succeed in his dream to establish NASCAR in the Antipodes.

Right Bob Jane's Thunderdome, a banked oval next door to the older circuit, is intended for AUSCAR (local equivalent of NASCAR) events. This pile-up at the inaugural meeting in 1988 featured visiting American stars as well as locals.

Above right Calder having burnt its fingers trying to host an F1 Australian GP in 1980, later attracted many top F1 stars to its Formula Pacific races. Here Alain Prost leads the 1982 event.

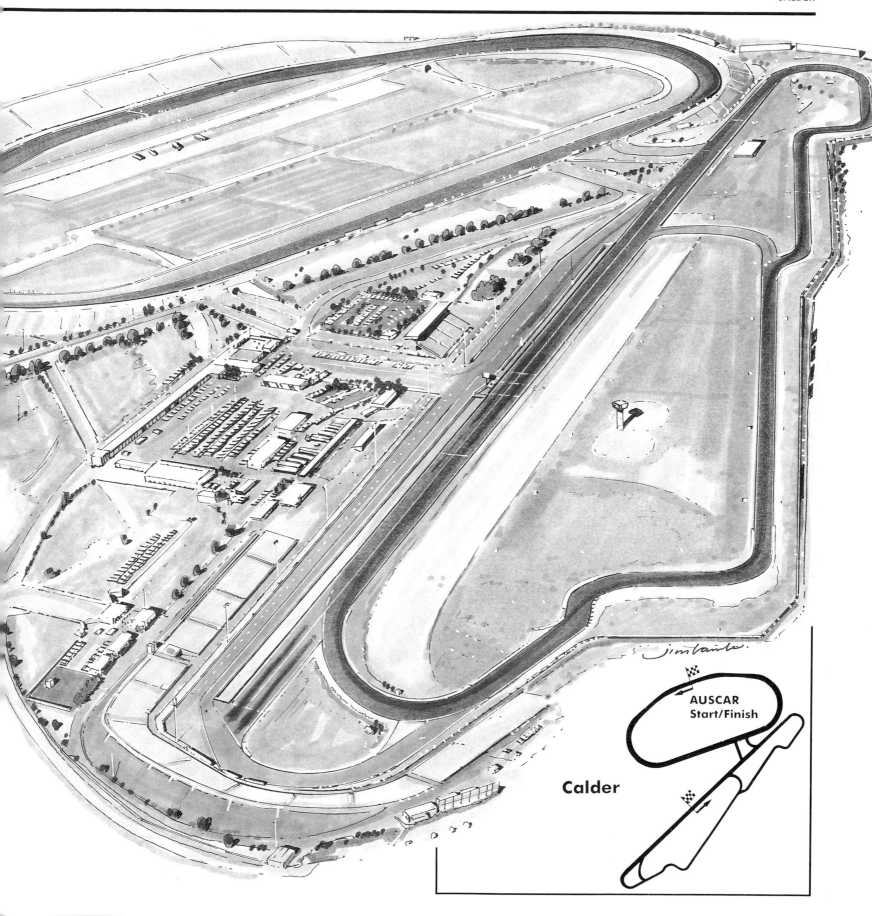

AUSCAR
Start/Finish

Calder

Other Australian Circuits

Today Australia is well served by permanent circuits but it hasn't always been like that. In the immediate post-war era, no such facilities existed and hence the Australian GP was obliged to begin a tour of temporary circuits, all now long gone: the airfields of Point Cook, Port Wakefield and Leyburn; road tracks at Nuriootpa, Narrogin and Southport. In many ways the history of the Grand Prix mirrors that of Australian racing as a whole in those post-war years as circuits came and went: airfields at Beverly, the gold mining town of Ballarat, Marsden Park, Altona, Strathpine and Schofields, and street tracks here and there.

There was **Mount Druitt**, near Sydney, opened in 1948, an old airstrip with a course laid out between rock-filled 44-gallon oil drums. Later a road course was built here, and proved popular with the drivers who were offered a share of the gate money — something unheard of in that era. It was here that a young Jack Brabham made his name in an MG and where the only 24-hour race in Australian history was held in January 1954. Through rain and mud, then heat and dust, the motley collection of cars lapped the 2.2-mile track, tearing up the surface. Though repaired, Mount Druitt closed in 1958, never having properly recovered from that hammering.

Closer into Sydney was **Parramatta Park**, an attempt to bring racing into the Sydney suburbs. It was absurdly unsafe and lasted only a couple of years. Down in Melbourne they raced on the runways of the Commonwealth Aircraft Corporation's airfield at **Fisherman's Bend** between 1948 and 1960 against the scenic backdrop of a large rubbish dump and the Melbourne docks. At Orange, in the Blue Mountains, there was an even stranger track at **Gnoo Blas**, a roller-coaster of a ride on farm roads around a lunatic asylum, with the inmates beckoning the drivers to join them.

In Western Australia, **Caversham** emerged as a major facility. Built in the Second World War, this was another airfield, 13 miles fom Perth. Caversham staged the Victory Grand Prix as early as 1946 but it took years of negotiation with the Royal Australian Air Force before a lease could be secured and development work begun. Finally in 1955 a deal was struck. Permanent pits were built and a PA system installed and at last, in 1957, the Australian Grand Prix paid its first call. Another would follow in 1962. Though fairly basic and with the unusual additional problem of errant kangaroos, Caversham survived until 1969 when the Department of Defence decided to take it back and turn it into a radio-communication centre. It was replaced by a new purpose-built facility at **Wanneroo**.

In the same exciting era for the sport there was **Longford**, to the south of Launceston in Tasmania. This track was first used in 1953 and closed 15 years later and was another roller-coaster ride over public roads, featuring the super-fast Flying Mile of straight, a viaduct and even a level-crossing. It became the favourite long weekend of the racing year, with the party beginning on the ferry across the Bass Straight. The itinerant Australian Grand Prix visited Longford in 1959, and was won by Stan Jones in his Maserati 250F, and as early as 1960 the circuit was able to attract international racers: Jack Brabham, Roy Salvadori, John Surtees and

Two Jaguar 3.4s and a Holden cross the Long Bridge in a Touring Car race at Longford (Tasmania) in 1959. Exciting but dangerous, the circuit disappeared in a major roadbuilding project at the end of the 1960s.

Bruce McLaren were among the winners in the early days. With the inauguration of the Tasman Cup, however, all the top guns of Europe visited, and Graham Hill, Jackie Stewart, and Piers Courage took turns at winning.

Longford, though a great track, was dangerous and there were some appalling accidents: Tim Mayer died in 1964 and a year later Rocky Tresise and a photographer also died. The decline of the Tasman Cup because of increasing F1 commitments and the beginnings of the safety crusades would probably have finished Longford off; but major road works arrived first and Longford closed for the last time in 1968.

The same year that Longford had opened, **Albert Park**, just south of downtown Melbourne, organised its first race. A 4.3-mile track around an artificial lake, it consisted of fast sweeping bends and was immediately successful in taking racing to the people. The Australian GP of 1953 was run there, won by Doug Whiteford. Albert Park went on to have a bright if brief career. Both the Grand Prix and the Australian Tourist Trophy took place at Albert Park in 1956, with the irrepressible Stirling Moss winning both. The following year Lex Davison won the Victoria Trophy in his Ferrari and in 1958 Moss returned to win a Formula Libre race, run under the title of the Melbourne Grand Prix. But that was it; political pressure was brought to bear and after just five years Albert Park reverberated to the sound of racing engines for the last time.

Up in Queensland, an old Liberator airstrip was establishing itself as the state's premier racing venue — **Lowood**, 43 miles west of Brisbane. Although used as early as June 1946, the track did not stage races regularly until 1956. On its fast swooping bends was fought the closest ever Australian Grand Prix finish in 1960 when Alec Mildren's Cooper held off Lex Davison's Aston Martin by a short nose. That was Lowood's moment of glory,

for a new generation of circuits rendered it obsolete and it closed in 1966.

New permanent facilities began to arrive, one after another, at the end of the 1950s. In quick succession came Baskerville, Amaroo Park, Symmons Plains, Warwick Farm, Lakeside, Mallala, Calder Park, Oran Park, Catalina Park and Sandown. By the end of 1962 Australia had more than enough permanent tracks. Two years later came the first Tasman Cup series, which proved to be a popular championship for Formula 1 teams in the winter period.

The first Tasman race in Australia took place at Sandown in 1964, won by Jack Brabham in a Brabham! Just what the fans wanted to see. Foremost among the Tasman tracks was **Warwick Farm**, which was very much the premier track of its day and the circuit by which all the others were measured. A racecourse in the suburbs of Sydney, Warwick Farm opened in December 1960, designed around the turf track by Englishman Geoff Sykes (formerly of Aintree) who managed it throughout its career. For the first time, racing became socially acceptable in Australia. The crowds picnicked around the course and the VIPs enjoyed themselves in the comfort of the clubhouse. The racing was good too. Brabham won in 1963-4 but for the next two seasons the Sydneysiders were treated to Jim Clark victories with a third coming just a few months before his death in 1968. In the interim fellow Scot Jackie Stewart popped up to win and in 1969 it was the turn of Jochen Rindt.

This was a happy era for Australian racing but with the Tasman Cup crumbling, to be switched to Formula 5000 regulations in 1970, Warwick Farm faded away, the victim of insufficient finance to make the necessary improvements and competition from the newer Oran Park. When the phantom bugler at Creek Corner played his own rendition of 'The Last Post' in 1973 an era of Australian

Adelaide

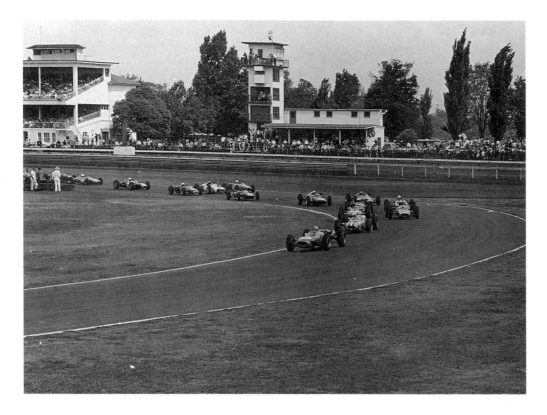

Finest of all the circuits used (as here) for Tasman Cup races, Warwick Farm was designed around an attractive racecourse in the Sydney suburbs.

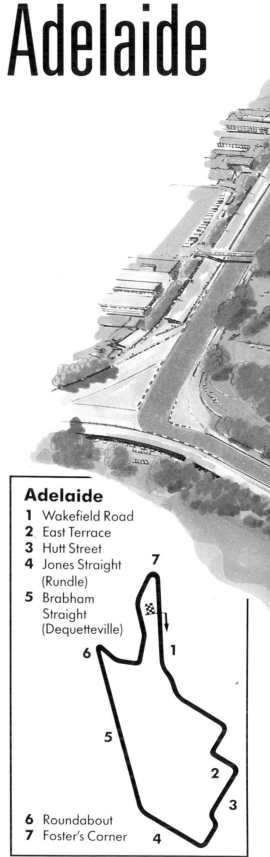

racing closed. Single-seater racing in the region would never again reach such heights as it did at 'The Farm'.

The third race in the original Tasman series of 1964 was held at **Lakeside**, a fast and daunting track, to the north of Brisbane in Queensland. Opened in March 1961, Lakeside was built on Sid Sakzewski's dairy farm at Petrie and as its name suggests it was alongside Lake Kurwongbah. Always challenging, Lakeside has deteriorated in recent years but in 1988 major improvements began to bring the track up to date. Of the other new tracks of the era, most survive today: **Baskerville** and **Symmons Plains** in Tasmania, both tiny and both anticlockwise; **Amaroo Park** in its natural amphitheatre, 25 miles (40 km) to the north-west of Sydney, the home of the Australian Racing Drivers' Club; **Mallala**, near Ade-

laide, another old airfield, closed in 1971 because of competition from Adelaide International, but recently in action again; and **Oran Park**.

Some did not survive: **Hume Weir** in a quarry near Albury; **Catalina Park**, in the Blue Mountains on the road from Sydney to Bathurst, a twisting 1.29-mile track set in a natural amphitheatre on the edge of the town of Katoomba; and **Surfers Paradise**, the ambitious track opposite the Ski Gardens complex on the Nerang River, Queensland, which opened with much fanfare and a Speed Week in 1966 but failed to attract the crowds away from the beaches despite a lap record of over 110mph. With land prices going berserk in the area, the track was sold to a Japanese property developer in 1988 and a replacement was planned. Add to the survivors the more recent tracks at Wanneroo, Winton and Adelaide International and you have the present Australian venues — with one notable exception: the streets of Adelaide, home of the modern Australian Grand Prix.

Adelaide

1 Wakefield Road
2 East Terrace
3 Hutt Street
4 Jones Straight (Rundle)
5 Brabham Straight (Dequetteville)
6 Roundabout
7 Foster's Corner

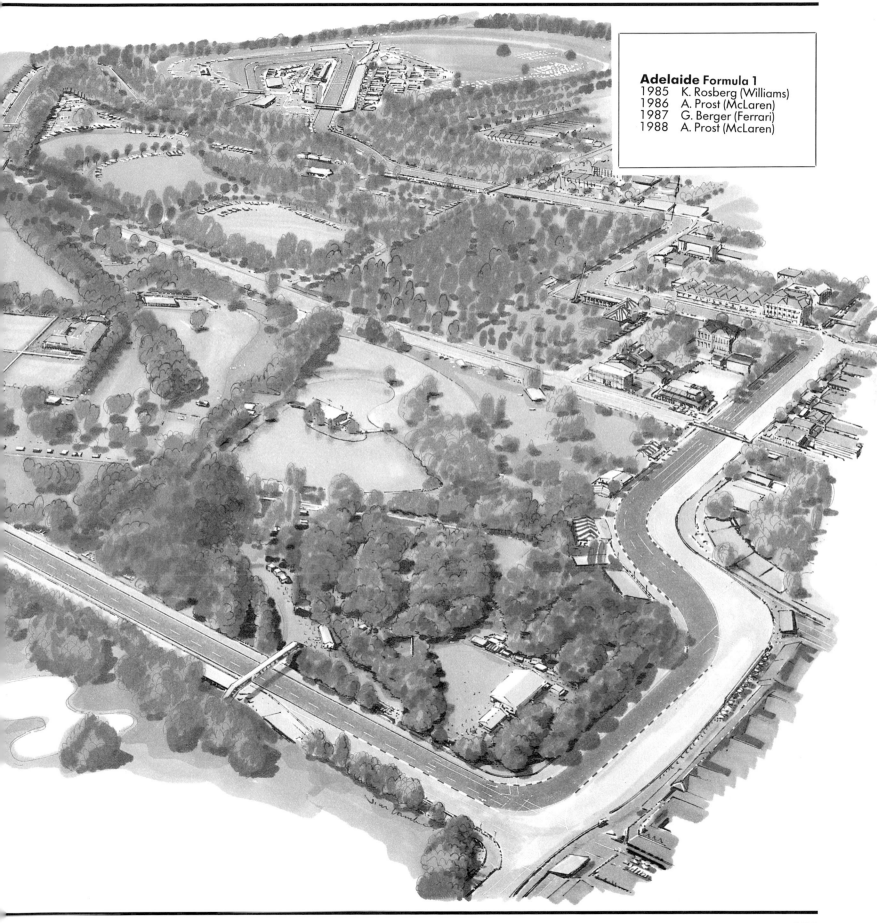

Adelaide Formula 1
1985   K. Rosberg (Williams)
1986   A. Prost (McLaren)
1987   G. Berger (Ferrari)
1988   A. Prost (McLaren)

Adelaide is the state capital of South Australia, the 'city of churches', and until recently was regarded as the sleepy cousin of the vibrant centres of Sydney and Melbourne. In reality, in the 1980s the city has undergone rapid industrial change and modernisation. The image problem, however, remained. The idea of a Grand Prix in Adelaide was a central part of the plan to change that image. It was intended to make Adelaide a little more 'racy' and to promote the state, its industries and the city itself. 'There are very few annual events which can focus the attention of the world on a city,' says the senior civil servant and Executive Director of the Australian Grand Prix Board, Dr Mal Hemmerling. 'We decided the Grand Prix could give the state a new image and make people proud of their city.'

The original idea for a race came from businessman Bill O'Gorman, who set about enlisting political support for the plan. South Australia's Premier John Bannon agreed that it was a good idea and negotiations for a race began with Bernie Ecclestone of the Formula One Constructors' Association (FOCA). That august body was not impressed until Bannon flew personally to London to discuss the matter with Ecclestone. The two negotiated a seven-year deal, beginning in 1985. The Director of the Cabinet Office, Dr Mal Hammerling was appointed Executive Director of the Australian Grand Prix Board and work began to have the necessary laws changed to enable a race to take place. Various federal and state grants were found to finance the work.

Adelaide is a parkland city, set between the sea and the rolling hills of the Mount Lofty ranges. The climate is Mediterranean, with long hot summers and short mild winters. Close by are the wine-making regions of the Barossa Valley, Coonawarra, and McLaren Vale, all fast becoming major names in the wine world. The plan was to build a track around one of the city's parks, and the result has proved to be very different from other modern Grands Prix: Adelaide is not merely a race but part of the huge 'Streets Ahead' festival. This gives the Adelaide GP a wonderful party atmosphere, helped by the fact that today it is the end-of-season event. As a result it is immensely popular with the teams, who need a rest by this stage of the year.

The incredible thing about Adelaide is that is completely lacks the feel of a temporary circuit. It is centred on Victoria Park Racecourse, and a new section of track was built, crossing the turf twice. Beyond that everything is put up and taken down each year, including an impressive pit complex, 2142 concrete barriers, over four miles of wire fencing and 54,000 grandstand seats. It is an incredible feat. The design of engineer Bob Barnard, the track sweeps away from the racecourse through a fast chicane and on to Wakefield Street. There follows a sequence of tight right-angle corners and a fast left-right sweep before the corner on to Jones Straight,

Above Adelaide, 1987 Grand Prix: winner Berger (followed by Piquet, Senna, Alboreto and Patrese) having turned right off Wakefield, is turning left past the first East Terrace grandstand.

Right Looking back down Jones Straight. Roberto Moreno's AGS negotiates the link leading on to the long Brabham Straight.

which leads to a fast kink on to the Brabham Straight, aka Dequetteville Terrace. Here the F1 cars of the 1980s reach top speed, something normally unheard of in the intimate confines of a modern street circuit. This is followed by a hairpin back on to Wakefield Street before the new racecourse section veers off left back to the pit hairpin.

Sir Jack Brabham, having lapped the track before it was first used for a Grand Prix commented, 'It's as good a street circuit as there is anywhere'. His opinion was backed up by those of the Grand Prix teams. They couldn't believe it!

Adelaide has staged some fine races too in the race's short history: there was Keke Rosberg's virtuoso performance in 1985 and the ultimate showdown the following year when Nigel Mansell lost the championship in a flurry of sparks and rubber when a tyre blew at high speed on Brabham Straight, allowing the championship outsider Alain Prost to defy the odds and snatch the title — just 19 laps from the flag. Hollywood could not have done better.

NEW ZEALAND

Racing in New Zealand is not what it once was. The era of Denny Hulme, Chris Amon and Bruce McLaren is long past, and today the heroes are increasingly the men who drive the touring cars. There is still an annual New Zealand Grand Prix, part of the Christmas Formula Pacific Championship but the blue riband racing event in New Zealand is the round-the-houses Labour Day touring-car event at **Wellington**. It's a race that Australian Peter Brook has won twice and he is fond of the place. 'Wellington,' he reckons, 'is certainly not boring! It's a really demanding track and very hard to put together a nice lap. I've always found the best way to deal with it is to have a go in qualifying and then sit down, have a cup of tea, check the car over, put it away and get your head together for the race.'

Driving around Wellington is like

Left Wellington: an Eggenberger-prepared Ford Sierra RS500 exits Ford Bridge in the 1988 event.

Above The large waterfront chicane precedes the short dash to the start/finish line at Wellington.

threading cotton through the eye of a needle. There is nothing much to hit apart from concrete walls — and a lot of people do that. The capital's street race is a relative newcomer in the international calendar and the track, which takes in the waterfront area and the fast blast along Jervois Quay, has been altered several times in its short history. The race was intended to attract attention to Wellington and to improve the image of the city and with major development planned, it has clearly been succesful. The track will undoubtedly be altered again but the developers — unromantic at best —

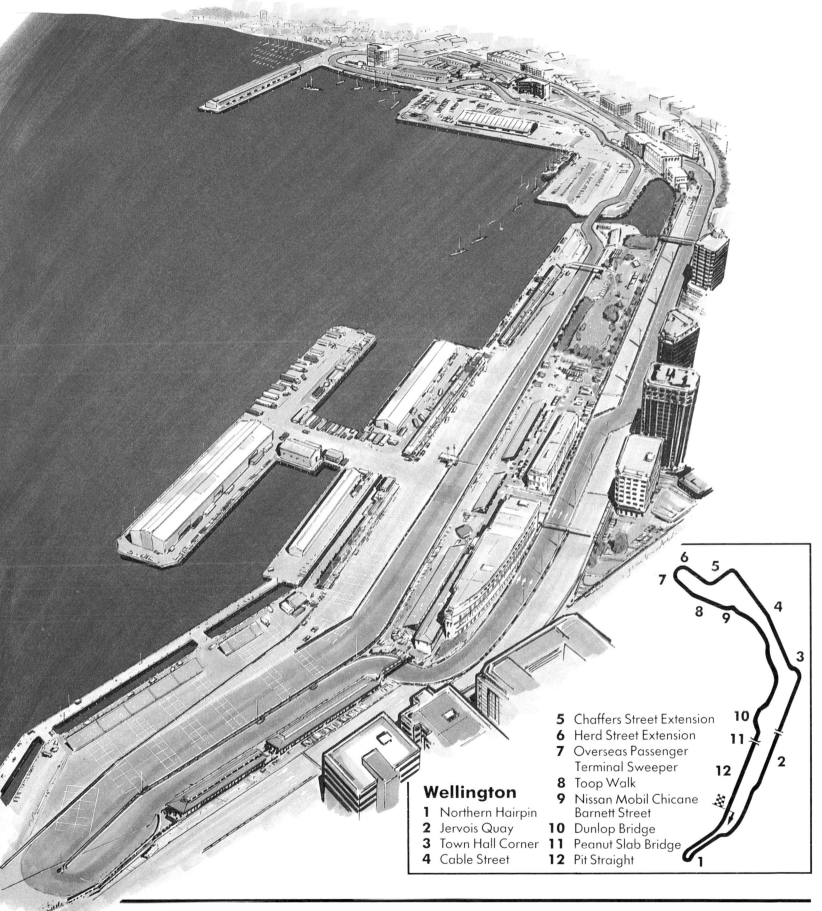

Wellington

1 Northern Hairpin
2 Jervois Quay
3 Town Hall Corner
4 Cable Street
5 Chaffers Street Extension
6 Herd Street Extension
7 Overseas Passenger
   Terminal Sweeper
8 Toop Walk
9 Nissan Mobil Chicane
   Barnett Street
10 Dunlop Bridge
11 Peanut Slab Bridge
12 Pit Straight

realise the value of the event and have included a circuit in their plans.

Racing in New Zealand began on the beaches; but in the post-war period it developed on airfields and racecourses. Initially there was a track laid out on the runways of the operational air force station on the outskirts of Canterbury, **Wigram**, which has staged an annual meeting since 1949. The track is high speed, flat and windy. **Ardmore**, the home of the New Zealand Grand Prix, was another airfield; it opened in 1954 with Australian Stan Jones, father of World Champion Alan, winning the first event. In later years it became an annual contest between Stirling Moss and Jack Brabham, the Englishman winning in 1956-59-62 and the Australian in 1958-60-61. The two-mile track was laid out on the disused airfield 20 miles south of Auckland, for one meeting a year and as with Wigram it was extremely fast. In 1962, however, Ardmore was reclaimed by the air force and the New

Zealand GP had to find another home at **Pukekohe**, close by in the rolling countryside south of Auckland. The track was opened in 1963, built

around the perimeter of a racecourse. It is flat, with a long straight feeding into a very tricky hairpin followed by a bumpy fast left. 'A great complex of

Above Pukekohe: coming out of the Elbow shortly after the start of the 1965 New Zealand Grand Prix. Winner Graham Hill leads Clark, Gardner (11), McLaren (47), Palmer (41), Davidson, Glass and Geoghegan.

Left A 1988 Touring Car race at Pukekohe: the cars are on the short circuit at Champion Corner, a fast right-hander which bypasses the Elbow.

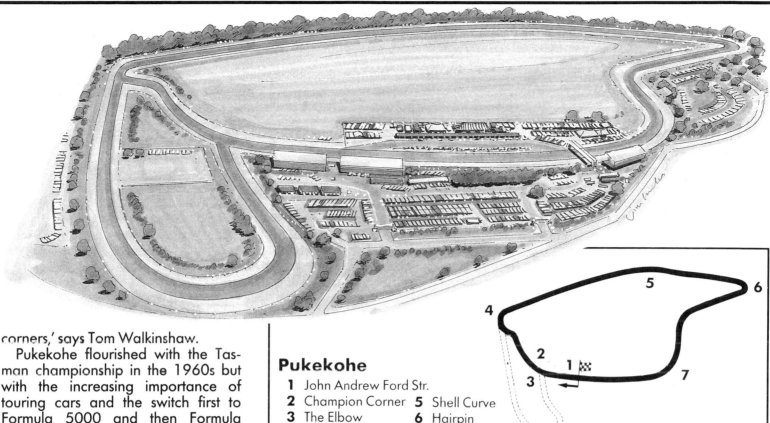

Pukekohe

1 John Andrew Ford Str.
2 Champion Corner   5 Shell Curve
3 The Elbow   6 Hairpin
4 Castrol Corner   7 Dunlop Curve

corners,' says Tom Walkinshaw.

Pukekohe flourished with the Tasman championship in the 1960s but with the increasing importance of touring cars and the switch first to Formula 5000 and then Formula Pacific it has faded from the international scene, though it still hosts the annual New Zealand Grand Prix for Formula Pacific cars. In recent years promoters have been trying to re-establish the international link, beginning a major rebuild in the hope of attracting a major FISA World Championship event.

Long before Pukekohe, however, New Zealand had its first permanent circuits at Levin and Teretonga Park. **Levin** is another racecourse but the tarmac track with its long, fast bends was laid out in 1956 and the circuit witnessed the early careers of Amon, Hulme and McLaren. It was the venue for the inaugural Tasman Cup race in 1964. Situated 30 miles from Palmerston on North Island on the Levin State Highway, it is the nearest thing to central there is in New Zealand.

The same cannot be said for **Teretonga Park**, opened in 1957 to replace the Ryal Bush course which had held races in 1956 and 1957. 'Terrible Tonga,' remembers David Hobbs, 'was the southernmost racing circuit in the world and cold as hell.'

Even local hero Denny Hulme finds it hard to be charitable. 'It was the nearest place to the South Pole, right on the tip of South Island. It was as flat as a biscuit and the track was always covered with sand, lupins and sheep droppings. It was anticlockwise and incredibly tough on tyres, having been built with a pebbly mixture of some sort. Actually, it wasn't a bad track, there was a big looped section where you would go off and get tangled up in wires and there was a long straight with a nice fast corner at the end.' Also known as Invercargill, Teretonga became a regular track in the Tasman Cup and Bruce McLaren, Jim Clark, Jackie Stewart and Piers Courage were among its most famous winners.

Neither Levin or Teretonga have been used for international races since the 1970s but New Zealand boasts three other permanent facilities: Bay Park, Manfeild and Levels Raceway. **Bay Park**, also sometimes known as Mount Manganui,

situated close to the major North Island resort of Tauranga, is a small and flat 1.33 mile track with long, oddly cambered sweepers, while **Manfeild Autocourse** is part of the agricultural showgrounds at Feilding, with no pits, but a series of good sweepers in the infield and a long straight.

Levels Raceway, for its part, is close to Timaru on South Island. It was built in the late 1960s to replace a street track at Waimate that had held races betwen 1959 and 1966 but was finally declared too dangerous. A similar fate befell racing in Dunedin, where races were staged from 1953 on three different street tracks, until its disappearance in the late 1960s.

The enthusiasm for racing is still strong in New Zealand but with its remoteness and dependence on Australia to share major series such as the Tasman Cup there is little hope that the great days of Kiwi racing will ever return.

ASIA

MACAU

Racing in Asia has been severely restricted since the dismantling of the European colonial system after the Second World War. Many countries have been unable financially or politically to support any form of regular racing track and, without the necessary circuits, international visitors have been few and far between.

One event has not only survived, but flourished — the Macau Grand Prix. Nowadays, this is the major international Formula 3 meeting of the year, an opportunity at the end of each season to see oriental drivers taking on those from the west and to see the best youngsters battling it out with Formula 1 drivers taking time off for some fun. A tiny Portuguese colony on the edge of mainland China, just a jetfoil ride from Hong Kong across the South China Sea, Macau has a faded colonial opulence. Pedicabs hustle between the gambling dens and 'hotels' and the colony has a curious eastern-western mix. It is a place where you can eat Chinese food and drink *viñho verde* and where it is wise not to argue with the gun-toting local police force. With each visit you find that a new building has popped up where previously there was nothing but wasteland, or wasteland where once there was sea.

The 3.8-mile Guia street circuit has an ambience of the old days of racing as it rushes madly between the houses and cliff edges — yet it too has a mix of the old and the new. The start area is along the seafront, under the imposingly modern Oriental Hotel. Then comes the flat Yacht Club Bend, where the F3 machines are right on the limit. The sea that used to be on your left on the run down to Statue Corner has been drained since 1986. Here is the

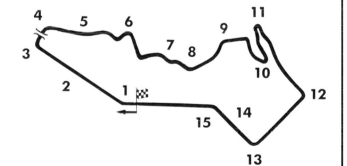

Above At Dona Maria Bend, near the end of the back leg of Macau circuit, the long left curve sharpens into a tight corner, the track dropping downhill.

Left F2 cars at the end of the seafront section at Macau, about to turn right at Statue Corner.

Macau

1 Yacht Club Bend
2 Yacht Club Straight
3 Statue Corner
4 Bridge
5 Hospital Hill
6 Maternity Bend
7 Solitude Esses
8 Faraway Hill
9 Moorish Hill
10 Dona Maria Bend
11 Melco Hairpin
12 Fisherman's Bend
13 R. Bend (Marlboro)
14 Reservoir
15 Reservoir Bend

major overtaking point on the track, under-braking for Statue, a tight right-hander — in the shadow of the Hotel

Lisboa — with nowhere to go if you get it wrong. There is a short straight to the righthander by the San Francisco Bar-

racks and then the track goes steeply uphill towards the hospital, between high stone walls, sweeping right-left-

Right F2 at Macau: coming on to the causeway at R., or Marlboro, Bend, with the sea on the left, the reservoir on the right, and Reservoir Corner and the pits straight ahead.

right to Maternity Bend.

Clinging to the hillside now, it passes race patron Teddy Yip's house — used as a garage by the teams he fields — before swerving through the Solitude esses and downhill to Faraway Hill and Moorish Hill. There follows a 90-degree right by the police workshops, and the long, long left Donna Maria Bend, dropping into Melco Hairpin, where it is inadvisable to attempt overtaking. In recent times this area of the track has featured a permanent yellow flag to stop the optimistic from trying to pass each other! The hairpin is taken in first gear, with a big drop at its exit. A few years ago before dispatching cars from England the TWR Jaguar XJS saloon car team telexed ahead for the measurements of the corner, to make sure the big cars could get through here without having to make a three-point turn!

Out of the hairpin, the track sweeps downhill left between houses, before emerging on to a causeway between the sea and a reservoir on the fast blast up to the fast right Fisherman's Bend, followed by another, R Bend (once called Rothmans), where if you get it wrong there is a danger of ending up in the South China Sea. Ahead is the fast left at Reservoir Bend which leads the track to the hydrofoil terminal pits and again into Yacht Club Bend. It is a place for compromise in set-up and no compromise in a driver.

The race developed as a rivalry between two local entrepreneurs, Bob Harper and Teddy Yip, but it did not reach its present level of international importance until 1983. Major changes had been made to improve the safety to allow the organisers to run the race according to Formula 2 rules; however, the plan fell through and F3 was adopted. In the 1970s each year saw a few international visitors for the Formula Atlantic races and they had had things comparatively easy with Riccardo Patrese, Vern Schuppan and Geoff Lees all picking up two victories apiece. The arrival of F3 opened the gates to teams from all across the world and the competition became increasingly intense.

That first F3 race in 1983 was dominated by a young Brazilian tearaway called Ayrton Senna, who defeated sometime Formula 1 driver Roberto Guerrero and another future Grand Prix star, Gerhard Berger. The Dane John Nielsen, after years in the doldrums in Formula 3, won the Macau GP in 1984 and found himself with drives in Formula 3000 and sportscar racing, while 1985 winner Mauricio Gugelmin was another to head to the Grand Prix scene with the Leyton House March team. The race has grown with each year and the talent spotters are always out in force to see how the new men cope with the demands of street racing as it used to be. Gerhard Berger sums up the place best of all. 'Macau,' he says, 'is a wonderful place!'

Other Asian Circuits

Wonderful Macau remains the exception to the rule in Asian racing. Other events, almost all street races of some form or another, have come and gone. In the 1960s and early 1970s **Singapore** ran a regular 'Grand Prix' on the north of the island, incorporating sections of Thomson Road, which had the unusual hazard of sticky oil tracks, dropped by the diesel buses in the course of the year. The Singapore organisers actually went as far as to build a link road through a forest to join Thomson Road but as Allan Grice, a regular visitor, remembers, 'it was always raining there!' In the course of 1988 plans began to emerge for a new circuit to be built in Singapore that is intended to host a Formula 1 Grand Prix in the 1990s. Across the water in **Malaysia** was another street track at Johore Bahru, an annual event left

over from the days of British rule, but with the disappearance of the British and their cars this too faded away.

Up country in Malaysia there were other races at Penang and at a road track near Kuala Lumpur named after the country's first Prime Minister, Tunku Abdul Rahman. This was abandoned with the construction of the new city of Pataling Jaya but a new facility was built in 1968 at Batu Tiga, 20 miles north-west of Kuala Lumpur on the main highway north. Owned by the Sultan of Selangor, whose palace overlooks the track, Batu Tiga's name was later changed to Shah Alam. In the early 1980s Formula Atlantic races took place on the 2.1-mile circuit and, in the hope of attracting major international competition, the track underwent major modifications and was extended to 2.3 miles in 1985. At the end of that year the

World Sportscar Championship visited with Jochen Mass and Jacky Ickx winning in oppressive humidity in their factory Porsche 962. The sportscars did not return in 1986.

In **India**, racing has been restricted to old British airbases, although the Bangalore and Madras Grands Prix have histories dating back to the 1950s, albeit for a bizarre collection of machinery. There has long been talk of a permanent racing track in India and in 1988 work began on the construction of an international specification motor sport complex at Irungattukutai, near Madras.

Thailand too has a permanent racing circuit at Pattaya, which has seen the occasional international visitor; plans for full-scale international races, however, have not come to fruition.

Batu Tiga, Malaysia: a heat of a hotly contested 1970s Formula 2 race at the circuit owned by the Sultan of Selangor.

JAPAN

With the major involvement in Formula 1 of Honda and other Japanese manufacturers in the 1980s, racing in Japan is becoming increasingly important on the international scene. The national championships in Formula 3000, Group C, touring cars and Formula 3 are no longer the backwaters they once were, with increasing numbers of international drivers basing themselves in the cosmopolitan quarters of Tokyo and racing full time in Japan. Some, like McLaren's recent test driver, the Italian Emanuele Pirro, pound around circuits developing new machines for the manufacturers, while others merely race at weekends to make a living. Such is the power of the yen.

But this is a recent development. Until the early 1980s when the first Europeans, Geoff Lees and Eje Elgh, arrived, Japan was isolated from mainstream racing, with only the occasional influx of foreign drivers. There was a brief flurry of international activity in the mid-1970s when Formula 1 visited Japan for two seasons but it was not until 1987 that the Japanese Grand Prix became a truly established part of the Formula 1 calendar.

Fuji

In 1976 and 1977 the Formula 1 teams visited the Mount Fuji circuit in the mountains to the south-west of Tokyo. Each visit was to prove dramatic. Situated in the foothills of the perfectly conical dormant volcano — a place of religious significance for the locals — the Mount Fuji circuit is today a fairly basic and dilapidated facility. The pits could never accommodate the modern Formula 1 circus with its endless caravans and trailers.

Fuji

Fuji Formula 1
1976   M. Andretti (Lotus)
1977   J. Hunt (McLaren)

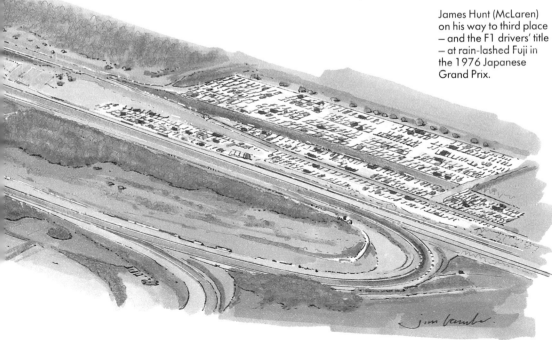

James Hunt (McLaren) on his way to third place — and the F1 drivers' title — at rain-lashed Fuji in the 1976 Japanese Grand Prix.

The international races at Mount Fuji have always taken place in the autumn, when the European racing season is over and the continental drivers turn their attention to Asia and the Pacific. Driving through the hills around Fuji at this time of year can be a marvellous experience, with the trees resplendent in their various shades of gold and green. The region around Mount Fuji and Hakone is actually a holiday area, dotted with lakes and spas. And after a weekend's racing, you can be guaranteed a healthy traffic jam as what seems like half the population of Japan tries to funnel on to the Tomei Expressway back to Tokyo. For racing fans, however, not far from Fuji is the world acclaimed Matsuda Collection of Porsches.

The circuit itself was opened in December 1965, built as a speedway with a long main straight beneath a huge, imposing grandstand. The original plan was for a 2.5-mile anti-clockwise superspeedway to match those in America. At the end of the straight the track originally dipped downhill and on to a stretch of daunting 30-degree banking. There was to have been banking at both ends of the track – the name Fuji International Speedway suggests a track in the American mould – but money ran out, leaving the circuit half speedway, half road course. The fearsome banking could not last for long and following several monumental accidents it was abandoned, although it can still be seen today.

From 1974 the demands of safety meant a clockwise course of 2.7 miles. Various other changes have been made since, with corners reprofiled and a chicane added to slow the cars coming on to the main straight. For a driver Fuji is a mish-mash of hidden apexes. The main straight ends with a deceptive downhill righthanded sweeper, leading on to a quick blast to a lefthander, followed by a series of rights feeding into a lefthanded hairpin, which can be seen down below the back of the rudimentary pits, before the road turns away right curling all the time. It used to continue on to the main straight – one seemingly endless power-down sweeper – but there is a chicane now, cutting speeds on to that high speed blast back past the pits. That straight gives you just too long to think about exactly what you are doing. No one ever had just a small accident on that piece of road.

All that is before you start worrying about the weather. It is said that if you can see Mount Fuji it will be a lucky day but since the volcano is constantly obscured by clouds this circuit is not one for the superstitious. On a good day, Fuji is a wonderful place to be; but when the weather is nasty, anywhere else in the world suddenly seems infinitely preferable to those misty slopes.

The most famous race at the circuit,

indeed one of the most famous races of the Formula 1 modern era, was dictated by the bizarre weather of Mount Fuji. It was 24 October 1976 and the Formula 1 World Championship finale was to take place at Mount Fuji. Niki Lauda, despite missing several races while he made a miraculous recovery from his awful accident at the Nürburgring, arrived just three points ahead of James Hunt in the points standings. Local hero Masahiro Hasemi had given everyone a shock in early qualifying by lapping his Dunlop-shod Kojima around with great gusto. A big crash meant the car had to be rebuilt, so by the time qualifying was over Mario Andretti had pole position for Lotus with Hunt's McLaren alongside and Lauda's Ferrari third.

On that Sunday morning the track was awash. After the warm up lap there were complaints from the drivers and the start was delayed in the hope that the surface would dry out. Finally, though many drivers were opposed to it, the cars went to the start. Hunt, from the front row, took off into the lead. Lauda did just three laps before withdrawing. The World Championship wasn't worth that kind of risk. He knew that better than anyone. Hunt led through the murk but as conditions improved his tyres began to go off. Finally one disintegrated, forcing James in to the pits. He rejoined in fifth place, one below that needed to take the title, with just four laps to go. Others, however, had similar tyre troubles and in those vital closing minutes Hunt forced his way past Alan Jones and Clay Regazzoni. Andretti had won but James Hunt was World Champion – not that he realised it at the time.

The following year the F1 men returned, though several teams elected to miss the race. This time Hunt won, although the celebrations were muted after Gilles Villeneuve had collided with Ronnie Peterson's Tyrrell and his Ferrari had crashed into a group of marshals and photo-

graphers, killing two of them.

Fuji was now finished as a Grand Prix track, though it would continue to be a venue for international showdowns as an important round of the World Sportscar Championship. An equally nail-biting finish occurred during the final round of the one and only FIA World Touring Car Championship in 1987 when the race leader, the Sierra Cosworth driven by Klaus Niedzwiedz and Klaus Ludwig, needed its sister car driven by Pierre Dieudonne to finish second in order to prevent Italian BMW star Roberto Ravaglia from taking the necessary points to clinch the title. With just a handful of laps to go Dieudonne had a puncture and had to visit the pits, leaving Ravaglia to take the title at the last gasp.

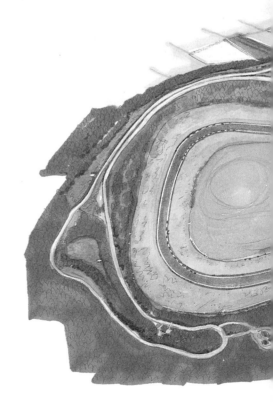

Suzuka

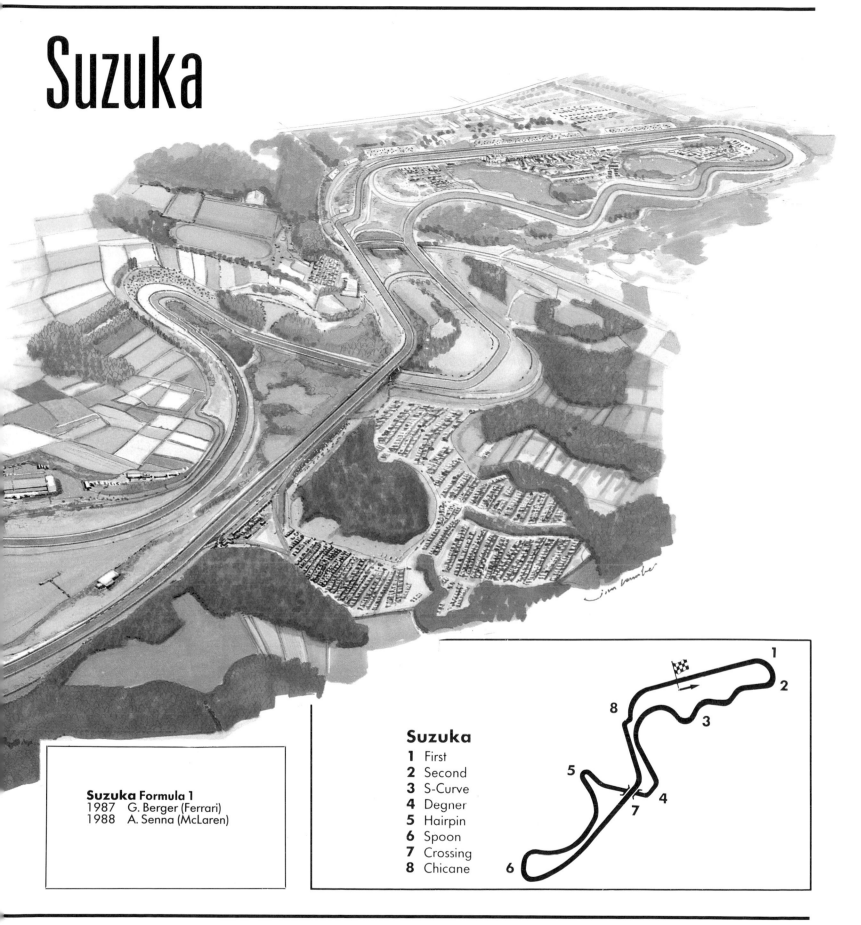

Suzuka Formula 1
1987   G. Berger (Ferrari)
1988   A. Senna (McLaren)

Suzuka
1 First
2 Second
3 S-Curve
4 Degner
5 Hairpin
6 Spoon
7 Crossing
8 Chicane

The very first Japanese GP had been held in 1963 at Suzuka, near Japan's third city, Nagoya. That was a sportscar race which was won by Peter Warr, who would go on to become the motive force in the Lotus F1 team after the death of Colin Chapman. The race was confined to sportscars until 1969 and then between 1971 and 1975 it was run for Formula 2 cars.

Built in 1962 as a test facility for Honda, Suzuka was designed by the Dutchman John Hugenholz, the man behind Zandvoort and, later, Jarama. It was to be part of a motorcycle sports land and as it developed, this combined amusement park and training centre carried various titles: Motor Sportland, Suzuka Circuitland, Techniland and ultimately Motopia – a motorcar utopia. And so it is, 2.48 million square metres of amusement parks with swimming pools, ice skating rink, monorails, big wheels, event halls, hotels, golf courses, restaurants, not to mention a motor racing circuit! Set in hilly country alongside the park, Suzuka has a strange feel to it. It must be like staging a race in Disneyland. You can see the funfair from the track and at various points around the circuit there are slip roads and parking spots for go-karts.

If the setting is slightly strange, the configuration of the track is equally bizarre, for Suzuka is not one circuit but two that can be used independently or combined. There is a separate control tower and pits at the back of the track on the straight forming the return leg to the Formula 1 pits, which are situated on a slight downhill. The first corner is fast and testing, sweeping right in a long arc rising around a pond then diving through a series of sweeps before disappearing from the main grandstand area through a fast

Right Testing but fast, Suzuka is liked by most F1 drivers. Here Patrese (Williams), pursued by Berger (Ferrari), comes to the end of the S curves behind the paddock.

Below Starting as, in 1988, they usually finished, Senna and Prost (McLaren) lead off in the Japanese Grand Prix at Suzuka. And track-owner Soichiro Honda, who supplied their engines, was there to see them complete a 1-2 victory.

lefthander. Suzuka is one of the very few figure-of-eight circuits, for the road cuts under itself after a pair of righthanders and bursts up to a left-hand hairpin. After that it heads to Spoon Corner, before dropping down on to the straight, past the secondary pits and over the track below to a fine sweeping lefthander which slingshots

the cars up the last corner, once long and fast but since 1983 disrupted by an extremely tight chicane.

To a man the Grand Prix drivers of the modern era like the track; it makes some ill because of the constant sweeps and changes of direction and elevation but all find it a challenge. Since it was licensed by FISA the track

has been modified from year to year, easing corners here, changing kerbs there. The major changes occurred in 1987 in preparation for the first Formula 1 Grand Prix at this venue, an event which saw Nelson Piquet take the World Championship in qualifying when his challenger and Williams-Honda team-mate Nigel Mansell crashed heavily. Ironically, having won 11 of the 14 GPs of that season, Honda engines were outpaced in their home race by the Ferrari of Gerhard Berger.

In true Japanese style, the same did not happen twice and in 1988 Ayrton Senna, who had made a dreadful start, put in the best drive of his career to catch and pass his McLaren teammate and championship challenger Alain Prost. Honda not only won the race with a 1-2 finish but they clinched the World Championship as well — and Soichiro Honda, the man who started the empire, was there to celebrate. A suitably happy ending for a race in Disneyland.

Below A Toyota comes into the pits at Suzuka during the Japanese round of the 1989 World Sportscar Championship.

Right The start of the 1989 Sportscar race. Leading off, from the right: Mercedes (winner), Toyota and Jaguar.

Other Japanese Circuits

Hi-Land Raceway at Nishi Sendai, 180 miles to the north of Tokyo, is another track that is part of a leisure complex including golf courses and skiing pistes. Skiing? Yes, Hi-Land Raceway really does live up to its name, located on a hilltop, at the top of a ski lift. The track is constant radius by design while also being very twisty. As such it has little international future.

Tsukuba, the closest track to Tokyo, is built on rich, flat agricultural land close to Science City, a futuristic place where every junction looks exactly like every other one and Westerners can be lost for weeks on end unless they can read Japanese. With land so valuable in Japan, the track is crammed into the smallest possible area, looping back on itself in a series of constant radius corners. **Sugo** is built on a grander scale: this 2.3-mile Yamaha test track near Sendai, situated halfway up a hill, has a fast downhill straight, sweeping corners and good facilities. The same cannot be said for **Nishi-Nihon**, to the South of Osaka. This too is set in hills but it remains a rather primitive facility, twisting anticlockwise and like many of Japan's circuits, crammed into too small a space.

In addition there are the smaller national level race tracks of HSP, in **Hokkaido**, **Nakayama**, west of Osaka and **Maze** on the west coast of Japan to the north of Tokyo. All are short and tight and unsuitable for international level competition.

INDEX